EDWARD MARSH

A Life of Poets,
Painters & Players

EDWARD MARSH

A Life of Poets,
Painters & Players

Sharon Mather

UNICORN

For Stephen

Published in 2023 by
Unicorn, an imprint of Unicorn Publishing Group
Charleston Studio
Meadow Business Centre
Lewes BN8 5RW
www.unicornpublishing.org

ISBN 978 1 911397 78 6
10 9 8 7 6 5 4 3 2 1

Design by newtonworks.uk
Printed in Malta by Gutenberg Press

Contents

THE THEATRE OF WAR

LEGACY

Foreword

In 1939, at the age of sixty-seven, Sir Edward Marsh – more commonly and affectionately known as Eddie – published his memoir, *A Number of People*. He had retired two years earlier from a distinguished career as a civil servant, for which he was awarded a knighthood in recognition of his services. Throughout Marsh's career he was at the heart of the establishment; he counted Prime Minister H. H. Asquith as a friend, and he served as Private Secretary to Winston Churchill, also a close friend. Despite difficulties and controversy, Marsh loyally supported Churchill in his diverse political posts, and their friendship endured until Marsh's death in 1953.

Marsh was a polymath and a scholar who led a remarkable life. He is mentioned in countless memoirs, biographies, diaries and collected letters of other well-known individuals of the period, so it is extraordinary that so little is known about him by the public at large. Marsh tended to live vicariously, more interested in other people than in himself; he worked industriously behind the scenes in order for others to succeed on the public stage. Many twentieth-century British writers and artists owe a debt to Marsh, who, beyond the considerable demands of his job, immersed himself in the literary and artistic circles of the day. His Visitors' Book from 1913 to 1937 includes the signatures of luminaries such as Rupert Brooke, E. M. Forster, Siegfried Sassoon, Robert Graves, T. E. Lawrence, Paul Nash, Stanley Spencer and Ivor Novello, to name but a few. A consummate networker and socialite, he was able to use his connections to forward the ambitions of his protégés – all of whom, through their various achievements, have stood the test of time rather better than Marsh himself, who remains an obscure figure.

Marsh's memoir, which he states at the outset is 'nothing so ambitious as an Autobiography',[1] is a veritable *Who's Who* of early twentieth-century intellectual, artistic and polite society. Through anecdotes about his family, friends and colleagues Marsh chronicles events in his life, but he is necessarily selective, and much is not said. His close friend Christopher Hassall was painstakingly discreet in his biography, *Edward Marsh: Patron of the Arts* (1959). Where Marsh's most intimate friendships are concerned, we are left to read between the lines. This book attempts to fill those gaps. It is the story of Marsh's life seen through the prism of his countless friendships with writers, politicians, poets, painters and players, an inexhaustible list that includes Rupert Brooke, Winston Churchill, Somerset Maugham, Patrick Hamilton, Dylan Thomas, H. G. Wells, Mark Gertler, Paul Nash, Stanley Spencer, Violet Asquith, Diana Mosley, Noël Coward, Ivor Novello and Christopher Hassall. What emerges in this account of Marsh's life is a story not only of love and loss but also of the vast scope of his influence and the importance of his legacy.

'A damnably clever child'

Edward Marsh was a precocious child, much loved by his domineering mother, Jane Perceval, the granddaughter of Spencer Perceval, the only British prime minister to have been assassinated. His parents had met at the Alexandra Hospital for Children with Hip Disease where his father, Frederick Howard Marsh, was a surgeon and his mother a nurse. Edward, affectionately known as Eddie, was born in London on 18 November 1872 (their first child, Mary, had died in infancy when Eddie was just eight months old), and his younger sister, Margaret, was born in 1874. Queen Victoria had been on the throne since 1837 and the British Empire was at its zenith.

Marsh, who was the focus of his mother's attention and ambition, was a gifted child. He had been introduced to Milton's poetry at the age of nine, and by the time he was twelve years old he could recite the first four books of *Paradise Lost*. As he said himself, he was 'a damnably clever child'.[1] In March 1883, at the age of ten, he entered Westminster School as an 'Exhibitioner' with a scholarship worth £30 (around £3,000 in today's money) a year. His mother was determined that he should not be out of her orbit for too long, so he was a day boy rather than a boarder. During his time at Westminster he was an active member of the Debating Society, he won a prize for English verse, and he was a House Monitor, a position of some responsibility.[2] By the age of fourteen Marsh had reached the top form at Westminster; his prodigious progress meant that for four years he had been taught directly by the Headmaster. He was also the youngest pupil from the school to attend Queen Victoria's Golden Jubilee in Westminster Abbey in June 1887.

Flora Russell (cousin of Bertrand Russell) recalled in a letter to Christopher Hassall how she had first heard of Eddie Marsh while he was still a schoolboy. She was walking past his family home in Bruton Street with her close friend, the distinguished archaeologist Gertrude

Bell, who remarked, 'Such a clever boy lives there. He is at Westminster and writes me the most brilliant letters.'[3] One can only guess what may have prompted the young Marsh to write to Gertrude Bell; but years later he would correspond with her (and T. E. Lawrence) in his official capacity as Private Secretary to Winston Churchill, then Secretary of State for the Colonies with responsibility for the Middle East. (After Gertrude Bell's death in 1926 Marsh and Flora Russell tried to get their letters returned, but they had been lost or destroyed.)[4]

Whereas Marsh's father was a somewhat remote figure, his mother was a strict and pervading influence. Under her direction Marsh spent most of his time as a youngster concerned with serious intellectual pursuits. As he recalled, 'My Mother was passionately fond of books, especially of poetry, and this taste she handed on to me, in a degree which was almost morbid: till I went to Cambridge I was nine-tenths bookworm.'[5]

There was, however, light relief for the teenage Eddie in the occasional company of his uncle, Norman Perceval, Jane Marsh's youngest brother. Uncle Norman would show Marsh the sights of London, which included visits to his club, 'the Rag' (the Army and Navy Club), as well as theatres and galleries. Thanks to him, Marsh absorbed the aesthetic of painting and acquired what would become a lifelong fondness for the raffish world of the theatre. Norman Perceval had fallen out of favour with the rest of the Perceval family, who deemed him to have married badly and considered him to be 'decidedly pagan and pleasure-loving'.[6] Jane Marsh was determined that her son should not become one of life's pleasure-seekers like her brother.

When applying for a place at university for her son loomed, Jane Marsh was convinced that if he went to Oxford it would encourage his propensity towards Anglo-Catholicism, and, equally worrying for her, that he would be destined for a literary career. This did not chime at all well with her hopes for him. In collusion with his Headmaster she urged Eddie to apply for an open scholarship at Trinity College, Cambridge. Marsh won his place, and in October 1892 he moved into his rooms in New Court, excited to be on the brink of his undergraduate life.

Cambridge was a transformative and emancipating experience for Marsh, not least because he was moving away from the suffocating influence of his mother. Her fears about Oxford paled into insignificance when she realised that her son's Cambridge friends were mainly agnostics, and, to her consternation, that he seemed to be turning away from religion altogether. Jane Marsh was shocked by what she regarded as his worldly behaviour.

Marsh made many lifelong friends at Cambridge, including Bertrand Russell ('Bertie'), Robert Trevelyan, Charles Sanger and G. E. Moore. Moore was very taken with Marsh, and thought him 'exceedingly handsome.'[7] The group of friends would often go away on reading parties to the Lake District, a popular destination at the time. On one such trip Marsh had overslept and rushed downstairs in his nightshirt to see if he had missed breakfast. According to Russell he looked 'frozen and miserable', which led to the bookish Trevelyan describing him as a 'cold white shape', a name that stuck to him for a long time.[8] Russell and Marsh corresponded regularly throughout their youth. Marsh was Russell's confidant, particularly in matters concerning his relationship with his fiancée, Alys Pearsall Smith. Russell told her 'I always speak the truth to Marsh',[9] and he sought Marsh's advice in cementing his relationship with her, although Marsh was hardly an expert in matters of the heart or relationships with women. Marsh was naive in many ways; as he recalled, Bertie had to explain to him why referring to their friend Michael Hunt as 'Mike Hunt' was considered a funny, if somewhat ribald, joke.[10] They spent much time in each other's company at Cambridge, often staying up talking until the early hours of the morning. Marsh was also a frequent guest at Russell's family home in Haslemere. Their lives and views diverged when Marsh was engaged in the political business of the First World War and Russell was imprisoned for being a conscientious objector, but their friendship was only temporarily broken off.

Whether or not his mother's fears concerning his worldly behaviour were justified, Marsh proved to be a model of academic brilliance, achieving a First Class Honours degree in Classics and winning the Senior Chancellor's Medal. Given his scholarly prowess, his parents were keen for him to forge an academic career and obtain a Fellowship at Trinity. Marsh had other ideas. He was intent on a career in the Civil Service, preferably something connected to the Foreign Office. He quickly learned that it was not sufficient for a civil servant to be possessed of a cultivated mind: it was also necessary for him to be correctly dressed. Marsh left the appearance of a provincial Cambridge scholar behind him and assumed the guise of an Edwardian man-about-town; the final touch was a monocle, a refinement with which he became synonymous. Throughout his adult life Marsh was an arbiter of style and impeccable manners that helped him to move easily into the circles to which he aspired. His appearance mattered to him a great deal. There are many conceited references in his correspondence to having been described as 'handsome'. He smugly recounted that the Duchess of Rutland 'did an extraordinarily good drawing of me [...] just flattering enough to please me mightily, without being ridiculous'.[11]

Marsh passed his Civil Service exams with flying colours, but just a few days before he was due to take up his new post on 24 September 1896 his mother suffered a heart attack and died. Marsh was shocked by the suddenness of her death, which occurred during a family dinner. He was also wracked with guilt that their special bond had weakened during his student days; they had often quarrelled, and he believed he had failed to live up to her expectations. Marsh had always been certain of his mother's love, and regretted that he had not shown her the love he felt towards her. He was not unusual in this regard: the Edwardian man was discouraged from displaying any kind of emotion. Being demonstrative was at odds with the essential trait of manliness. Marsh came to terms with his loss in private and threw himself into his new job. He entered the Colonial Office as a Second Class Clerk; he was Assistant Private Secretary to Joseph Chamberlain from 1900 and then to Alfred Lyttelton from 1903. In 1905 he was promoted to the position of First Class Clerk when he became Private Secretary to Winston Churchill.

Fortunately for Marsh he had a great many friends to provide a convivial distraction from the demands of work. One of those was the writer and critic Edmund Gosse. Marsh had first met him at a tea party in Cambridge hosted by his tutor, the Classicist A. W. Verrall. After graduation he was reintroduced to Gosse by his Cambridge friend Maurice Baring; Gosse and Baring were 'devoted to one another',[12] and through their friendship Marsh became a regular attendee at Gosse's salons and New Year's Eve parties. Gosse's home, in Delamere Terrace and later in Hanover Terrace, was one of London's cultural centres, where Marsh mingled with 'the literary company of [his] dreams'[13] which included Thomas Hardy, Max Beerbohm, W. B. Yeats and Sidney Colvin, Director of the Fitzwilliam Museum. Gosse took Marsh under his wing and made many introductions on his behalf, including securing his membership of the Reform Club.

Most significant for Marsh was the introduction to the novelist Henry James. They first met at one of Gosse's grander dinner parties, and Marsh described their subsequent occasional meetings as 'always a delight'.[14] Later on they were to become closer through their shared admiration of Rupert Brooke. Notwithstanding his high regard for James, Marsh would often entertain friends with stories and irreverent comic impersonations of him. Siegfried Sassoon, for one, delighted in Marsh's 'evergreen imitation of the great man enunciating – with immense effort – one of his convoluted sentences'.[15] However Marsh was careful to keep these antics well hidden from the Master.

By the end of 1896, at the age of twenty-four, Marsh had not only embarked on a responsible career in the Civil Service but, by virtue of his good looks, intelligent conversation and reputation as an accomplished Cambridge scholar, he was also a fixture on the London literary scene. He had the combined advantage of a youthful appearance and a mature intellect – as Henry James reportedly remarked, 'the Flower of Youth with the Fruits of Time!'[16]

In addition to the highbrow literary salons that he frequented, Marsh also immersed himself in the London season. Writing to Pamela Lytton, the wife of Victor (Bulmer-)Lytton, who like her husband was to be a close friend throughout his life (as well as an early flame of Winston Churchill's), he confessed 'how tremendously I have enjoyed the season and how flat I feel now it is over'.[17] It was a remarkable time of great luxury and decadence for the upper classes. Edward VII, who ascended the throne in 1901, was described by Henry James as the 'arch vulgarian', 'a corpulent voluptuary'. As the Prince of Wales, Edward (Bertie) had been the playboy prince of pleasure and embodied the spirit of his era. In Marsh's youth the hectic and often unseemly social life of upper-class Edwardian London was his principal pleasure, although in his memoir he was keen to distinguish pleasure from dissipation. Conrad Russell, his friend and colleague at the Colonial Office, was concerned about his excessive socialising and gave him dire warnings to 'beware of the Smart Set!'[18] Marsh was enjoying himself too much to take note of his friend's wise counsel. His advice to Russell was to 'drink champagne at dinner parties, "because it makes one more amusing." "It only makes you *think* you're more amusing," was Russell's grave reply.'[19] Nonetheless, Marsh did take to heart Russell's observation that 'one's first duty is to make life as pleasant as one can for the people one is thrown with',[20] and this became a guiding principle in his life.

At this early stage of his career Marsh was content to work hard at the office during the day and party equally as hard at night. He could not have imagined how his professional life, tied to Winston Churchill, would make him instrumental in affecting the course of British history. Nor could he have foreseen how his personal life would be transformed by his association with a succession of poets, painters and players.

THE POETS

Chapter One

Cambridge Heralds

My friendship with Rupert Brooke was certainly one of the most memorable things in my life. In his combination of gifts, of body, character, mind and spirit, he was nearer completeness and perfection than anyone I have known; intellect and goodness, humour and sympathy, beauty of person and kindness of heart, distinction of taste and 'the common touch', ambition and modesty, he had them all.[1]

Marsh first set eyes on Rupert Brooke on 30 November 1906, during Brooke's first term at King's College, Cambridge, when he was playing the part of the Herald in the *Eumenides* with 'grace invincible'.[2] Marsh lived in Raymond Buildings in Gray's Inn but was a regular visitor to Cambridge long after his graduation and many of his Cambridge friends were also present at the performance, including A. C. Benson, later Master of Magdalene College. Benson gave a cursory mention of Brooke's fleeting appearance in his diary: 'A herald made a pretty figure, spoilt by a glassy stare.'[3] In contrast, Marsh had been completely bowled over by Rupert Brooke's extraordinary physical beauty: he described Brooke's performance as 'one of the successes of the evening. His radiant, youthful figure in gold and vivid red and blue, like a Page in the Riccardi Chapel'.[4] Brooke had written to his friend and mentor the writer St John Lucas (St John Welles Lucas-Lucas) and given a rather different account of his part in the play:

If you come to Cambridge at the end of the month you will see
a performance of the Eumenides, in which an aged and grey

haired person called Rupert Brooke is wearily taking the part of
the Herald. I put a long horn to my lips and pretend to blow and
a villain in the orchestra simultaneously wantons on the cornet. It
is very symbolic.[5]

Brooke's friendship with Lucas had begun in 1905 when Lucas, who
lived in Rugby, was twenty-five years old and Brooke was still a pupil at
Rugby School where his father was a schoolmaster. Brooke would send
Lucas drafts of his poems to critique, and Lucas in turn would recommend reading material to the aspiring poet. Coincidentally, Marsh was
an admirer of Lucas, and thought his novel *The First Round* was 'simply
fascinating and couldn't bear its coming to an end'.[6]

Brooke gave his mother yet another version of the *Eumenides* performance: 'The idea of my playing Hermes fell through, but they have
given me the equally large part of the Herald. I stand in the middle of
the stage and pretend to blow a trumpet, while somebody in the wings
makes a sudden noise. The part is not difficult. The rehearsals are very
amusing.'[7]

Brooke's interest in putting on plays and acting continued throughout his undergraduate career, and he went on to co-found the Marlowe
Dramatic Society with his friend and fellow undergraduate Justin
Brooke (no relation). In July 1908 Lytton Strachey gave the Society's production of Milton's *Comus* a modestly favourable review in the
Spectator, writing to Virginia Stephen in April of that year, he said, 'I
daresay you would have found the jokes a little heavy – as for me, I
laughed enormously, and whenever I began to feel dull I could look at
the yellow hair and pink cheeks of Rupert.'[8]

It would seem that Brooke's attractive appearance outshone his
acting talent. Much to Brooke's annoyance, his good looks were often
the only thing that people noted. David (Bunny) Garnett, who had
met Brooke through the Fabian Movement summer camps, thought
him 'extremely attractive. Though not handsome he was beautiful. His
complexion, his skin, his eyes and hair were perfect.'[9] Henry James,
'very unforgettingly', met Brooke on a visit to Cambridge in early June
1909.[10] There is an apocryphal story that James asked his hosts whether

Brooke was a good poet. On receiving a negative response he replied, 'Well, I must say I am *relieved*, for with *that* appearance if he had also talent it would be too unfair.'[11] Four years after his brief reference to Brooke's appearance in *Eumenides*, A. C. Benson wrote about him again in more fulsome painterly detail:

> He was far more striking in appearance than exactly handsome in outline. His eyes were small and deeply set. It was the colouring of face and hair which gave special character to his look. The hair rose very thickly from his forehead, and fell in rather stiff arched locks on either side – he grew it full and over long, it was of a beautiful dark auburn tint inclining to red, but with an underlying gleam in it. His complexion was richly coloured, as though the blood was plentiful and near the surface; his face much tanned, with the tinge of sun-ripened fruit.[12]

Brooke is usually described as blonde but curiously Benson gives the impression that he was auburn or 'strawberry blonde'. Almost every reference to Rupert Brooke in Benson's diary comments on his handsome appearance (Benson is not so flattering about Brooke's other attributes). Women were also smitten by Brooke's beauty. The poet Frances Cornford in her poem 'Youth' hails her friend as 'A young Apollo, golden-haired'[13] – an image that was to stay with him beyond the grave. Frieda Lawrence said of him that 'He was so good-looking, he took your breath away.'[14] No photograph of Brooke could do justice to his good looks and his flawless complexion.

It is not surprising that Marsh was drawn to Rupert Brooke. It was no secret among Marsh's circle that he enjoyed the company of attractive young men. Some of his closest friends were homosexuals, necessarily discreet, and, in his own case, probably non-practising. As a teenager he had contracted mumps, complicated by German measles, which seems to have affected his voice: in its peculiar falsetto it became one of his most distinguishing features. The painter Graham Sutherland said on meeting Marsh for the first time, 'I was unaware of much except the high, light, slightly lisping, withdrawn, yet infinitely persuasive voice.'[15] A. C. Benson described him as having 'an almost prim old-maidish voice'.[16] Somerset Maugham described it as a 'shrill voice'.[17] And Marsh said of his own voice, 'if my choice lay between squeaking and gibbering like a ghost in the streets of Rome and growling like Hamlet's father I preferred the former. Perhaps this is because I can't hear myself talk – my voice sounds to me quite normal.'[18] In his later years Marsh recalled asking the composer Ivor Novello, 'I don't think my voice is so very bad, do you?' Novello replied: 'Well it *is* rather a drawback.'[19] According to Marsh's friend and biographer Christopher Hassall, there were consequences of the illness beyond the effect on his maturing voice:

> The disease had determined the colour of his personality and the course of his life so fundamentally that one cannot wish it to have been otherwise, although the result was a disability. So early in life did it happen, and the knowledge of it came so gradually, there are no grounds for supposing he grieved that he was to be incapable of the act of love, or minded at all that he was destined from then on to live and die as chaste as the day he was born. It enabled his affections to grow more intensely in the mind, and as a result he cultivated a capacity for friendship which, untroubled by physical desire, could develop into a devotion characteristically feminine in its tenderness.[20]

Writing in the late 1950s, Hassall was careful not to say anything contentious about Marsh, hence his euphemistic and sentimental account of the effects of Marsh's childhood illness. It was also an attempt to protect both their reputations. Given Marsh's senior position in the Civil Service, and the fact that at the time homosexual acts were illegal and carried a prison sentence, discretion was vital. The Wolfenden Report dealing with homosexual offences and prostitution was not published until September 1957, and the changes to the law to decriminalise homosexual behaviour between consenting adults were not implemented until a decade later in the Sexual Offences Act 1967, eight years after Hassall's biography was published. As a young man Marsh would have been only too aware of the public scandal that surrounded the imprisonment of Oscar Wilde for indecency and homosexual acts. In Marsh's milieu homosexuality, lesbianism and bisexuality were often open secrets. Most men in the public eye were discreet, but others were less so. Marsh's contemporaries in the Blooms-bury Group, which included Lytton Strachey and his younger brother James, Duncan Grant, John Maynard Keynes, Virginia Woolf and Vita Sackville-West, were well known for their complicated, gender-fluid relationships.

Referring to Marsh's time at Cambridge, Hassall simply said 'he con-sidered his companions singularly blessed in their freedom from the obsession of sex. "We had no known affairs," he wrote, "and I can only remember two of my intimates even falling in love."'[21] But the ration-ale of mumps being the cause of Marsh's lack of 'physical desire' did not satisfy Geoffrey Keynes, a medic and Rupert Brooke's close friend, who wrote to Hassall after the publication of his biography and said, 'Milo [Keynes] and I have discussed your explanation of Eddie with mumps, and we think you have it all wrong! A complicated affair.'[22] A tantalising comment; unfortunately Keynes did not elucidate further – at least not on paper.

Unlike Marsh, Rupert Brooke was not 'untroubled by physical desire'. While a schoolboy at Rugby many of his schoolfellows were infatuated with him, and he indulged in romances with boys includ-ing Charles Lascelles, Michael Sadleir and Denham Russell-Smith, the younger brother of his school friend Hugh Russell-Smith. At this time boyhood romances such as Brooke experienced were a common feature of public school life. In his posthumously published novel *Maurice*, E. M. Forster, another of Marsh's young friends, explored homosexual love from public school to Cambridge and beyond. Simi-larly Christopher Isherwood, in his semi-autobiographical novel *Lions and Shadows: An Education in the Twenties*, recounts his relationships with boys and young men. Public school boys were taught Classics – Latin and Greek – and Greek culture promoted boy worship based on Plato's *Symposium*, which endorsed 'brotherly' love, with its inher-ent ambiguity of spiritual versus physical love. The historian Bettany Hughes asserts that in ancient Greece 'increasingly sex with all women was seen as a distraction from a truly fulfilling life, from male compan-ionship and from the manly business of fighting and empire-building'.[23]

Empire-building was a powerful drive in the Victorian age, so it is not surprising that the notions of manliness and male friendship were also prevalent. William Johnson Cory was famously dismissed from his post as a schoolmaster at Eton for encouraging intimacy between teachers and their pupils. A. C. Benson, who was a teacher at Eton before being appointed a Fellow and Master of Magdalene College, wrote: 'But if we give boys Greek books to read and hold up the Greek spirit and the Greek life as a model, it is very difficult to slice out one portion which was a perfectly normal part of Greek life [homosexual love], and to say that it is abominable.'[24]

On hearing of the unexpected death of his friend Denham Russell-Smith in July 1912, Brooke wrote to James Strachey and gave a candid account of their relationship:

> We had hugged & kissed & strained, Denham & I, on & off for years – ever since that quiet evening I rubbed him, in the dark, speechlessly, in the smaller of the two Small Dorms. An abortive affair, as I told you. But in the summer holidays of 1906 & 1907 he had often taken me out to the hammock after dinner, to lie entwined there. – He had vaguely hoped, I fancy … But I lay always thinking of Charlie [Lascelles].

Brooke went on to tell Strachey that in 1909 Russell-Smith was his overnight guest at The Orchard, Grantchester. He described in detail how they had sex, despite having discussed the subject of sodomy earlier in the evening and Russell-Smith having 'thought it *was* wrong'. Brooke had his reasons for seducing his friend:

> But I wanted to have some fun, &, still more, to see what it was *like*, and to do away with the shame (as I was taught it was) of being a virgin. At length, I thought, I shall know something of all that James & Norton & Maynard & Lytton know & hold over me.[25]

Brooke's intimate revelations to Strachey confirm that he was attracted to men. He was also attracted to – and conducted many relationships with – women, sometimes concurrently. James Strachey had been infatuated with Brooke since their Hillbrow prep school days, and was indefatigable in his pursuit of him while at Cambridge, but without success. Frustrated by Brooke's lack of interest in his advances, Strachey described Brooke in a letter to their mutual friend the artist Duncan Grant as 'a *real* womanizer'.[26] Not all of Brooke's relationships with women were consummated, as in the case of the actress Cathleen Nesbitt and Noel Olivier.[27] Brooke certainly had a sexual relationship with his Tahitian beauty, Taatamata. He wrote to Marsh from Tahiti on 7 February 1914 describing his daily routine: 'I spend my time between swimming, working, & having astonishing medieval adventures with Tahitian beauties.'[28] He acquired an infection and fever after coral-poisoning to his leg and on 7 March he wrote: 'I have been nursed & waited on by a girl with wonderful eyes, the walk of a goddess, & the heart of an angel, who is, luckily, devoted to me. She gives her time to ministering to me, I mine to probing her queer mind. I think I shall write a book about her – Only I fear I'm too fond of her.'[29] Brooke addressed his poem 'Tiare Tahiti' to her, and there is an unproven claim that she bore his child.[30]

Brooke's emotionally tormented love affair with Ka Cox whom he had met at Cambridge resulted in her becoming pregnant. She suffered a miscarriage, after which Brooke ended their relationship. Their liaison has been well documented by Brooke's biographers, and is referred to obliquely by Cathleen Nesbitt in an interview with Michael Elliot published in *The Listener* on 20 January 1972:

> But in that day and age, in his class, men knew as little about sex really as women did. He fell in love and induced a woman to live with him and then grew out of love with her. He thought she was with child by him, and then she had a miscarriage, and the whole thing put a terrible guilt complex in him.[31]

During Brooke's three years at King's College, long before his complicated love life became apparent, Marsh 'went to Cambridge pretty often' and 'saw him from time to time'.[32] They were both members of a Cambridge elite, ostensibly secret, intellectual society known as the Apostles, which had been formed in 1820. 'Brothers', as they were known, were elected mainly from King's, Trinity and St John's colleges.

The historian Hugh Trevor-Roper waspishly described the Apostles as 'the egregious secret society of self-perpetuating, self-admiring narcissi'.[33] Their sphere of influence extended well beyond Cambridge and into British public life. Bertrand Russell, John Maynard Keynes and Lytton Strachey were all Apostles. Like Marsh they became 'Angels' after graduation and continued to be very much connected to the society.

The Apostles met to discuss and debate subjects such as truth, ethics and God. In 1903 one of the Edwardian Apostles, the philosopher G. E. Moore, published *Principia Ethica*, which like Plato's *Symposium* identified the love between men as 'true love'.[34] This concept was espoused by the Apostles (including Marsh) almost as a manifesto. Much of their discussion related to 'higher sodomy', the spiritual and emotional love between men, versus 'lower sodomy', the physical expression and sexual act between men. A well-established homosexual clique existed at Cambridge when both Marsh and Brooke were undergraduates, and its members colluded to protect one another's privacy and reputations. Initially an advocate of 'higher sodomy', Brooke later distanced himself from the idea of homosexual love altogether, and in particular from James (and Lytton) Strachey. He wrote to Noel Olivier on 28 August 1912:

> You are rather mistaken about James. I didn't 'take offence with' him. It had been coming inevitably to this for months & months & months. It's complicated & bound up with things you can't understand – [sodomy]. It's part of my new view of things, that I find creatures like that, Stracheys & so forth, not only no good but actually dangerous, spots of decay, menaces to all good. Even if one doesn't mind rats *qua* rats, one has to stamp out carriers of typhoid.[35]

At the outset of their friendship, the Apostle gatherings afforded Marsh and Brooke an opportunity to meet. In a letter to James Strachey dated 28 November 1908 Brooke wrote, 'No real news. Eddie is here again for the weekend.'[36] A meeting of the Apostles had been fixed which Marsh planned to attend after dinner with his friends the

Verralls, and he also arranged to meet Brooke for breakfast in King's College the following day.[37] There was 'an exchange of postcards' between them during November 1908, but they were still on quite formal terms.[38] However by March 1909 arrangements were made for Brooke to stay overnight with Marsh in London on his way back to Cambridge from a family holiday in Devon. Marsh's excitement at the plan is palpable: borrowing from Lewis Carroll's nonsense poem 'Jabberwocky' he enthuses: 'My dear Brooke, or may I say Rupert and will you do likewise? I am delighted that you will come on the 23rd, Shakespeare's birthday, oh frabjous day – I will keep it jealously – so if you want to change it, or could stay more than one night, let me know in goodish time.'[39]

In fact Brooke did alter their arrangements, and came to stay on 22 April instead.[40] They met for dinner at Brooks's, one of Marsh's London clubs, after which they went to see a play together.[41] This was the first of what were to become frequent visits for Brooke to Marsh's home in Raymond Buildings. Here Marsh's housekeeper tended to Brooke's needs: 'Mrs Elgy was delighted, in spite of the extra work, for Marsh was out all day and Brooke she said was the "stoojius [studious] type," who caused no trouble.'[42] Brooke was just one of the protégés who enjoyed Marsh's hospitality.

Brooke had moved out of King's College to the village of Grantchester, just south of Cambridge, where he could emulate the life of a Neo-Pagan and be close to nature. Marsh arranged to visit; on 21 July 1909 he wrote to Brooke, 'Your orchard [Brooke's house was called The Orchard] was the making of my Sunday.'[43] In the same letter he mentioned that he was going to visit Mells, near Frome in Somerset. Intent on moving in the highest ranks of fashionable society, Marsh would be staying at Mells Manor, as the guest of Sir John and Lady Frances Horner. Their daughter Katherine was married to Raymond Asquith, the son of the Prime Minister, H. H. Asquith. Marsh described her brother, Edward Horner, as one of his 'greatest friends'.[44]

Edward Horner was another beautiful young man. Like many of his privileged circle he craved excitement, and was 'brilliant, restless and dissatisfied'.[45] In order to keep in touch Marsh visited him regularly during term-time at Balliol College, Oxford. Although Marsh was much older, Horner admitted him to his group of old-Etonian friends, which included Patrick Shaw-Stewart, Duff Cooper, 'Tommy' Lascelles, and brothers Julian and Billy Grenfell (Marsh described the latter as having 'the body of a Greek god and the face of a water baby'). They frequently played poker, which Marsh hated, not least because he always lost, but he had prowess in their other favourite activity, which was to drink copious amounts of champagne. At their invitation he attended a Bullingdon dinner which he described later as 'the nearest I ever got to an Orgy'.[46] On a hot summer night Marsh would occasionally join them at Wharf House, owned by the Asquith family, to sleep in the garden under the stars – a regular event described by Violet Asquith as the 'crowded male Sunday at the Wharf'.[47]

That summer Brooke's parents had rented a large house in Clevedon, near Mells, and Marsh planned to take Horner along with him to visit Brooke. Brooke responded eagerly, saying that 'Tuesday to Saturday will be admirably suitable.' Less encouragingly, he said, 'This is a quite dreadful place. One cannot stir outside the garden. And my family are too detestable for words.'[48]

Mrs Brooke was not overly keen on her son's friends. 'The Ranee', as Brooke called his mother, was a forthright matriarch with a pervasive influence on her son. Geoffrey Keynes wrote, 'She could not really approve of her son's friendship with people whom she regarded as dilettanti *littérateurs* such as St John Lucas.'[49] They would have included Marsh, who found his dealings with her very difficult. He described her as having 'a keen intelligence in practical things, and a certain grim humour in her own sense – not the kind of humour that makes people tolerant and self-critical', and went on to say, 'of artistic perception I never saw the smallest sign.' He pronounced: 'She was extremely autocratic and extremely puritanical, rigid and conventional in her notions of decorum, living most strictly up to her ideals of duty; and passionately devoted to Rupert, with whose mind and view of life she was completely out of sympathy.'[50]

Where their mothers we concerned Marsh and Brooke had much in common. Jane Marsh had been formidable and determined to stay very close to her son; Marsh described her as 'the all-pervading influence in my early life'.[51] She was a member of the Catholic Apostolic Church, popularly known as the Irvingites: 'the evangelical form of religion which became the mainspring of her life was also the source of her extraordinary strength, and nobility, as well as narrowness of character.'[52] She determined what books Marsh was permitted to read and the plays he was allowed to see, and emphasised the importance of church-going. In respect of her faith, Marsh recalled:

> She was an eager student of Prophecy, and I suspect her favourite book in the Bible was *Revelation*. Her studies led her to suppose that the End of the World was at hand, and her dearest ambition for my sister and me was that we might be unsuccessfully tortured by the Antichrist, and win through to be caught up to Heaven at the Second Coming.[53]

Although Marsh had never been particularly close to his father, he was dismayed when he remarried, and he was disparaging about his stepmother. When Howard Marsh became Master of Downing College, Cambridge, on at least two occasions A. C. Benson dined with them all at the Master's Lodge, and observed:

> Eddie rather *sniffy*; he might have been a smart young officer dining rather petulantly and impatiently at a country vicarage – not nice to his father, horrid to his stepmother. […] Mrs Marsh was I think a nurse, but she is a nice woman, tho' I think not highly born enough for Eddie, whose mother was a Walpole [she was also a Perceval].[54]

Benson was clearly unimpressed with Marsh's behaviour and overt snobbery. However, his predilection for the upper echelons of society and the *beau monde* were to work in Rupert Brooke's favour. As Brooke spent more time with Marsh and mingled with his social set in London, his ambition to become a famous poet drew closer to realisation.

Chapter Two

Private Secretary and Private Passions

Marsh had been thirty-four years old when he first met Rupert Brooke. He had recently been appointed as Private Secretary to Winston Churchill (recommended to him by Pamela Lytton), then Under-Secretary of State for the Colonies. On hearing the news of his appointment in December 1905 Marsh recalled:

> By an irony, I was not particularly pleased. I had assimilated myself comfortably to the West African Department; I was two years older than my prospective master – and furthermore, I was a little afraid of him [...] and though I had thought him the most brilliant person I had ever come across, he struck me as rather truculent and overbearing.[1]

Marsh wrote, 'I can see what he will expect from his P. S. and it's *simply* terrifying – all so utterly beyond my capacity.'[2]

Once in post, however, he soon put aside his trepidation, and a great partnership was forged; Marsh became 'an inseparable adjunct' of Churchill's life.[3] They were an incongruous pair, not least because Marsh was not interested in politics or world events unless they affected him, or those he loved, personally. However being Private Secretary to Churchill suited him, and he gave full rein to his capacity for empathy, attachment and desire to be of service. From late 1907 to early 1908 he accompanied Churchill on his visit to Cyprus, East Africa, Uganda, Sudan and Egypt. Churchill was an accomplished horseman: Marsh learned to ride a horse especially for the expedition, and was taught by Wilfrid Scawen Blunt on one of his Arab horses from the famous Crabbet Park Stud. The writer and Orientalist Blunt was a controversial and radical figure. He had been a good friend of Winston's father, Lord Randolph. After Randolph's death he formed a friendship with Winston, and encouraged him to espouse liberal views on imperial matters. Both men enjoyed dressing up in Arab costume on their occasional meetings.

In Africa Churchill and his entourage went on safari; they camped out in tents, trekked twelve to twenty-five miles a day, and shot big game. Churchill was in his element and cheerfully exclaimed 'safari sogoodi' at the end of each day's march.[4] Despite sunburn and blisters Marsh also enjoyed the experience, although he was a bad shot. He declared, 'I don't shoot the big game, I only shoot at it.'[5] He was obviously confident in his chief's shooting prowess, however: he accompanied him on one expedition in search of rhinoceros armed with nothing more deadly than a pink umbrella.[6]

Marsh was very pleased that in addition to his diverse duties as Private Secretary he had been given a lucrative commission by the *Manchester Guardian* to write a series of articles about their African trip to entertain its readers.

Marsh followed Churchill when he was appointed to the Board of Trade from 1908 to 1910, moved on to the Home Office in 1910, and then to the Admiralty from 1911 until 1915. Churchill was a demanding chief, but showed great affection towards Marsh. On 20 August 1908 he wrote to him: 'Few people have been so lucky as me to find in the dull and grimy recesses of the Colonial Office a friend who I shall cherish & hold to all my life.'[7] In 1910 Marsh had been offered the position of Private Secretary and Master of Ceremonies to Herbert Gladstone, appointed Resident in Government House, Pretoria. He declined, on the basis that 'It would mean chucking Winston for good, and that would simply be too great a wrench. We have got peculiarly attached to one another in the four years we have been together, and I do want to stay with him so long as he is in office.'[8]

Marsh became increasingly close to the Churchill family too. Lady Diana Mosley, a cousin of Churchill's wife, recalled that 'Eddie was very often at Chartwell. He was kind, gentle and witty, everything he said in his high-pitched squeaky voice sounded specially amusing.'[9] He was a regular correspondent with Winston's mother, Lady Randolph Churchill, who had urged him to 'Be happy and enjoy yourself, and look after my Winston – he is very precious to me.'[10] Clementine

Hozier, soon to become Mrs Winston Churchill, wrote to Marsh saying, 'He [Winston] is so very fond of you, & I am glad you will let me be your friend too.'[11] Winston and Clementine were married on 12 September 1908; Marsh's wedding gift to Winston was the complete works of Sainte-Beuve, the nineteenth-century French writer and literary critic.

Winston and Clementine invited Marsh to be godfather to their daughter, Sarah, and he became close to their son, Randolph. In 1928 Randolph was at school when he heard that Marsh, on a walking holiday in Corsica with his niece, Nancy Maurice, had collapsed and fallen badly. Following his Corsican misadventure, later diagnosed as due to nephritis and uraemia, Marsh divided his six-week convalescence between London, Chartwell and Redroofs (Ivor Novello's home in Maidenhead). While at Redroofs Marsh received a letter from Randolph, who was at nearby Eton, referring to the 'frightful adventure' and asking him to visit: 'Do come if you can manage it, as I am most anxious to see you again, and here [*sic*] all about your experiences. Your loving, Randolph.'[12]

Unlike Marsh, Rupert Brooke had not set his sights on a career in the Civil Service after graduation. His father died of a stroke on 24 January 1910, and he went back to Rugby to take over his father's former role (and salary) as a housemaster temporarily and to help his mother move house. A career in teaching was not on his agenda either: he told Marsh, 'I am glad I am not going to be a schoolmaster forever. The Tragedy would be too great.'[13]

Following William Parker Brooke's death the family's financial circumstances were reduced, and Brooke relied on a quarterly allowance of £150 dispensed by his mother. He augmented his income with freelance writing and winnings from poetry competitions run by the *Westminster Gazette*, which provided cash prizes in the region of two guineas (£2 2s). Brooke's firmly held Fabian principles led him to believe that an artist should be supported. In a talk he gave to the Cambridge Fabians he expounded on the idea of the state providing a fund which would be administered to provide an income for artists in the region of £250 (around £24,000 in today's money). 'It is impossible to know how much more Milton or Marvell would have given us if they had had enough money to live on.'[14] Brooke was fortunate that Marsh was very willing to help in this regard: his patronage provided Brooke with a place to stay in London, an active social life, and access to an established literary network.

Brooke wrote to Marsh on 26 September 1909, 'I shall be in London sometime between Monday Oct. 11th & the next Thursday. Will you be there then? Or still in … is it *Russia* this time? I want to see Lear, if they keep on at it.'[15] Marsh was indeed in Russia with his friend the writer Maurice Baring, visiting the Russian Ambassador to London, Count Benckendorff; but on his return he obediently accompanied Brooke to see *King Lear*.

On 3 March 1910 Brooke, while still acting housemaster at Rugby, wrote to Marsh inviting him to Grantchester, 'Next term I'll be at the Orchard again. It will be a pink Paradise of blossom. Will you come & have lunch in a bower of apple blossom there?' This was followed by yet another request to stay with Marsh in London: 'During the third week in April I shall be in London for a day or two. Will you be there & able to put me up for a day or two?'[16] On 12 April Brooke wrote again, this time from Lulworth Cove: 'I am sorry I have been so vague about my visits. […] On Tuesday the 19th, I come up to London. Can you put me up for Tuesday & Wednesday nights? And will you be free to see *Trelawny of the Wells* on either evening?'[17] In addition to Brooke's requests for a bed in London and theatre trips, Marsh treated Brooke to dinner in fashionable restaurants and clubs, and introduced him to the cream of high society. Marsh had become infatuated with Brooke, and his generosity was rewarded by having a beautiful young man in tow. In May 1910 he offered to take Brooke abroad for a fortnight, but his invitation was declined: 'I wish I could have come. It would have been lovely. Grantchester's lovely, though, too. When are you coming?'[18] Brooke reciprocated Marsh's largesse and hospitality in a rather less glamorous fashion:

> That week-end, the 23rd, turns out to be perfectly all right. You'll find me quite wild with reading and the country. Come prepared

for bathing and clad in primitive clothes. Bring books also:
one talks eight hours, reads eight, and sleeps eight. The food is
extremely simple and extremely unwholesome.[19]

In between their meetings Marsh, in spite of 'having a dog's life' and 'hardly a minute to read' (he had accompanied Churchill, who appeared to have limitless energy, on a hectic election campaign for the seat of Manchester North-West), would write long, descriptive letters to Brooke. Brooke's response to these missives would often be just a brief postcard.[20] Brooke was certainly a prolific letter writer, but most of his letters were directed to his contemporaries and various love interests and not, at this point in their relationship, to his patron and mentor.

As well as furthering his own ambition, Brooke (persuaded by his mother) was also bold enough to ask Marsh to exert his influence on behalf of his younger brother, Alfred, a Liberal who was interested in pursuing a political career. Rupert Brooke reported back to his mother:

I asked E. M. about Alfred. He didn't know much personally. But he promised to talk to the head of the – isn't it called the Whip's Office? – Jesse Herbert: and get him to see Alfred some time, and advise him what to do. […] For they'll give Alfred special attention with Eddie Marsh's influence: and it appears to be the central place from which all political activity starts out.[21]

Brooke was taking his ambition to be a poet seriously. His desire had been formed early on, and he was encouraged by his success as a schoolboy in winning poetry competitions and seeing one of his early poems, 'The Sea', printed in the *Westminster Gazette* in September 1906. He wrote to Frances Cornford from Rugby on 7 July 1910, exclaiming 'I am slowly recovering from Work. Henceforth I am going to lead what Dudley Ward calls "a Life Dedicated to Art." Hurray!'[22] However, a life dedicated to writing poetry also proved to be hard work. As Brooke described to his girlfriend Ka Cox, 'I'd been working for ten days alone on this beastly poetry. Working at poetry isn't like reading hard. It doesn't just tire and exhaust you. The only effect is that your nerves and your brain go.'[23]

The first manuscript poem that Brooke showed Marsh was 'Day That I Have Loved'. Initially Marsh had been reluctant to read Brooke's verse because he liked him so much and 'should have hated not to like his work'.[24] He was happily reassured when he read the poem, and it was published in the *Westminster Gazette* on 1 June 1910.

On 4 December 1911 Brooke's first volume of poetry, containing fifty poems written between 1905 and 1911, was published by Sidgwick & Jackson. Brooke had approached Frank Sidgwick, who agreed to publish but had doubts about one poem in particular, 'A Channel Passage' (written in December 1909), which he wanted to omit from the volume. The poem linked seasickness with lovesickness; he warned Brooke: 'we feel bound to advise you very strongly that the majority of your reviewers will pounce upon it to your disadvantage'. Brooke was having none of it and the poem stayed put.[25]

A Channel Passage

The damned ship lurched and slithered. Quiet and quick
My cold gorge rose; the long sea rolled; I knew
I must think hard of something, or be sick;
And could think hard of only one thing – *you*!
You, you alone could hold my fancy ever!
And with you memories come, sharp pain, and dole.
Now there's a choice – heartache or tortured liver!
A sea-sick body, or a you-sick soul!

Do I forget you? Retchings twist and tie me,
Old meat, good meals, brown gobbets, up I throw.
Do I remember? Acrid return and slimy,
The sobs and slobber of last year's woe.
And still the sick ship rolls. 'Tis hard, I tell ye,
To choose 'twixt love and nausea, heart and belly.

The publisher was right to be concerned about the critics:

Almost all the critics seem to have given their chief attention
to those few poems which came to be known as 'unpleasant,
notably *A Channel Passage*. […] Criticism ranged from J. C.
Squire's complaint in the *New Age* that 'the appalling narrative of

a cross-Channel voyage should never have been included in the volume.[26]

The *Times Literary Supplement* wrote, 'His disgusting sonnet on love and seasickness ought never to have been printed: but we are tempted to like him for writing it.'[27] In this particular poem Brooke had demonstrated a new realism, in both the subject and the language – a new kind of aesthetic which was to become a feature of Georgian poetry. Marsh of course loved it, and wrote to Brooke when the book first appeared:

> I've been living on your book since I got it a few days ago, and
> I must write and tell you [...] I had always in trembling hope
> reposed that I should like the poems, but at my wildest I never
> looked forward to such magnificence. You have brought back
> into English poetry the rapturous beautiful grotesque of the 17th
> century.[28]

Brooke was 'unrepentant about the unpleasant poems', and delighted by Marsh's response to his work: 'Your letter gave me great joy. [...] God! It's so cheering to find someone who likes the modern stuff, & appreciates what one's at. You can't think how your remarks & liking thrilled me.'[29] Buoyed up by Marsh's validation, understandably Brooke later declared: 'I know that I can be the greatest poet and writer in England. Many know it.'[30]

There had been and would be a hiatus in their meetings, as Brooke explained to Marsh on 22 December 1911:

> I'm so sorry I never saw you again. The last part of November
> & the first part of December I spent in writing my dissertation
> in Grantchester. As I had a Soul Crisis as Insomnia [*sic*] &
> other things, I couldn't do it at all well. I came to London in a
> dilapidated condition for a day or two after it was over. Now I'm
> here [Rugby] over Christmas. About the 27th I go to Lulworth
> with a reading-party for a fortnight. Then to the South of France,
> then Germany ... & the future's mere mist. I want to stay out of
> England some time. (1) I don't like it. (2) I want to work – a play,
> & so on. (3) I'm rather tired & dejected. So I probably shan't be

in London for a long time. If I am I'll let you know … I'm going to try to do scraps – reviewing, etc. – in my spare time for the immediate future. I suppose you don't edit a magazine? I might review Elizabethan books at some length for *The Admiralty Gazette*, or T. A. T. (Tattle Among Tars), or whatever journal you officially produce? … At least I hope you'll issue an order to include my poems in the library of all submarines.[31]

At this time Marsh was working with Churchill at the Admiralty. Their stint at the Home Office had been eventful, not least with the Tonypandy Riots and the Battle of Sidney Street, but the Admiralty was to prove even busier and more action-packed. Marsh complained to Lady Gladstone on 30 November 1911, 'I have been frightfully hard at work here ever since we came, Winston stays till at least 8 every day […] So all the usual writing times have been cut off. Even Sundays are no longer my own.'[32]

Marsh's social life did not abate, however, and it was augmented by his latest enthusiasm for contemporary verse. In his memoir Marsh credits his new-found interest in contemporary verse to meeting the poets Francis and Alice Meynell. He said of Francis Meynell, 'His chief preoccupation was with contemporary verse, a field which I had hardly entered – for till then I had preferred my poetry vintage; but he poured the new wine into my old bottle, and I drank deep.'[33] It may be true that Marsh had once preferred his 'poetry vintage', but it was a little disingenuous of him to say that his change of heart was due to meeting the Meynells. It is much more likely that his affection for Brooke, and the appearance of Brooke's *Poems* in print, were the factors that effected his conversion from the 'vintage' to the 'new'.

On the basis of Marsh's enthusiasm for Brooke's *Poems*, Francis Meynell suggested that he might like to write about it for the Poetry Society's magazine the *Poetry Review*, which would help it reach a larger audience. Meynell's friend Harold Monro had accepted the role of editor of the *Poetry Review* with the aim of bringing younger poets to the fore, not only among Poetry Society members but also among a more general audience. According to Joy Grant, Monro 'believed the English were a poetic race, waiting only to be released from an effete tradition to regain their inheritance'.[34] Marsh's article on Brooke's *Poems* appeared in the April 1912 issue. Monro had specified that it should be 'rather in the nature of an appreciation than a criticism';[35] Marsh was happy to oblige (though later in life he professed to 'hate the Poetry Society').[36] Described by Joy Grant as 'an alert, perspicuous, pedantic appreciation', it was a fervent endorsement of Brooke's poetic talent. Marsh expounded passionately: 'it will be surprising if the book does not come to be looked on as one of the stations of the fiery cross which the Muse now seems to be sending out through England.'[37]

James Strachey wrote to Brooke on 24 February 1912 after having unexpectedly bumped into Marsh: 'Who should be there, coming out, but Eddie [...]. We took tea at Barbellion's – and Eddie brought out of his tail pocket (where it always lies) his review of your poems. He's *most* anxious for a word from you. Such a *nice* man, I thought.'[38] Marsh had already sent a draft copy of his article to Brooke, accompanied by yet another long letter. He explained:

> The long and the short was, that the pages of the *Review* were open to me! I was rather frightened, never having written a line of any sort since I left Cambridge – but anyhow, I thought, I can do better than say that Mr Brooke's trumpet sounds the authentic note – and I *might* be able to give you a leg up – so I consented. [...] At this moment I am rather pleased with it, and I hope that on the whole you will like it – and above all that it may induce some of the 4,000 to purchase.[39]

Spurred on by Strachey's note concerning Marsh, Brooke wrote a tardy letter of acknowledgement from Rugby on 25 February 1912 explaining why he had not been in touch:

> God! How one can suffer from what my amiable specialist described as 'nervous breakdown'. [...] I tottered, being too tired for suicide, to Cannes, not because I like the bloody place, but because my mother happened to be there. I flapped slowly towards the surface there; & rose a little more at Munich. [...] I detail all this to account for my recent silence.[40]

The review for the Poetry Society was just the first of Marsh's concerted efforts to promote Brooke's work. He made use of his most influential literary contacts, and reported to Brooke:

> I must say, my dear, that the more I study your poetry the more I like it. I showed the book on Friday to Edmund Gosse and Austin Dobson – and I was really delighted with their reception of it. E. G. read a lot of it out loud, with every grace of diction – and after about three poems said 'I declare *contra mundum* that he is a poet' and that you were far the most interesting of the new people I had introduced to him. […] They asked me to convey to you the admiration of two elderly poetasters.[41]

Marsh was also at pains to stress the importance of his connection to Gosse, whose friendship he valued enormously, 'By the way Rupert dear, if you meet Gosse I beg you for my sake to be nice to him – also he is a good backer and may be useful to you! And a little kindness does wonders with him.'[42] Marsh was clearly lining up the literary doyens for Brooke's benefit. He also contacted the poet Robert Bridges, whom he had first met when he was fourteen years old while recuperating from his bout of German measles. Determined to solicit Bridges' support for Brooke's work, he asked:

> Would you look at a few of the poems in the book I am sending? It is by a very great friend of mine, about two years down from Cambridge (he is trying for a fellowship at King's with a dissertation on Webster about whom he has found some interesting things –) […] I think he has such a great talent that I feel almost justified in asking you to take an interest in his work.[43]

(Brooke achieved his fellowship. In 1913 he was elected a Fellow of King's College on the strength of his dissertation, *John Webster and the Elizabethan Drama.*)

It is perhaps ironic that Brooke later wrote to Marsh, 'You know I don't rate Bridges so highly. I think Yeats worth a hundred of him.'[44] Notwithstanding Brooke's opinion, a year later Bridges was to become Poet Laureate. Brooke had considered the pending appointment with

Marsh, writing from America on 29 June 1913, 'The Laureateship is discussed ardently and continually. [...] I say, do just see that the Laureateship is kept. It would be a *frightful* scandal if it were abolished. Why not Bridges?'[45] Plainly Brooke was fickle.

Brooke was immensely pleased with Marsh's review of his work, and recognised his 'skilful advocacy' with regard to Gosse. But Marsh was perturbed when Brooke went on to tell him pensively, 'I suppose I shall see you some day. I can't say what I'm going to do after I leave Rugby' (Brooke was staying with his mother at the time); 'I expect I shall go abroad again.' He continued, 'I'm vaguely thinking of writing a few articles & reviews & things in intervals to keep myself going.' Ever hopeful that Marsh would be able to assist him, Brooke asked, not entirely tongue-in-cheek, 'I suppose you don't know of any editor who requires occasional absolutely true & infinitely brilliant accounts of books & things, written by a man of immense learning?'[46]

The dismal thought of not seeing Brooke for some time prompted Marsh to propose to visit: 'I should like to know if it would be too exciting for you or too depressing (you can *think* whichever you like, but please *say* too exciting) if I came and put up at the Rugby Inn for a Sunday?'[47] Marsh visited Brooke on 23–24 March 1912, but by the end of April Brooke was back in Germany. He had gone to recover his health and equilibrium after suffering what some have described as a nervous breakdown. The decline in his mental and emotional health had been brought on by developments in his complicated love-life: his ardent advances had been rejected by Noel Olivier, and his relationship with Ka Cox had broken down after she had suffered a miscarriage. The absence from England also afforded him a break from his mother's cloying attention.

Throughout this time Marsh was kept busy by Churchill with frequent trips to naval bases around the country on the Admiralty's yacht, *Enchantress*. He was also mediating between Churchill and Admiral Lord Fisher, who was overseeing the expansion and modernisation of the Royal Navy. In addition he accompanied Churchill on a trip to Belfast in February 1912, occasioned by the growing controversy over the Irish Home Rule Bill. Even so, Rupert Brooke and poetry were never far from his mind.

While in Berlin Brooke composed what was to become one of his most famous and most loved poems, 'The Old Vicarage, Grantchester'.

At the end of May he wrote to Frances Cornford telling her about the poem: 'I scrawled in a Café a very long poem about Grantchester, that seemed to me to have pleasant silly passages. I sent it to the King's May week Magazine Basileon: so, if it got there in time, you may have seen it.'[48] Originally entitled 'The Sentimental Exile', was published in June 1912 in *Basileon*.[49] The poem expresses Brooke's romantic feelings towards nature and his longing for an idealised Neo-pagan existence. Towards the end of June Brooke spent his first night back in England with Marsh at Raymond Buildings so they could attend a London meeting of the Apostles the next day. Once back home in Grantchester he sent Marsh a copy of *Basileon*: 'Here's this hurried stuff [the poem]. Will you send it back to me sometime? It's my only copy.'[50] Marsh copied out the poem, returned the magazine, and was gushing in his response to Brooke: 'It's lovely, my dear, […] it's the most human thing you've written, the only one that has brought tears to my fine eyes. […] I showed it to my two old pundits, Gosse and Dobson. They were enraptured and begged me to assure you of their continued admiration.'[51]

Notwithstanding his rapturous response, Marsh was a critical copy-editor; he suggested a few changes that Brooke might make to improve the poem, and later convinced him to change the title from 'The Sentimental Exile' to 'The Old Vicarage, Grantchester'. In 1939, long after Brooke's death, Marsh was still waxing lyrical about the poem: 'I can't imagine a poem which would better combine "the moralizing, the pastoral-descriptive and the satirical poem" than *Grantchester*.'[52]

By August 1912 the spare room in Marsh's flat was now Rupert's room. In September 1912, having settled into his London pied-à-terre, Brooke introduced Marsh to his new acquaintances, the writers John Middleton Murry and Katherine Mansfield, who happened to be living nearby off Chancery Lane.

Middleton Murry and Mansfield were just two of many literary connections that Brooke and Marsh were to make at this time. With Brooke as the catalyst, a group of poets had begun to emerge giving rise to 'Georgian Poetry'.

Chapter Three

Becoming Georgians

John Middleton Murry and Katherine Mansfield were the editors of *Rhythm*, an avant-garde literary and arts review. They invited Brooke to contribute, and on his return from Germany in August 1912 he called on them in person. Murry later recalled how that led to an introduction to Marsh:

> The visit ended by his inviting us to lunch, somewhere in Soho. Eddie was there. We were at first distinctly shy of him: he was so immaculate, so aloof behind his enviable monocle, so evidently from another sphere, that it was with a shock of pleasant surprise that we discovered in him a bubbling spring of dry and delightful humour. […] we had enjoyed our lunch so well that we rather diffidently asked Eddie if he would care to come and see us. To our surprise, he evidently would, and he fixed the evening there and then.[1]

The friendship with Marsh was soon established, and both Brooke and Marsh were visitors to Murry and Mansfield's small cottage in Runcton, West Sussex. Murry described Marsh 'standing cheerfully and patiently under an old apple-tree while I stood on his shoulders to throw down the fruit to Katherine. He was so obviously not dressed for such an enterprise', and he went on to remark on 'the essential sweetness of the man'.[2] Marsh was a saviour to Murry and Mansfield, who were encumbered by mounting debts with no money to live on. Murry recalled, 'so far as substantial meals were concerned, we practically lived off Eddie':[3] he would invite them both to breakfast and lunch. Marsh followed this with a gift of £100 (around £9,000 in today's money) in order to help cover their debts and the cost of producing *Rhythm*. Years later Murry had further evidence of Marsh's 'essential sweetness' when in 1940 he wrote to him asking for his assistance in getting a Civil List pension. Marsh had not realised at first that it was Murry who had written the letter, signed simply as 'Jack'; but then he lobbied on his behalf, as Murry was in dire straits with 'four children to educate, & a serious illness – & hardly any money'. Marsh thought him a 'very strong case'.[4]

Through *Rhythm* Murry and Mansfield (Brooke nicknamed them 'the Tigers') had created a network of aspiring young poets. One of them, Wilfrid Gibson, had moved from his home in Hexham to London in order to make his way in the literary world. Murry and Mansfield introduced him to Marsh, who in turn introduced him to Brooke on 17 September 1912 when they went to fetch Gibson from his lodgings, 'to show him a spectacular fire which had broken out at Kings Cross'.[5] Together they watched the conflagration until it was under control then returned to Raymond Buildings to discuss poetry. Brooke told Frances Cornford, 'I've been meeting a lot of poets in London. They were so nice: very simple, and very goodhearted.'[6] He enthused, 'In them is more hope – more fulfilment – than in the old-world passion and mellifluous despair of any gentleman's or lady's poetry.'[7] This was the beginning of a devoted friendship between Brooke and Gibson, described by Marsh as 'wholesome and innocent and tweed-clad personalities'.[8]

The discussion that took place between Brooke and Marsh the day after the King's Cross fire was to be of great significance. It revolved around the question of how to persuade the public to take more interest in contemporary verse. Brooke had the idea of writing several poems, adopting different pseudonyms, and presenting them in an anthology of talented new poets. Marsh quickly dismissed Brooke's ruse, since talented new poets already existed within their circle. They acted promptly and invited Harold Monro to publish the anthology. Brooke was happy to contribute poems to the enterprise, but was not at all keen to compile the anthology. It fell to Marsh to take on the task of editor, though Brooke was not above kibitzing: 'I'll see you in the evening & at breakfast: & talk about the Georgian poets then. I find myself believing I can make a rival better selection from the same poets! Of course I can't set up to advise you; but I can taunt.'[9]

Marsh came up with a title: 'Georgian Poetry'. Brooke was not enthusiastic, but on this occasion Marsh prevailed. He later explained, 'My proud ambiguous adjective "Georgian" (which I had maintained against some opposition because it was the only way of marking my belief that a new era had begun – Eras are always christened after Sovereigns)'.[10] It was agreed to publish an edition of five hundred, with half the proceeds from sales going to the *Poetry Review* and the remainder to be distributed among the contributing poets. Marsh would not benefit financially: quite the reverse, he was to underwrite the entire project. His aim was 'to provide a means by which writers whose work seemed to me to be beautiful and neglected might find a hearing from the reading public'.[11] According to the poet Walter de la Mare,

> Poetry was his passion. [...] In September 1912 I had four letters
> from him in three days. Every one of them was aflame with
> enthusiasm over his new project – Georgian poetry: 'there's
> something I particularly want to talk to you about. I want to do
> something to make people realize the quality of the work being
> done nowadays in poetry. [...] I merely want to throw the poems
> hard at the public's head.'[12]

Marsh expressed his feelings rather more decorously in his preface to the first volume, *Georgian Poetry 1911–12*, which he wrote in October 1912:

> This volume is issued in the belief that English poetry is now once
> again putting on a new strength and beauty. Few readers have the
> leisure or the zeal to investigate each volume as it appears; and
> the process of recognition is often slow. This collection, drawn
> entirely from the publications of the past two years, may if it is
> fortunate help the lovers of poetry to realize that we are at the
> beginning of another 'Georgian period' which may take rank in
> due time with the several great poetic ages of the past.
>
> It has no pretension to cover the field. Every reader will notice
> the absence of poets whose work would be a necessary ornament
> of any anthology not limited by a definite aim. Two years ago
> some of the writers represented had published nothing; and
> only a very few of the others were known except to the eagerest

'watchers of the skies'. Those few are here because within the chosen period their work seemed to have gained some accession of power.[13]

Among the poets whose work appeared in this volume, in addition to Brooke, were Lascelles Abercrombie, W. H. Davies, Walter de la Mare, John Drinkwater, James Elroy Flecker, W. W. Gibson, D. H. Lawrence and John Masefield. They did not represent a literary movement as such, but within their work was a reaction against what had gone before. As Robert Ross said, 'In 1911 British poetry had almost no place to go but upwards.'[14] It was felt that poetry should be more vital, more true to life and more stimulating than in the Edwardian era, when dramatists and novelists had flourished but poetry had declined. There was a resurgence of interest in poetry among the reading public, and the Georgians were considered to be modern in their poetic realism. Ross observed: 'Brooke was perhaps the most significant single influence which led Georgian Poetry almost from the start to exploit one major phase of the poetic renaissance, the new realism.'[15] It was not 'modern' in the sense in which the poetry of Ezra Pound or T. S. Eliot is regarded as modern, as it focused on nature and retained an essentially pastoral, English quality. Among the younger Georgian poets a genuine coterie was formed, and the opening of Monro's Poetry Bookshop in December 1912 gave them a place to congregate.

Monro, like Marsh, wanted to popularise the work of up and coming poets. The premises, at 35 Devonshire Street in Bloomsbury, would provide not only a shop but lodgings, an office space for Monro's publication projects, and importantly a space for public poetry readings. Several poets lodged there, including Brooke's friend Wilfrid Gibson. Brooke gave the first public reading from his *Poems* at the official opening on 9 January 1913, after which he gave regular readings at the bookshop. He wrote to Noel Olivier on 12 February 1913, in whimsical vein, 'I gave a reading at the Poetry Bookshop, from the poets. Thousands of devout women were there, & some clergymen, perhaps I told you. An elderly American female cried slightly, & shook me by the hand for some minutes.'[16] Monro's friend the poet A. K.

Sabin recalled Brooke's performance as 'beautiful as an annunciating angel'.[17]

Brooke was just as eager as Monro and Marsh to promote 'Georgian Poetry'. He wrote at length to Marsh:

> When I lie awake o' nights – as I sometimes do – I plan advertisement for 'Georgian Poets'. I hope you're going to get it reviewed on the Continent. Certainly the *Nouvelle Revue Française* ought to be urged to write about it. Gosse could write a note to one of the people connected with the N.R.F. – he must know them all – to draw their attention to it. Or you could get at Coppeau, who's in London just now, through Roger Fry. Or I could get round at them through people I know. I expect there are one or two more French papers. I'll try to see if there are any German papers any good. I'll mention it in the paper I write for [the *Westminster Gazette*], if they'll admit me. I'm sure with a little pushing, a good hundred copies could be sold in Germany & France. I hope you're getting Gosse to do *The Times*, & Hewlett, & the others you spoke of – getting hold of Northcliffe, & so forth. […] You'll be able to found a Hostel for poor Georgians on the proceeds.[18]

Brooke wrote to Ka Cox to tell her about the publication: '*Georgian Poets* 3s. 6d. net ready in December. Brooke, Abercrombie, Masefield, Gibson, Chesterton, S. Moore, & the rest. He's [Marsh] really got too many rotters in. But we all think our fortunes will be made.'[19] Brooke was not far wrong. 'The sales of *Georgian Poetry* went astonishing well from the very first. […] Marsh estimated in 1939 that in the final reckoning *Georgian Poetry I* sold 15,000 copies.'[20]

Poetry had become a mainstay of Marsh's life, even to the extent that he said 'I really think if I were rich the very first thing I would do is to become a publisher.'[21] He told Brooke: 'Patrick [Shaw-Stewart] always laughs at me for finding a poet wherever I go' and Frieda Lawrence 'rather hurt my feelings by saying that she simply couldn't believe from my appearance that I cared for poetry!'[22] In Marsh's case appearance was clearly deceptive. Now, in his capacity as an editor of poetry, he engaged in debate with D. H. Lawrence concerning 'the formal deficiencies of his poems', and the outraged Lawrence described him as the 'policeman of poetry'.[23] Lawrence and his wife, Frieda, had been introduced to Marsh by Middleton Murry and Katherine Mansfield. Marsh wasted no time in promoting Lawrence. The writer Catherine Carswell, a contemporary and close friend of Lawrence, recalled: 'When Mr. "Eddie" Marsh, always on the spot when fresh genius was about, introduced Lawrence and Frieda to Herbert and Cynthia Asquith, and the Asquiths invited the Lawrences to Broadstairs, where Mr Marsh also was, Lawrence would have it that Murry and Katherine must come too.'[24]

Marsh certainly seemed to have a nose for 'fresh genius', and was determined to make useful introductions for his protégés.

During Brooke's sojourn in Berlin Marsh royally entertained the other poets in London. He wrote to Brooke on 29 November 1912 telling him he had met James Elroy Flecker and had seen John Masefield receive the Polignac prize (awarded by the Royal Society of Literature for Masefield's poem 'The Everlasting Mercy'). Finally, he recounted, 'I took Wilfrid [Gibson] and introduced him to Gosse, Hewlett, Newbolt, Sturge Moore, Masefield, de la Mare – I wonder if anyone had ever been introduced to so many poets at once.'[25] Marsh was clearly enthusiastic about his new friends, with the names of the London literati spilling on to the page, but he also wanted to let Brooke know exactly what he was missing during his absence from London.

Throughout the months that followed Brooke's return from Germany he and Marsh once again enjoyed a busy social life. There were countless dinners, visits to the theatre and music hall, exhibitions, and meetings with various poets and painters, including a visit to Ditchling to meet the sculptor and typographer Eric Gill,[26] who described them in his diary as 'Atheistical beggars'.[27] On 15 April 1913 Marsh and Brooke attended Violet Asquith's twenty-sixth birthday party at 10 Downing Street. She had first met Brooke at one of Marsh's supper parties at Raymond Buildings just before he had embarked on his journey to America and she recalled how they instantly "fell" into friendship.'[28] During this time Marsh also introduced Brooke to the actress Cathleen Nesbitt, who was to become a significant romantic interest in Brooke's life. In turn, Brooke introduced Marsh to a friend from his Rugby School and Cambridge days, the musician and composer William Denis Browne – a friendship that 'Marsh came to cherish second only to that with Brooke himself'.[29] According to Hassall, in Brooke's absence 'the friendship with Denis Browne had become more intimate. He had entertained Marsh in his lodgings' and 'whenever Brooke was away Browne was the evening companion, or they would form a trio in Soho restaurants or at the theatre'.[30]

Brooke also became more closely involved with his fellow Georgian poets Abercrombie, Drinkwater and Gibson, who had moved out to the Gloucester village of Dymock, and he joined in their scheme to publish a poetry periodical to be called *New Numbers*. Generously supportive as ever, Marsh agreed to guarantee the first two issues against financial loss.[31] Marsh ventured out to Dymock, and on 17 August 1913 he wrote to Brooke from the Abercrombies' cottage, 'The Gallows': 'Here I am at last, it's the most delicious little house, black and white, with a stone courtyard, and crimson ramblers, and low-beamed rooms. […] I've spent most of this morning […] cutting up French beans and peeling potatoes, I love domestic occupations.'[32] Marsh had no experience of domestic chores and he relished the novelty. Many years later in an article for *The Listener* Catherine Abercrombie remembered:

> Sir Edward Marsh was the good friend of us all, and a most delightful visitor he was. Though our cottage was of the most primitive, you would not have known from his manner that he was not in a stately home of England with servants and amenities galore. The only time he was at all put out was when several wasps attacked him in the bathroom, which was only a curtained-off recess by a huge chimney-stack in the courtyard – and he dared not flee from them until he had got his monocle firmly fixed in his eye and was able to find his clothes.[33]

Brooke was also affected by the bucolic existence in Dymock among the poets. When he visited the Gibsons and the Abercrombies in 1914 he enthused, 'Abercrombie's [cottage] is the most beautiful you can imagine: black-beamed & rose-covered. And a porch where one drinks great mugs of cider, & looks at fields of poppies in the corn. A life that makes London a very foolish affair.'[34] Brooke's words reflected his inner conflict between living close to nature barefoot in the Old Vicarage in Grantchester, and the necessity of being in London where he could make useful connections in order for his literary career to flourish.

At the end of May 1913 Brooke set off for New York as a correspondent for the *Westminster Gazette*, commissioned to write a series of travel articles based on his impressions of America. He was supremely confident of success, and told his mother, 'I have no fear about being able to make a living now, for there are so many papers that'll print anything by me whenever I like.'[35]

Meanwhile earlier in May Marsh found himself on board the *Enchantress* again for a month-long cruise in the Mediterranean combining work with play. Also on board, as well as Mr and Mrs Churchill, were Prime Minister Asquith, his wife and their daughter Violet. Card games were a particular favourite with Marsh, although he was an indifferent player. Violet described their nightly games of bridge when Marsh would be 'transformed', sitting 'erect with a square jaw and glittering eyes, holding his cards in trembling hands and breathing heavily. He took his own performance very seriously.'[36] His misfortune was to partner Churchill, who played a maverick version of the game. The serious purpose of the cruise was Churchill's meeting with Lord Kitchener in Malta in order to 'discuss the future balance of British sea-power between the Mediterranean and the North Sea'.[37] *The Times* reported that the purpose of the voyage was 'to make an official inspection of the naval establishments at Malta'.[38]

Marsh wrote to Brooke on 16 May when the *Enchantress* was anchored off Corfu, anxious that his letter should catch him before he departed for America: 'Do take care of your precious self and have a glorious time, to make up to me for your not being in England! and try not to stay away for too long. I shall feel the want of you.'[39] The cruise was, according to Marsh, 'a tremendous success', and he went on to describe the frantic social life he was leading.[40] He confessed, 'the small hours of Monday morning are the worst imaginable – I'm always dog-tired with tennis and drunk with champagne.'[41]

Marsh's workload at the Admiralty increased significantly as Britain continued to expand its Royal Navy in response to Kaiser Wilhelm II's rapid expansion of the German navy. 'Certainly there was plenty to do at the Admiralty, and I have never lived such a concentrated life […] We began the day about nine o'clock, and went on usually till one or two next morning.'[42] Marsh was also under pressure from Admiral Lord (Jackie) Fisher, who was as determined as Churchill to modernise the Royal Navy. Fisher wrote several letters to Marsh marked 'Secret & Private'; recognising that he was the trusted conduit to Churchill, he was eager to push forward the transition from a coal-powered to an oil-powered Navy.[43]

Between Brooke's departure for New York on 31 May 1913 and his return to England on 5 June 1914 he and Marsh corresponded regularly – or rather Marsh wrote frequently to Brooke, especially concerning the Georgian poets and the anthology. He also sent him what he considered to be the best of the latest novels, including D. H. Lawrence's *Sons and Lovers*, which he thought was a 'masterpiece'.[44]

On hearing that Brooke planned to lengthen his stay in America and to include a trip to the South Pacific islands, Marsh could not help expressing frustration at his extended absence: 'Have you any idea when you're coming back Rupert, it's really very serious. Your letters are very jolly but I do want to see you – and life is very short and quick, I shall be 41 next month – I hope you'll write some poetry in the South Seas.'[45] Later he wrote, 'I do miss you.'[46] Brooke, feeling guilty, confessed, 'I'm ashamed that I write so spasmodically. My way, I assure you. I write regularly to no one – not even my four young women.'[47] One letter that Marsh received from Brooke caused him a great deal of concern: in contrast to the self-possessed young man who had set off to America, he appeared vulnerable and seemed to be suffering a crisis of confidence about his ability as a poet: 'Plan out a life next year for me, Eddie, […] But my dear, I doubt if you'll have me. The Game is Up, Eddie. […] I tried to be a poet. And because I'm a clever writer, & because I was forty times as sensitive as anybody else – I succeeded a little. […] I'll never be able to write anything more, I think.'[48] Marsh was swift to encourage Brooke and allay his fears:

I just got your I suppose last letter from Tahiti announcing your complete change of character and our consequent probable incompatibility. God forbid, but I'm not much alarmed, from Gauguin-land what Avatar? I think I'm prepared to love you under whatever transformation. [...] You have achieved your instrument, and I expect a time will come when you will want to play on it again. It will be the bitterest disappointment of my life if you aren't 'among the English poets when you die' as Keats said. [...] I'm only afraid you will find *me* changed beyond bearing. I seem to myself to have grown terribly dull and unattractive lately.[49]

Prior to his imminent return to London, Brooke wrote to Marsh from New York: 'I got hundreds & hundreds of lovely letters yesterday, & most of them from you. Yours were all very nice to read.' He then went on to tell him, 'I can't sleep for thinking of England.'[50] Not for the first, or the last, time Brooke referred to England in his writing; it was not simply the country of his birth, but a recurring symbolic theme in his poetry, elemental and inextricable to his perception of himself, and what he believed he represented.

Brooke had considered turning up in London unannounced, but then thought better of it. He told Marsh, 'I've just cabled you, to find out if you *will* be in London then. For the agony of doubt conquered my deep and secret desire to wander in on you, all unexpected, one lovely June morning.'[51] Marsh, relieved and apprehensive, wrote to Brooke on 10 May: 'I should like to arrange for being here when you come – it seems much more than a year that you have been away. I shall be dreadfully shy and afraid of comparisons with cowboys and beachcombers, so you must make allowances at first.'[52] He went on, 'you mean to arrive like a thief in the night – make an exception for me. I won't tell anyone else – but it would be so disastrous if you came and I wasn't here, or couldn't give you a bed!'[53] Despite his diffidence, Marsh was thrilled at the prospect of Brooke's homecoming: 'It's splendid to think that you're really on the way back Rupert dear. I do long sometimes to see you. Every now and then it comes over me, how much more I should be enjoying everything if you were here.'[54]

Brooke was met from the train in the early hours of 6 June 1914 by a welcoming committee comprised of Marsh, Denis Browne and Cathleen Nesbitt; many years later she recalled the ever-attentive Marsh, 'looking for coffee for Denis Browne and me at Paddington station in the small hours of the morning of Rupert's return from America'.[55]

Marsh was elated to have his cherished protégé once more under his wing. He hosted a homecoming party for Brooke at which 'Hugh Walpole and Desmond MacCarthy were among those who stayed on late and watched Brooke demonstrating a Samoan *Siva-siva* dance under the sober plane-trees as dawn broke over Holborn.'[56] In tow with Marsh once again, another intense London social season began for Brooke comprised of dinners at Downing Street, plays, performances by the Russian Ballet, and more introductions to literary figures, including D. H. Lawrence, J. M. Barrie, George Bernard Shaw, Gerald du Maurier and Siegfried Sassoon. Despite the busy season a shadow loomed over the frivolity that summer as war with Germany threatened. The ominous entry in Marsh's engagement diary for 24 July 1914 read 'WAR CLOUD'.[57]

Chapter Four

The Soldier Poet

During August 1914 the partying stopped and Marsh was overwhelmingly preoccupied with Admiralty business. Brooke wrote to him on 2 August, 'I feel you're the one link I have with the heart of things at this bloody time. Send me a card, once, to say how things are.'[1]

At one of the many Downing Street dinner parties Marsh had introduced Brooke to Winston Churchill, who had offered to help him to a commission should the threatened war with Germany become a reality. Churchill was keen to create a new land force unit under the auspices of the Admiralty and under the command of Major-General Paris; subsequently the Royal Naval Division (RND) was formed from Royal Navy and Royal Marine reservists and volunteers. In tandem Churchill also established a flying combat unit, the Royal Naval Air Service (RNAS). Little wonder that Marsh was working flat out at the Admiralty.

Brooke wrote to his friend the painter Stanley Spencer on 31 July 1914 expressing his intention to get involved in the action: 'If fighting starts, I shall enlist, or go as a correspondent. I don't know. It will be Hell to be in it; and Hell to be out of it. At present I'm so depressed about the war, that I can't talk, think, or write coherently.'[2]

Brooke did not have long to wait. When German troops invaded Belgium in the summer of 1914 the British Government could not tolerate the violation of Belgian neutrality. Prime Minister Asquith's ultimatum to Germany to withdraw its forces from Belgium by midnight on 3 August was ignored, and on 4 August 1914 Britain declared war on Germany.

On 2 August 1914 Brooke had written to Marsh, 'Now the thing has really come, I feel as if I *can't* sit still. I feel I must go as a correspondent, if I can't as a fighter. Tell me if you hear of any jobs.'[3] Marsh told Brooke that he would recommend him and Denis Browne to Churchill for a place in the RND. His advocacy with Churchill, who in any case had already promised Brooke an appointment, was successful, and no official application or interview was required. Marsh wrote, 'I'm glad I could do it for you since you wanted it, but I feel I'm "giving of my dearest", as the newspapers say.'[4]

Brooke was commissioned on 14 September 1914. On 27 September Marsh waved Sub-Lieutenants Brooke and Browne, initially of the Anson Battalion, off from Charing Cross as they departed for the Kent coast. By 4 October the Ansons were en route to Antwerp. Brooke and his cohort were inexperienced, ill-equipped and hardly prepared for battle. H. H. Asquith, whose own son Arthur – 'Oc' – was with them, blamed Winston Churchill and vented his frustration at 'the *wicked* folly of it all' and described it as 'like sending sheep to the shambles'.[5] Antwerp fell to the Germans, and the British troops were ordered to withdraw. Marsh wrote to Brooke and Browne, 'I do trust you're coming back unscathed. I've been racked with anxiety all this week as you can imagine, and I haven't yet got any definite news of you two.'[6] On his return Brooke gave an evocative account of his experience as a witness to the dehumanising effect of war:

> I marched through Antwerp, deserted, shelled, and burning, one night, and saw ruined houses, dead men and horses: and railway-trains with their lines taken up and twisted and flung down as if a child had been playing with a toy. And the whole heaven and earth was lit up by the glare from the great lakes and rivers of burning petrol, hills and spires of flame. That was like Hell, a Dantesque Hell, terrible. But there – and later – I saw what was a truer Hell. Hundreds of thousands of refugees, their goods on barrows and hand-carts and perambulators and wagons, moving with infinite slowness out into the night, two unending lines of them, the old men mostly weeping, the women with hard white drawn faces, the children playing or crying or sleeping. That's what Belgium is now: the country where three civilians have been killed to every one soldier. [...] It's queer to think one has been a witness of one of the greatest crimes of history. Has ever a nation been treated like that? And how can such a stain be

wiped out? [...] But it's a bloody thing, half the youth of Europe blown through pain to nothingness, in the incessant mechanical slaughter of these modern battles. I can only marvel at human endurance.[7]

Brooke was palpably affected by what he had witnessed. It was as though he had now found a moral purpose in participating in the war: the feeling of patriotism, the notion of rectifying a moral wrong, combined with the prevailing sense of the period of 'manliness' and duty informed his view. He wrote to Cathleen Nesbitt: 'I'm rather disturbed, my dear one, about the way people in general don't realize we're at war. It's – even yet – such a picnic for us – for the nation – and so different for France and Belgium. The millions France is sacrificing to our thousands. I think – I *know* – that *everyone* ought to go in.'[8]

At this early stage of the war the general public and the generals (with the exception of Kitchener) believed that it would be over in a matter of months. The full impact of the horror of trench warfare which had begun with the first Battle of the Aisne in September 1914 when both sides began to construct trenches, and the subsequent Battle of Ypres in April–May 1915, had yet to reach home. Brooke's anger at the injustice and horror of the effects of war impelled him to act: 'now I've the feeling of anger at a seen wrong – Belgium – to make me happier and more resolved in my work. I know that whatever happens I'll be doing some good, fighting to prevent *that*.'[9]

In December, thanks to Marsh's influence, along with Arthur (Oc) Asquith, Patrick Shaw-Stewart, and eventually Denis Browne at Brooke's behest, Brooke was transferred to the RND Hood Battalion based in Blandford, Dorset. Marsh sent a telegram to Brooke informing him that 'All is changed again and you are all to go to Hood, which is splendid, it will be done a little gradually, but all will come right in the end.'[10]

Brooke was a socialist at heart. He firmly believed in the principles of liberty and equality of opportunity and wealth, and while based with the Hood Battalion at Blandford he 'tried to enlist Marsh in a campaign for getting an increase in pay for the lower ranks'.[11] Sadly there is no evidence to suggest that he was successful in this particular enterprise.

Early in December 1914 Brooke wrote to Marsh, 'I hear Winston's expected. *Insist* on coming with him.'[12] Naturally Marsh obliged. Violet Asquith, the Prime Minister's daughter, was also a visitor to the camp, wanting to see not only her brother but Brooke.

Eventually Brooke managed to get leave from the camp and stayed with Marsh in London, where he enjoyed the luxury of hot baths and the usual round of dinners and theatre trips. For brief spells they put Admiralty business and war to one side. They took in a performance of *Peg o' My Heart* starring Laurette Taylor, who never forgot Marsh and Brooke singing the title song together – a curious duet.

Notwithstanding his military preoccupations poetry was still at the forefront of Brooke's mind, and he contributed newly penned poems, his war sonnets, to *New Numbers*, published in January 1915. The last account of Brooke visiting the Poetry Bookshop around this time is by Harold Monro, who described him after the foray to Antwerp as sitting 'mostly on the corner of the table, in his new uniform, looking haggard and discouraged, and talking almost entirely about the war'[13] – a very different picture from the 'annunciating angel' of two years earlier.

On 28 February 1915 Brooke and the Hood Battalion set off for Gallipoli to assist in the bombardment of the Dardanelles, taking part in Churchill's ill-conceived campaign to join the Russians in fighting the Turks. The strategy was designed to overcome the stalemate on the Western Front by a gigantic flanking manoeuvre. Brooke told his mother about the mission:

> What follows is a dead secret (as is our day of starting). We
> are going to be part of a landing force to help the fleet
> break through the Hellespont and the Bosphorus and take
> Constantinople, and open up the Black Sea. It's going to be one
> of the important things of the war, if it comes off. We take 14–16
> days to get there. We shall be fighting for anything from 2 to 6
> weeks. And back (they reckon) in May. [...] At any rate, it will be
> much more glorious and less dangerous than France.[14]

If only Brooke's last sentence had proved to be true. Before the Hood's departure Marsh wrote to Patrick Shaw-Stewart, Denis Browne, and, most significantly, the following to Brooke:

> Denis promised to take care of you, and you must take care of him – I shall live in a shadow, Rupert, till I see you and him safe and well again – you know I'm glad and proud that you are going, and I don't think it's particularly dangerous as things go – but it's where you and he come in that I feel what the war can do to me as a person. I expect you know what you are to me – certainly the thing I'm most proud of.[15]

Prior to their departure for Gallipoli, Violet Asquith wrote in her diary: 'Poor little Eddie was heartbroken at losing the "Hood" – & a rather pathetic figure.'[16] Of all Brooke's friends and intimates, she was the only one who stood on the quayside at Avonmouth and waved him and her brother off on their expedition to Turkey. Another entry in her diary describes how shortly beforehand 'Rupert walked with me along the narrow crowded decks – down the little plank stairs – then I said goodbye to him. I knew by his eyes that *he* felt sure we should never see each other again. […] I saw Oc's [her brother's] face to the last – Rupert's not at all – I think he purposely stayed away.'[17] Brooke wrote to her on 8 March in a fatalistic mood: 'Do not care much what happens to me or what I do. When I give thought to it all, I hate people – people I like – to care for me. I'm selfish. And nothing but harm ever seems to have come of it, in the past. […] I think, there's bad luck about me.'[18]

The *Grantully Castle*, commandeered as a troop carrier, set off on its mission, stopping in Malta and then on to the Greek island of Lemnos. Although Brooke was suffering from seasickness, he still wrote fragments of poetry on the voyage. On 18 March they set off for the Dardanelles expecting to engage in military action. In the end they did not make a landing or see any action; unbeknown to them at the time they had taken part in a military ploy or manoeuvre. Much had to be reorganised in terms of the ship's armaments. They returned to Lemnos, then went on to Port Said in Egypt, where they set up camp. Officers were allowed brief leave in Cairo, but the conditions at the camp were dire and the British men were not equipped to deal with conditions so foreign to them. Brooke said, 'We ate sand and drank it, and breathed and thought and dreamed it. And above all a fierce torrid sun.'[19]

At this point Brooke suffered sunstroke and dysentery. He was also troubled by a small sore on his lip which was thought to be a mosquito bite. By 10 April he was back at sea and anchored once more at Lemnos. His health was fragile and he suffered headaches but managed to carry out light duties and participate in military exercises on shore. Meanwhile his lip had gradually become more swollen, and by 20 April he had a high fever and was suffering pain in his chest, back and head. The ship's doctors diagnosed acute blood-poisoning, and it was decided to transfer him to a nearby French hospital ship. He was escorted by the battalion's medical officer, Dr Schlesinger, and his friends and fellow officers Asquith and Browne. In the absence of modern-day antibiotics Brooke's condition worsened and he lapsed into unconsciousness; he died from septicaemia at 4.46 p.m. on 23 April 1915 – ironically, St George's Day. He was twenty-seven years old. Browne had kept vigil at his bedside throughout. Later he wrote to Marsh:

> I sat with Rupert. At 4 o'clock he became weaker, and at 4.46 he died, with the sun shining all round his cabin, and the cool sea-breeze blowing through the door and the shaded windows. No one could have wished for a quieter or a calmer end than in that lovely bay, shielded by the mountains and fragrant with sage and thyme.[20]

Brooke was buried later that day in an olive grove on the Greek island of Skyros. The burial party included Asquith, Browne and Shaw-Stewart. They lined his grave with branches of olive and sage, covered it with large white stones, and positioned two makeshift crosses. Within a few hours they were back on board the *Grantully Castle* heading for Gallipoli.

Chapter Five

'Rupert Brooke is dead'

Brooke's sonnet 'The Soldier'[1] was read out by Dean Inge from the pulpit of St Paul's Cathedral on Easter Day, 4 April 1915. A report on the sermon was printed in *The Times* the following day. Written in these early days of the war, the poem conveyed a feeling of courageous, passionate idealism; the beauty of sacrifice in dying for the country one loves; an innocent mood not yet obliterated by the brutality of trench warfare on the Western Front revealed in the later poems of Wilfred Owen and Siegfried Sassoon. It shows that 'the Georgians were the last of the Romantics, even in war. These poets, and the poems they wrote, could have no place in a post-war Modernist agenda.'[2] Lascelles Abercrombie later explained Brooke's attitude:

> the outbreak of war made him realise what England meant to
> him – not merely the idea of patriotism, and the culture and
> tradition of English nationality, but the actual physical fact
> of England, 'England's green and pleasant land'. This was in
> danger: this he must help to defend: this, in the intervals of
> military training, gave him the poetic theme he was looking for.
> Hence that note of welcome with which he accepted the War;
> that note to us, who lived through the war into its disillusion, the
> peace, may nowadays perhaps sound somewhat strangely.[3]

The poet and novelist Vera Brittain recalled in her memoir *Testament of Youth* how in 1915 her English tutor at Oxford

> showed us her latest acquisition from Blackwell's – the newly
> published first edition of Rupert Brooke's *1914*. Those famous
> sonnets, brought into prominence by the poet's death on the eve
> of the Dardanelles campaign, were then only just beginning to
> take the world's breath away […] For the young to whom Rupert
> Brooke's poems are now familiar as classics, it must be impossible

to imagine how it felt to hear them for the first time just after they were written. With my grief and anxiety then so new, I found the experience so moving that I should not have sought it had I realised how hard composure would be to maintain.[4]

But what of Marsh at this time? Burdened by his duties at the Admiralty, his faint hope that Brooke might have accepted an offer of a staff appointment, keeping him safe by avoiding the struggle in the Dardanelles, had been dashed by Brooke's solid refusal to leave his battalion. Early on 23 April 1915 Marsh had taken a telephone call from Churchill informing him that Brooke's condition was 'grave'. Weakened by dysentery and sunstroke, Brooke was losing his battle to fight off the septicaemia that had set in from the infected mosquito bite. Churchill asked Marsh to pass the news on to Brooke's mother, which he duly did. He also sent a telegram to Violet Asquith giving her the news of 'our beloved Rupert'.[5] A month later Marsh sent Violet another letter which contained a string of beads and Brooke's compass which he had asked Marsh to give her if he were killed.[6] Virginia Woolf reported to her sister, Vanessa Bell, that 'Violet Asquith says she loved him [Brooke] as she has never loved any man'.[7]

Marsh was desolate at the loss of Brooke. Years later he said, 'Rupert Brooke's death in April 1915 was the worst blow I have ever had, and it changed everything for me.'[8] Browne had written to Marsh about Brooke's death on 25 April, saying 'I thought you would care to have the facts as they happened' (see above, p. 47). Browne was dear to Marsh, being his companion and vicarious connection to Brooke during Brooke's absence on his travels in Germany and America. In June 1915 Marsh received another poignant letter which Browne had written in anticipation of his own death: 'My dear, I've gone now too; not too badly I hope. I'm luckier than Rupert, because I fought. But there's no one to bury me as I buried him, so perhaps he's better off in the long run. [...] Good-bye, my dear, & bless you always for all your goodness to me.'[9]

On 8 May 1915, while still fighting in the Dardanelles, Browne had been wounded in the neck and evacuated to Egypt to receive treatment and to recuperate. He returned to the fighting before he had fully recovered, and during the second battle of Krithia he was fatally shot in the shoulder and stomach on 7 June. He gave his wallet, containing the note for Marsh, to his fellow officer who was unable to save him. Browne was left on the battlefield, reported as 'wounded and missing', and his body was never found.[10]

Patrick Shaw-Stewart wrote to Marsh after Browne's death: 'I feel very much for you in this additional shock. You will feel you have put your friends into the Hood to be killed – but indeed this is a bloody campaign. […] That fourth of June was a fearful day – I don't suppose I ought to write it, but there is very little of us left, only 4 now.'[11] Reading these words, which articulated Marsh's part in their demise, was excruciating for him and only added to his burden of misery and guilt. His melancholy was exacerbated when the last letters he had written to Brooke and Browne were returned to him, neither of which had been read.

Churchill admired Rupert Brooke: Violet Asquith remembered that 'his imagination was caught by Rupert's eagerness and beauty and by his romantic sense of dedication'.[12] Churchill's eulogy appeared in *The Times* on 26 April 1915:

> Rupert Brooke is dead. […] The thoughts to which he gave
> expression in the very few incomparable war sonnets which he
> has left behind will be shared by many thousands of young men
> moving resolutely and blithely forward in this, the hardest, the
> cruelest, and the least-rewarded of all the wars that men have
> fought. They are a whole history and revelation of Rupert Brooke
> himself. Joyous, fearless, versatile, deeply instructed, with classic
> symmetry of mind and body, ruled by high undoubting purpose,
> he was all that one would wish England's noblest sons to be in the
> days when no sacrifice but the most precious is acceptable, and
> the most precious is that which is most freely proffered.[13]

The obituary, steeped in sentiment, along with Dean Inge's sermon, reached a wide audience; it captured the imagination of the general public with its rhetoric of idealism, patriotism and sacrifice, and provided the perfect instrument to convey the State's wartime propaganda. The canonisation of Brooke had begun. Violet Asquith wrote to Churchill the same day that the obituary appeared in the newspaper:

I must write to tell you how beautiful I thought your tribute to
our beloved Rupert in today's Times. All those who loved him
must be grateful to you for it. I feel heartbroken. He was the most
radiantly perfect human being I have ever known – so flawless
that one sometimes wondered whether he quite belonged to this
ragged scheme of things – whether he hadn't strayed here out of
some faery land. He obviously belonged to the 'pre-destined' – so
obviously that one could not but hope that even fate might shrink
from so cruel a platitude as his destruction. […] Poor Eddie – my
heart aches for him – his whole life pivoted on Rupert.[14]

Her sentimental tone and flowery language, typical of her class and
the Edwardian era, to a contemporary reader may seem exaggerated,
but her last remark concerning Marsh was not so far from the truth
of the matter: Marsh was an emotional man and his happiness, now
his unhappiness, certainly 'pivoted on Rupert'. An entry in her diary
describes Marsh as 'stricken' by the news and 'quite broken'.[15] James
Strachey, who had written to his friend the Cambridge mathematician
Harry Norton on 3 May 1915 about Brooke's death, observed, 'Poor
Eddie, whom I interviewed at the Admiralty the other day, seemed
almost done for.'[16]

Brooke's death affected many people. H. H. Asquith wrote:

I can't tell you what I feel about Rupert Brooke's death. It has
given me more pain than any loss in the war. We have seen a
great deal of him all this autumn and winter, he & Oc being
fellow officers, & the closest companions & friends. And Violet &
he had a real friendship – perhaps the germ at any rate […] of
something more. He was clean-cut & beautiful to look at, and had
a streak of something more than talent: his last Sonnets struck a
fine note.[17]

His wife Margot Asquith (Violet Asquith's stepmother) wrote in her
diary about Brooke on hearing of his death:

Hearing from Bongy [Maurice Bonham Carter, Violet's future
husband; they married in November 1915] that he was ill I sent
him a wire by Eddie Marsh in the afternoon 'My love thinking

of you', but he would never have got it. If one can dare say it, Rupert's death seems an awful, terrible waste! He had all the qualities I love – Goodness and real Temperament, Freshness, Candour and brains. He had charm and sympathy, immortal youth and no touch of that devastating cleverness that exorcises Holiness, dissects Love and despises God.

I took a copy of *New Numbers* with me for him to write my name in it the last time I saw him. He put his hands on my shoulders and looked at me with his beautiful eyes and kissed me in Oc's little wooden tent at Blandford on 26th Feb. 1915.[18]

The last publication of *New Numbers*, in December 1914, included Brooke's five war sonnets, written in November and December 1914. Catherine Abercrombie recalled, 'when Rupert died [...] we closed down the publication – it was too heartbreaking to go on without him.'[19] Wilfrid Gibson, also mourning the death of his friend, wrote the following poem:

To the Memory of Rupert Brooke 23rd April 1915
He's gone.
I do not understand.
I only know
That, as he turned to go
And waved his hand,
In his young eyes a sudden glory shone,
And I was dazzled by a sunset glow,
And he was gone.[20]

John Masefield, Lascelles Abercrombie and John Drinkwater were also inspired to compose poems in tribute to Brooke which they sent to Marsh. Even Duff Cooper was moved to pen a poem: 'Saw in the paper this morning that Rupert Brooke had died of sunstroke at Lemnos. Terribly sad. I knew him very little, but he was a very good poet and a very beautiful man. I wrote some verses and sent them to Eddie Marsh who was devoted to him.'[21]

Siegfried Sassoon sent his condolences to Marsh: 'I won't write anything about R. B. except that I know how much his loss means to you,

– (as indeed to us all).'[22] The French writer André Gide, who had met Brooke through Jacques and Gwen Raverat, wrote to Marsh following Brooke's death to discuss translating Brooke's war sonnets into French.

Bertrand Russell also had something to say about Brooke, though long after his death:

> On one occasion he [Professor Ralph Barton Perry of Harvard University] met, in my rooms, Rupert Brooke, of whom he had not heard. Rupert was on his way back from the South Sea Islands, and discoursed at length about the decay of manhood in these regions produced by the cessation of cannibalism. Professor Perry was pained, for is not cannibalism a sin? I have no doubt that when Rupert died, Professor Perry joined in his apotheosis, and I do not suppose he ever realized that the flippant young man he had met in my rooms was identical with the golden-haired god who had given his life for his country.[23]

Henry James had written a long letter of condolence to Marsh the day after Brooke's death:

> My dear dear Eddie. This is too horrible and heart-breaking. […] Why do I speak of my pang, as if it had a right to breathe in the presence of yours? […] I value extraordinarily having seen him here in the happiest way (in Downing Street, etc.) two or three times before he left England, and I measure by that the treasure of your own memories and the dead weight of your own loss. […] You won't have again any relation of that beauty, won't know again that mixture of the elements that made him. And he was the breathing beneficent man – and now turned to this! But there's something to keep too – his legend and his image will hold.[24]

Spurred on by James's words, Marsh, whose devotion to Brooke was undiminished by his passing, set about fulfilling his dream that Brooke should be remembered 'among the English poets' like Keats, Shelley and Byron.

In the event of his death, Brooke had instructed Marsh: 'You are to be my literary executor. But I'd like mother to have my MSS till she dies – the actual paper & ink I mean – then you.'[25] In many of his letters to various people Brooke referred to Marsh as being the person to deal with his literary affairs. But after Mrs Brooke's death in 1931 Brooke's wish was ignored, and Geoffrey Keynes was named as the literary trustee for the Rupert Brooke Estate together with Dudley Ward, Walter de la Mare and Jack Sheppard, then Provost of King's College, Cambridge. Marsh recalled in his memoir:

> when she died and her will was read, it was found that she had appointed three executors, of whom I was not one. […] She had only mentioned me to leave me *for my life* the manuscripts which Rupert had meant me to have, after her […] On my death they were to go to King's College, Cambridge […] I did not care to have them on these terms […] so I gave them straight to King's.[26]

Brooke had also asked Marsh to assist Dudley Ward in destroying correspondence relating to any of his love affairs of which his mother was unaware; what, if anything, was destroyed is unknown. Violet Asquith wrote to Mrs Brooke after his death and both Ka Cox and Cathleen Nesbitt were visitors. Marsh began the task of collecting and collating correspondence between Brooke and his circle.[27] He was operating under the assumption that he was indeed Brooke's literary executor, and began to write a memoir of Brooke as a preface to a collection of his poems. He was not prepared for the battle that ensued:

> When I sent her [Mrs Brooke] my manuscript, the storm broke. I had no business to write without consulting her. Rupert was hers, not mine, and it was outrageous that a single one among his friends, especially one of comparatively recent standing, should take on himself to determine the manner in which he should be presented to the world.[28]

When the painter Mark Gertler heard from Marsh about Mrs Brooke's reaction he guilelessly asked, 'I wonder why exactly Mrs Brooke objected to the memoirs being published?'[29]

The correspondence in 1915 between Brooke's friend Frances Cornford and Marsh reveals the protracted and tetchy negotiations between Mrs Brooke and himself. Cornford, who had become Mrs

Brooke's confidante in the matter, tried to explain to Marsh: 'I feel that in a way she understood Rupert in the roots of her heart more than any of us – Gwen & Jacques agree with me but I don't know if you would?'[30] Cornford tried to assuage the tension between the two of them; later she reflected upon how she endeavoured to 'mediate between this fantastically opposed couple, though I doubt if an archangel could have succeeded'.[31] Writing to console Marsh, she attempted to justify Mrs Brooke's response: 'I'm sure however deliberate & collected Mrs Brooke's letters seem that her nerves are really strained desperately. That state of nerves will make even gentle people – which she would never be – cruel. So once again you mustn't be miserable.'[32] Mrs Brooke's 'nerves' would also have been cruelly affected by the news that Rupert's younger brother, Alfred, who had enlisted with the Post Office Rifles, was killed in France on 14 June 1915, not two months after Rupert's death. But Marsh was not unsympathetic towards her. Frances Cornford reported that Mrs Brooke had greatly appreciated Marsh's kindness towards her immediately after Rupert's death, and quoted her:

> Eddie helped me unpack all Rupert's things when they came
> back from the Mediterranean. There were his books, and his
> clothes, and a lock of his hair. It was like seeing Rupert's body on
> the floor in front of me. And I will say that if Eddie had been my
> own son he could not have been more good to me.[33]

The main concern of Brooke's mother and his friends was reiterated by Cornford: 'The more you write yourself the more the memoir will be your picture.'[34] 'My criticism isn't new; I believe Katherine [Cox] felt & said almost the same thing, it is that only one side of R is represented so much more fully than the others.'[35]

The memoir and poems were finally published in April 1918. A review appeared in the *The Times Literary Supplement* on 8 August 1918, unsigned, but written by Virginia Woolf (as she admitted in a letter to Ka Cox). Virginia Woolf treasured her own memories of Brooke, and described him in a letter to his mother as 'a wonderful friend'.[36] She was five years older and recalled having spent childhood holidays in St Ives with the Brooke family; more recently, she had seen him in London and stayed with him in Grantchester. Privately she described the memoir as 'one of the most repulsive biographies I've ever read', though she went on to say, 'this of course is a little over-stated!'[37] However her review represented and made clear the views of Brooke's friends: 'It is inevitably incomplete, as Mr Marsh, we are sure, would be the first to agree, if for no other reason because it is the work of an older man. [...] The incomplete version which must in future represent Rupert Brooke to those who never knew him.' It ends with 'One turns from the thought of him not with a sense of completeness and finality, but rather to wonder and to question still: what would he have been, what would he have done?'[38]

Who can say what Brooke would have done? Perhaps, given the success of his *Letters from America*, he might have followed a career in journalism, or he might have published a novel. In the summer of 1919 in a shed in the garden at the Old Vicarage among dusty artefacts Marsh's young friend Lance Sieveking came across a pile of canvasses and 'a fat bundle of manuscript';[39] although tempted to take the paintings and the manuscript, he had left them there. By the time Dudley Ward had bought the house the shed and its contents had been destroyed, but Ward confirmed that Brooke had at one time been working on a novel.

Vera Brittain had thoughts similar to those of Virginia Woolf: 'How would Rupert Brooke have written, I wonder, had he lived until 1933? [...] Would he still have thought that Holiness and Nobleness and Honour described the causes for which those sacrifices of youth and work and immortality were offered?'[40] If Brooke had survived beyond the early days of the war it is probable that his poetry like that of his fellow Georgian poet Siegfried Sassoon would have reflected the disillusionment and pain that the First World War inflicted on his generation of young men. In June 1916 Sassoon had been awarded the Military Cross for gallantry in action; a year later, on 30 July 1917, his statement against the continuation of the war was read out in the House of Commons and published in *The Times*. Sassoon had sent copies of the statement to a select list of individuals who included Arnold Bennett,

Thomas Hardy, H.G. Wells, and Marsh. He believed that 'the war is being deliberately prolonged by those who have the power to end it. […] I believe that War, upon which I entered as a war of defence and liberation, has now become a war of aggression and conquest.'[41] Marsh responded swiftly: 'My dear Siegfried, Thank you very much for telling me what you have done. Of course I'm sorry about it, as you expect. As a non-combatant, I should have no sort of right to blame you, even if I wanted to. But I do think you are intellectually wrong – on the facts.' He went on to exhort him:

> But now my dear boy you have thrown your die, and it's too late to argue these points. One thing I do beg of you. Don't be more of a martyr than you can help! You have made your protest, and everyone who knows that you aren't the sort of fellow to do it for a stunt must profoundly admire your courage in doing it. But for God's sake stop there.[42]

Virginia Woolf wrote to Mrs Brooke following the publication of her review of Marsh's memoir:

> I am afraid that I gave the impression that I disliked Mr Marsh's memoir much more than I meant to. If I was at all disappointed it was that he gave of course rather his impression of Rupert than the impression which one had always had of him partly from the Stracheys & other friends, of his own age. But then Mr Marsh could not have done otherwise […] Rupert was so great a figure in his friends' eyes that no memoir could possibly be good enough.[43]

Virginia Woolf did not hold Marsh in high regard. It is clear that her antagonism towards him went beyond her reaction to his memoir of Brooke, as three years later she noted in her diary: 'We saw George Moore [the writer, not the philosopher] talking to Eddie Marsh, on some steps; a little obese, dim eyed, weak, inconsiderable.'[44] It is clear that she was talking about Marsh, not Moore. 'Poll' was Cambridge slang for a student who goes down with only a pass degree, i.e. without honours. Woolf's jibe was certainly not true of the scholarly Marsh.

Lady Ottoline Morrell was viciously critical of the memoir and of Marsh and his 'set':

> We have Rupert Brooke's memoir by E. M. and it is *sickening* – so sentimental and one-sided, only giving his own 'soppy' view of him – only as he was to that silly fashionable set – and never even a hint of the very interesting, complicated side of him. It is a cruel thing to be put on the screen for the world to see – E. M. as the photographer.[45]

Marsh's memoir was an unapologetic paean to Brooke. This was not surprising given his feelings for him: as he wrote to Denis Browne on hearing the news of Brooke's death, 'I feel that my whole plan of life has broken down – he was so bound up in nearly all the things I cared for – his friendship was the only thing that I was very proud of.'[46] And Cathleen Nesbitt described how tears were 'falling down his face while he selected some of Rupert's letters for his memoir'.[47]

Marsh's affection for Brooke had manifested itself in both public and very private ways. Geoffrey Keynes related how he had received a small brown paper package from Marsh's estate after his death in 1953 which contained Brooke's necktie. Marsh had slept with this small token of love placed under his pillow since Brooke's death. Keynes lacked Marsh's romantic attachment to his old schoolfriend and promptly burned the tie.[48]

Friendship is a constant theme in Marsh and Brooke's lives. Theirs was not a sexual relationship. Geoffrey Keynes said that Marsh 'had been deeply attached to Rupert, […] but lived himself in a sexual no-man's-land'.[49] Marsh was undoubtedly in love with Brooke; his friends were aware that he was 'devoted' to him. Meanwhile, Brooke fell in and out of love with women. One biographer claimed that 'Apart from the platonic relationship with Cathleen Nesbitt, later in 1912, all the young women who mattered to Rupert were kept secret from Eddie.'[50] That this is not true is evident in the correspondence between Brooke and Marsh. Marsh had introduced Brooke to Cathleen Nesbitt and she remembered him 'leaving us to ourselves with a little tour of the kitchen to show us where we could find the Earl Grey

Tea and Tiptree jam'.[51] But Marsh also introduced Brooke to Violet Asquith and Lady Eileen Wellesley; Brooke had a sexual relationship with the latter and Marsh's flat was the location for their trysts, as was also the case during his liaison with Phyllis Gardner. Years later Marsh reflected on Brooke's relationships with women:

> Rupert had a lot of 'inspirations' – first a bevy of Oliviers (whose house was the scene of *Dining Room Tea*) then Ka Cox, who married Will Arnold-Foster & died last year – I should have said she was the chief one till Cathleen Nesbitt came along – but P. G. [Phyllis Gardner] was certainly one of them.[52]

Although Marsh's love for Brooke was not reciprocated in the same way, Brooke valued his relationship with Marsh enormously – not simply because Marsh was able to use his influence and connections to further his ambition, but because Brooke placed great importance on friendship. He told Jacques Raverat, 'I know what things are good: friendship and work and conversation. [...] Friendship is always exciting and yet always safe. There is no lust in it, and therefore no poison.' He concluded the letter with an admonition: 'When you go through London, see that man [Marsh] – although Gwen's so bloody supercilious about him. It's eccentric, I admit, to conceal a good heart beneath good manners, but forgivable surely. And he'd love to see you. He's really so nice, and deserves well.'[53]

Both Jacques and Gwen Raverat were suspicious of Marsh since he was much older than Brooke and a member of establishment circles. According to one of Brooke's biographers, Jacques Raverat was 'fiercely homophobic'[54] and that may have accounted for his dislike of Marsh. Another biographer describes Marsh's 'epicene manner, monocle, and snobbish devotions' which made him an object of derision among Brooke's friends and goes on to say that Jacques Raverat called him 'a valet to his heroes'.[55] Even so, Brooke encouraged Marsh to purchase Gwen Raverat's woodcuts; while in Canada he had reminded him, 'Don't forget those woodcuts of Gwen's you were going to buy.'[56]

To many people Marsh and Brooke must have seemed like an odd couple. Phyllis Gardner reflected:

I never saw a worse-assorted pair. To this day, I cannot think how they managed to exist together at all; R[upert]with his wild golden hair and keen blue eyes and habit of going about in grey flannels and soft collars: Eddie with his man-of-the-world face and manners and his evident preoccupation with things of this life. They seemed to look upon one another with a sort of friendly amused toleration.[57]

Brooke's valuation of his friends was acknowledged by his mother, who wrote to Violet Asquith, 'Perhaps my Rupert has been spared much by going now. His tender heart would have been torn in pieces if he had seen his friends wounded or killed.'[58]

Stanley Spencer told Marsh that Brooke 'used to inspire me' and enthused, 'I think friendship is a wonderful thing […] the exact purpose of which is to cause one another to bring forth the joy of Heaven.'[59]

Marsh explained his own views on friendship to Walter de la Mare: 'The wish of my heart is to do anything I can to help my own personal friends, whose work is work that I care about.'[60] Although he did not consider himself to be particularly wealthy, he extended generous patronage to his poets, enabling them not only to achieve much more in literary terms but in some cases simply to survive. This was certainly true in the case of Rupert Brooke and the Georgian poets. While Brooke had initially given Marsh the vehicle of Georgian poetry, it was Marsh who drove it forward long after Brooke's death. Georgian poetry, easy to understand with its celebration of truth, beauty and moral innocence, was, according to the writer Penelope Fitzgerald, 'the last body of English poetry to be actually read by ordinary people, for pleasure'.[61] Its success was short-lived, since it became yet another casualty of the First World War. Young poets lost their lives and poetry lost its optimism. The optimism of Georgian poetry seemed inappropriate after the bleakness of war, and it was criticised for its escapism and lack of vigour. Even so at the outset it was deemed to be new and provided a literary stepping-stone to Modernism. Modernist writers such as T. S. Eliot followed on the coattails of Robert Graves, Siegfried Sassoon and D. H. Lawrence, all of whom had earlier been published in *Georgian Poetry*.

Frank Swinnerton later wrote of Marsh, 'He did more, from 1911 to 1922, to further the cause of modern poetry than any other man.'[62] Robert Graves commented, 'Poetry was not a game to him, or a field for exploitation; it was the source of deeply felt emotion.'[63] Marsh could be moved to tears by the beauty of an enigmatic line of poetry, and ever since he was first apprised of Brooke's ambition to be a poet, poetry and emotion were inseparable for him. Sadly, Marsh's desire to elevate Brooke's reputation as a poet did not always achieve a positive outcome, as poet and critic James Reeves aptly summed up:

> the idealistic raptures expected of [Brooke] held him back. Neither Marsh nor Brooke's older admirers, men like Gosse and Dobson, wholly accepted the 'unpleasant' element in Brooke, whose powers of self-criticism were somewhat blunted by his friend's easy praise. [...] Brooke was somewhat deflected from his purpose as a rebel by premature adulation, and his subsequent canonization entirely obscured the mixed and contradictory character of his real promise and achievement.[64]

Despite his noble intentions, Marsh's memoir of Brooke served to detract from the man and harmed his posthumous reputation as a poet. His endeavours to place Brooke the poet like the beautiful Greek god Apollo on a pedestal was too much for Brooke's contemporaries. Even in Brooke's lifetime the way others perceived him had been affected by Marsh's enthusiasm for him. Siegfried Sassoon recalled being introduced to Brooke: 'I was unprepared to find him more than moderately likeable. Eddie's adoring enthusiasm had put me somehow on the defensive. [...] From the first I got the impression that the great Rupert Brooke was quite a modest chap after all.'[65] Sir Alan Lascelles also recalled after Brooke's death, 'I wish I had known him. The only time I met him, I thought "here is another of Eddie's young Cleverclevers" and passed him by on the other side.'[66]

Paradoxically, Marsh's friendship and patronage of Brooke had bestowed a dubious legacy. Marsh had helped to ensure Brooke's place in history as a poet, but Brooke the person had been lost in the process of glorification. Until comparatively recently Marsh's memoir had set

in stone Brooke's saccharine mythical image. Marsh's view had suffered from bowdlerisation by interested parties, particularly Brooke's
mother. In a letter to Marsh Geoffrey Keynes illustrated the inherent
problems of reaching an objective view of Brooke, and described what
he eventually hoped for in terms of a record of Brooke's life:

> I liked very much hearing your memoir of Rupert which I think
> gives a very good picture of such parts of him as can be put in a
> memoir – at any rate according to his mother's standard by which
> anything the slightest bit 'shocking' has to be suppressed. And
> obviously a really true picture of Rupert would have to include
> lots of light hearted blasphemy and hard knocks all round. [...]
> But if this memoir is published I think a much amplified and
> quite unexpurgated version should exist in MS and be put aside
> for an indefinite number of years, to await the verdict of another
> generation which wouldn't feel the knocks or mind the supposed
> 'shockingness'. I feel rather acutely about this myself because I
> don't like the idea of too *mild* a Rupert being given irretrievably
> to a complacent world. This is not meant to imply an adverse
> criticism of your memoir, which, as I told you at the time is jolly
> well done; but I frightfully want it not to be final.[67]

Keynes later described Marsh's memoir of Brooke as an 'elegantly
written trifle', 'totally inadequate as a portrait of its subject'.[68] His wish
for an 'amplified' and 'unexpurgated' study of Brooke's life has since
been fulfilled by modern biographers. Ironically, though, Keynes and
his fellow trustees of the Brooke Estate authorised Christopher Hassall
to write a biography of Brooke published in 1964 which is hardly
an 'unexpurgated' account of Brooke's life. Noël Coward said that
he had read the book carefully and thought that 'He – the soldiers'
poet – emerges as a rather tiresome young man, too preoccupied with
being "open-air" and tramping through England's green and lovely
land. Unmistakeably a good poet. The book is too long and his letters
are also too long. A fascinating but curiously irritating character.'[69]
Undoubtedly Hassall's version of Brooke's life was influenced by his
own close friendship with Marsh; and certainly if Marsh had still been
alive in 1964 he would have challenged Coward's view.

The publication of Marsh's memoir of Brooke in 1918 had coincided with widespread disillusionment about the war intended to end war. The critics and the reading public eventually considered that Georgian poetry should be 'hushed in grim repose'.[70] While to a modern audience that embraced Eliot's *The Waste Land* Brooke's poems appeared too conventional or traditional, sales of his work continued to grow steadily. His poems are read by those who wish to connect with a romantic past and those who, whatever fashion in literature might dictate, appreciate his work for its sensuous, emotional and expressive language. Brooke's poems, particularly the war sonnets, are representative of their moment in time, written by a young man whose life was cut short at one of the most significant periods in British history.

Long after the publication of his memoir Marsh was concerned to promote Brooke's work and to protect his posthumous reputation. He was dismissive of Timothy Rogers, who edited collections of Brooke's writings and wrote about the Georgian poets: referring to Rogers' proposal for *A Richer Dust*, he commented 'I don't think it will be much of a book.'[71]

In 1947 Marsh was contacted by Maurice Browne, who with his wife had founded the Chicago Little Theatre and who had been met by Brooke on his trip to America. Shortly after Brooke's death, in November 1915 Browne had staged a production in Chicago of Brooke's play *Lithuania*, but the reason for his letter was that he had become aware of a rumour circulating in the USA that Brooke was a homosexual and his death was caused by syphilis. Marsh referred the enquiry to Geoffrey Keynes, who firmly negated the claims, but before doing so he replied to Browne:

> let me say most positively that during all the years when I knew
> him I never saw the slightest reason for thinking that he had a
> 'homosexual streak'. I can't of course answer for him as a school-
> boy, but there is nothing I am more certain of than that if he ever
> had one he had completely outgrown it by the time I got to know
> him. Moreover the only time I ever saw or heard it suggested was
> in a review in some yellow rag or other which turned out to have

> based itself on the phrase in *The Great Lover* about 'the rough
> male kiss of blankets'![72]

Marsh appears to concede that Brooke may have had homosexual
encounters as a schoolboy (which Brooke admitted in his letters to
James Strachey); however, he was steadfast in refuting the rumour that
Brooke was homosexual and was adamant that he did not die from a
syphilitic infection. He went on to remark: 'I am still old-fashioned
enough to think that even geniuses have a right to a reasonable privacy
about their sexual affairs, though I recognize that there is a case for
the contrary.'[73] His comment is as relevant today as in 1947.

Marsh's objections to inferences of homosexuality concerning
Brooke arose again in 1952 when Patric Dickinson's *Apollo's Laurel
Bough: A Sketch of Rupert Brooke* was broadcast on the BBC's Third
Programme. After listening to the broadcast Marsh wrote to Dickinson complaining about the 'tiresome contemporary penchant for
finding homosexualism everywhere'. Dickinson was forthright in his
rebuttal:

> My dear Eddy, simple heterosexuals like my humble self don't
> have to look very far, or hard, in the world of the Arts. It *is*
> everywhere, […] I daresay the present state of intellectual society
> caused me to over-brutalise the case […] the fact is, that very
> many people believe Brooke to have been homosexual and I took
> the most obvious and empathetic way of saying he was NOT. […]
> my only object in writing such scripts is to try and discover the
> truth. Do you think – and most of it was Brooke's own words –
> that my script was untruthful? If it was I am deeply sorry. If it was
> not, I feel I have made a contribution towards understanding a
> remarkable person who is, very largely, misunderstood.[74]

Brooke was indeed 'a remarkable person', and perhaps Marsh would
have had to accept some criticism and responsibility for his being 'very
largely, misunderstood.' Misunderstood or not, Brooke's relationship
with Marsh and the Georgian poets more widely clearly demonstrated
the immense value of friendship and patronage to impecunious
writers.

Brooke would rather have had a subsidy from the state than be indebted to a patron (albeit an enlightened one), true to his Fabian principles and his plea 'we must provide for Art'. The paper that he read to the Fabian Society in Cambridge around 1909, *Democracy and the Arts*, was essentially a blueprint for the Committee for the Encouragement of Music and the Arts (CEMA) that Maynard Keynes chaired in 1941, and was reconfigured in 1946 as the Arts Council. But he himself provided philanthropic care. His will ensured financial security for the less well-off among his fellow Georgians: Lascelles Abercrombie, Wilfrid Gibson and Walter de la Mare received the royalties from the sales of *Poems*. He had said, 'If I can set them free [...] to write the poems and plays and books they want to, my death will be more gain than loss.'[75]

Marsh emphatically disagreed that Brooke's death could ever be more gain than loss, but he was keen that young poets would be encouraged and stimulated by Brooke's legacy to do their 'best in poetry'. With that in mind he made use of his 'Rupert money', the royalties accrued from his memoir of Brooke, to help other young poets such as Robert Graves and his friend Edmund Blunden. Blunden had also been published in the *Georgian Poetry* series. Marsh insisted on giving him money: 'I should want you to look upon the help as coming from R.B. and not from me personally, and needless to say it would be quite between ourselves.'[76]

But it was not only poets whom Marsh was keen to promote and assist. Another group of creative young men also benefited from Marsh's patronage: he was to become the saviour of several emerging painters making their way in the precarious world of contemporary art.

THE PAINTERS

Chapter Six

The Conversion

Throughout his intense friendship with Brooke and his involvement with the Georgian poets, Marsh was also a significant patron of the young British artists of his day – '*les jeunes*', as they were called by the artist and critic Roger Fry. In addition to his love of poets and poetry, picture buying was one of his 'principal delights'.[1] Marsh's influence on and contribution to British art culminated after his death in January 1953 in the bequest of his prestigious collection of paintings to the Contemporary Art Society;[2] it was a substantial gift to the nation, and the pictures now hang in our public galleries such as Tate Britain.

In May 1953 the Contemporary Art Society published *Sketches for a Composite Literary Portrait of Sir Edward Marsh*, a compilation of tributes from Marsh's friends and representatives from the arts. The booklet was produced to accompany a memorial exhibition of some of the pictures which formed part of his bequest; they included works by Christopher Wood, Duncan Grant, Mark Gertler, Henry Moore and Augustus John. However, the story that led to this valuable and generous gift began many years earlier.

While still an undergraduate at Cambridge Marsh had been introduced to the freshman Victor Bulmer-Lytton, 2nd Earl of Lytton, and his younger brother, Neville. The three of them were to become dear friends. (Quite how dear one can only imagine, as Pamela Lytton, Victor's widow, was not happy to have the 'early boyish letters' of Eddie to Victor published.[3]) Marsh spent considerable time over many years at Knebworth with the Lytton family. Most significantly, it was Neville Lytton who changed Marsh's life by putting it into his head to collect paintings. Prior to that, Marsh confessed, 'if I went to an exhibition of pictures, it no more occurred to me to buy one than it occurred to me to buy a monkey if I went to the zoo.'[4]

Neville Lytton, unlike his brother Victor, had declined the academic route of university; he showed promise as a painter and embarked on an artistic career instead. He went on to Paris where he studied at the Ecole des Beaux Arts with Léon Bonnat. After leaving Cambridge Marsh often stayed with him in Paris, enjoying a holiday from his duties at Whitehall. They became close companions; 'Neville was ever-lastingly grateful to Eddie for reading aloud to him long hours whilst he painted – he said it made a great contribution to his own literary education.'[5]

Neville invited Marsh to be best man at his wedding to Judith Blunt, daughter of the poet Wilfrid Scawen Blunt and Lady Anne, Baroness Wentworth, which took place in Cairo on 2 February 1899, but it coincided with Marsh's sister's wedding in London, so he was unable to accept. Marsh fostered a friendship with Judith too; she became 'a cherished acquisition in his life',[6] and he wrote to them both regularly. Perhaps Marsh felt that being close to Judith helped to cement his relationship with Neville Lytton. Whether he was aware of the strain that existed between the two from the outset of their relationship is not clear, nor is it clear whether Marsh contributed to that tension.

In 1887, at the age of twenty-five, Judith had fallen in love with Victor Lytton, who despite their having spent time together during the Cambridge May Week in 'blissful solitude'[7] did not propose to her. She believed she was lucky with horses and unlucky in love, but she did not lack marriage proposals. Victor's brother Neville, who was six years her junior, had fallen madly in love with her and was persistent in his passion. In the end Judith, whose resolve was weakened by his tearful entreaties, and pressure from her parents who wanted her married off, capitulated. She did not love Neville. She broke off their engagement twice, and on the eve of their wedding wrote poignantly in her diary 'Goodnight to my Dreams.'[8] They went on to have three children, but divorced in 1923, after which Judith was estranged from her husband and from her children.

Shortly after the Lyttons' wedding Marsh took rooms with them at their London *pied-à-terre*, 3 Gray's Inn Place. He also spent most weekends with the couple at their home in Surrey. The three of them welcomed the dawn of the twentieth century together at a New Year's Eve dinner hosted by Marsh's father. Marsh lived with the Lyttons until early in 1903, when he moved into his own home nearby. Years later, when Christopher Hassall was writing his biography of Marsh, Judith – who had inherited the title Lady Wentworth in 1917 – told him that Marsh's letters to Neville were 'ardent and enthusiastic' and 'mostly of too intimate a nature for publication'.[9] Shortly before her death in 1957 she said of Marsh, 'He worshipped N [Neville] with an almost unbelievable extravagance of devotion as an idol of his own creation which he assumed could not best be shared by me.'[10]

Marsh and Lytton would scour the London galleries and art sales together looking for English Old Masters. Lytton favoured watercolour painting and the English tradition typified by the works of Cotman, Cozens and Girtin, even though these artists were deeply unfashionable at the time. Marsh's first purchase was a Thomas Girtin watercolour; that was followed by his acquisition of Herbert Horne's collection of two hundred drawings by English School luminaries including William Blake, George Romney and Thomas Gainsborough.

It was not as if Marsh could afford to indulge in such an expensive pastime solely on his Civil Service salary. After the assassination of his maternal great-grandfather, Prime Minister Spencer Perceval, in 1812, a grant of £50,000 (around £2.8 million in today's money) had been settled by the Government to benefit the Perceval family, and after his mother died in 1896 he intermittently received annuities from what he referred to as the 'murder money'. He confessed, 'It never seemed quite large enough to be worth investing in those tedious belongings stocks and shares; and I usually blued it on a picture.'[11]

A fervent admirer of Marsh's collection was the young French sculptor Henri Gaudier-Brzeska; they had been introduced by their mutual acquaintances John Middleton Murry and the poet and critic

T. E. Hulme. Henri wrote to his lover Sophie Brzeska on 14 November 1912: 'I called on Marsh last night, and there saw the most magnificent examples of Girtin's work – it impressed me immensely, and Constable and Turner and Cotman – in fact, all the best 18th to 19th century English landscape. I am still enchanted with it all.'[12]

Marsh went on to collect oil paintings too, a particular treasure being *Llyn-y-Cau, Cader Idris* by the eighteenth-century Welsh painter Richard Wilson. Diana Mosley reminisced, 'I loved being invited to luncheon with him in his flat at Gray's Inn. The walls and even the doors were stuck all over with pictures and drawings. He showed me the first picture he ever bought, a landscape by Richard Wilson; for the most part his collection was by living English painters.'[13] When Kenneth Clark, Director of the National Gallery, told Marsh that the Trustees wished to secure this painting as part of its collection, he altered his Will accordingly. (It is now in Tate Britain.)

However, Marsh's desire to acquire Old Master paintings came to a halt, much to Lytton's dismay, when he 'experienced Conversion'.

> Buying Old Masters in shops began to seem a sheeplike, soulless conventionalism. How much more exciting to back what might be roughly called one's own judgement, […] to go to the studios and the little galleries, and purchase, wet from the brush, the possible masterpieces of the possible Masters of the future! Besides, to buy an old picture did nobody any good except the dealer; whereas to buy a new one gave pleasure, encouragement and help to a man of talent, perhaps of genius.[14]

Lytton was not the only person who took a dim view of Marsh's change in taste from Old Masters in favour of contemporary art. His housekeeper, Mrs Elgy, greeted each new acquisition 'with some genial or downright disparaging remark […] or howls of derisive laughter'.[15] Her bedroom walls were completely covered with pictures from his collection and she would conveniently drape her dresses over them, much to his vexation. Marsh was undeterred, and having already bought an example of Roger Fry's work from his London exhibition in 1903 he went on to purchase one of Duncan Grant's early paintings,

Parrot Tulips, from an exhibition by young painters at the Carfax Gallery in 1911.

Marsh's epiphany caused an acrimonious split in his friendship with Neville Lytton. Their divergence of artistic appreciation was sealed when Lytton damned *Parrot Tulips* as 'a disgraceful picture'.[16] He further criticised Marsh as 'the kind of person who might easily come to have an influence on young artists, and it was deplorable that [he] should give [his] countenance to such a slovenly piece of work'.[17] Years later their opposition was still apparent. In a letter dated 15 December 1945 Lytton congratulates the painter Philip Connard on being appointed Keeper of the Royal Academy Schools and hopes he will have 'a powerful and beneficial influence on this post-war youth, [...] to counteract the influence of the false shepherds – the Kenneth Clarks, the Eddie Marshs'.[18]

Marsh's preference for contemporary art might also explain why his meeting in 1901 with Bernard Berenson, the preeminent authority on Renaissance painting and owner of the Villa I Tatti in Florence, did not develop into a friendship. They had acquaintances in common, not least Kenneth Clark, and both were collectors of art, but Berenson had a marked distaste for modern art.

According to John Middleton Murry, Marsh himself occasionally suffered doubts concerning his latest purchase. 'Every week almost he had a new picture in his breakfast room, and he was always saying: "and now I'm not quite sure whether I really like it. But I certainly did when I bought it. Perhaps I am safer with old English watercolours."'[19]

One contemporary watercolour in his collection, which he described as 'one of my treasures',[20] was a cartoon by Max Beerbohm painted while Marsh was working with Winston Churchill at the Board of Trade. Marsh is portrayed standing by the door wearing his signature monocle and holding his briefcase. Marsh and Churchill were immortalised by Beerbohm again in *A Study in Dubiety*, which appeared as the frontispiece of the *Blue Review* (a short-lived literary magazine run by John Middleton Murry and funded by Eddie Marsh) in July 1913. Marsh contributed an essay on Beerbohm's parody and caricature to that edition.

Marsh and Churchill were both interested in painting, but, as with Neville Lytton, they did not always see eye to eye. Diana Mosley remembered 'Winston Churchill inveighing against a large picture by Stanley Spencer of Cookham war memorial which hung on the staircase [at the Mosleys', 96 Cheyne Walk], and Eddie Marsh defending it against his onslaught'.[21] They did however agree upon the merits of Walter Sickert. Sickert was recognised as an important artist in his own lifetime, and since his death has been acknowledged as one of the most influential figures in twentieth-century British art.

Marsh had met Sickert's younger brother, Oswald, while still an undergraduate. Oswald was in the year above him, and he found him 'the gentlest being I have known'.[22] Oswald Sickert 'attracted to Cambridge the exotic and charming figure of the French painter, Auguste Bréal'[23] and, more significantly for Marsh, he also introduced him to his brother, Walter. The Café Royal in London was a popular Bohemian haunt for artists, and after lunching there with the Sickert brothers in April 1892 Marsh was taken to Walter's studio where he had his first encounter with a Sickert painting in progress. He was impressed with Walter, who was then 'in the fine dandy flush of his elegant and witty prime, and full of Anecdotes of Painting'.[24] He had a mischievous sense of humour. At a private view at the Leicester Galleries he introduced Marsh to an American couple, cheerfully regaling them with 'I want you to know Eddie Marsh – I was madly in love with him when he was a choir-boy.'[25] Marsh was thoroughly embarrassed. Marsh and Walter Sickert remained friends, not least through their shared connection to Winston Churchill. Sickert gave Churchill, a keen amateur, painting lessons, and in 1927 painted his portrait. Unfortunately Churchill was not taken with his teacher's effort, and gave the portrait away.[26]

Marsh had two of Sickert's pictures in his collection which he lovingly described:

The New Bedford, a masterpiece of his early period, and the recent *Her Majesty's*, a heavenly vision of sky-blue and honey-colour which is to me the loveliest of the discoveries made by that wonderful veteran on the new leaf which he turned over a few years ago. It is a weakness of mine, I hope an amiable one, to think my specimens the best of their maker's handiwork.[27]

Notwithstanding his obvious pride in owning two of Sickert's paintings, after the artist's death in 1942 Marsh rather dismissively wrote, 'I'm in the middle of [reading] the life of Walter Sickert (I'm sorry he has left us, but I don't suppose he would have *done* much more).'[28]

But true to form Marsh had helped Sickert with an anonymous benefaction when, despite the success of his exhibitions, he had found himself impecunious. In 1934 Sickert was approaching his seventy-fourth birthday and was far from well when Marsh received a letter from Sickert's friend Sir Alec Martin, Director of Christie's, who was concerned about his 'serious, almost desperate, financial position'; things were so bad that he would 'be forced into immediate bankruptcy'. Martin and a group of friends who included Gerald Kelly, Sylvia Gosse, John Cooper, Professor Henry Tonks and Sir William Llewellyn PRA had formed a committee 'to raise a substantial sum, such as will enable Mr Sickert to continue his work which he cannot do at present harassed as he is by many creditors'.[29] Marsh alerted Churchill immediately: 'Have you heard of Walter Sickert's desperate position? I'm afraid he has been very improvident, thinking when he had a good break that it would last for ever. But he's a great artist, & must be forgiven. [...] I hate to bother you, but I'm obliged to do what I can for the old boy.'[30]

Churchill, who was 'very grieved to hear of his plight', responded to Marsh's plea with 'A thousand thanks. It is absolutely okay' and donated a cheque for £10 to the Walter Sickert Fund.[31] Sickert's debts were settled and he regularly drew on the fund. By the summer of 1939 some £200 were left in reserve (around £10,500 in today's money). At this point Sir Alec decided to lobby the Prime Minister's office to give Sickert a Civil List Pension. Supported by Gerald Kelly and Kenneth Clark, the application overcame initial resistance, and in March 1940 'Sickert was granted a pension of £170 per annum, payable – on Kelly's advice – in quarterly instalments'; as Sickert's biographer, Matthew Sturgis, points out, it was 'a godsend as well as an honour'.[32] Even with

Eddie Marsh at
Cambridge by Hollyer

Rupert Brooke

Eddie Marsh with Winston Churchill on a visit to Africa in 1907

Eddie Marsh and Winston Churchill, 1907

Royal Naval Division poster

Rupert Brooke in uniform,
Blandford, 1914

C

Violet Asquith, aged 19

Siegfried Sassoon by
Glyn Warren Philpot,
1917

D

Grave of Rupert Brooke

The Honourable Neville
Lytton, photograph by
Frederick Hollyer, 1893

Draughting a Bill at the Board of Trade, cartoon by Max Beerbohm, Winston Churchill with Eddie Marsh in the doorway, 1909

A Study in Dubiety   Max Beerbohm
    Mr. Edward Marsh wondering whether he dare ask his Chief's
leave to include in his anthology of " Georgian Poetry " Mr.
George Wyndham's famous and lovely poem : " We want eight
            and we won't wait."

A Study in Dubiety by Max Beerbohm, *c*.1913

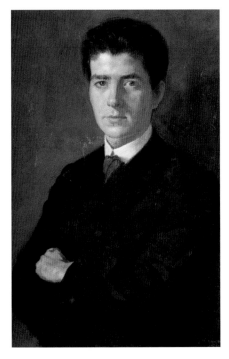

John Currie, *Self-portrait*, 1905

John Currie, *Mark Gertler*, 1913

the additional income, Sickert's financial situation remained precarious; 'Winston Churchill, who had become Prime Minister in 1940, was anxious to help his friend and arranged for the Civil List Pension to be supplemented from the Royal Bounty Fund.'[33]

Churchill and Marsh were pleased to help Sickert towards the end of his life, but Marsh was far better known for his effect on the lives of young artists at the beginning of their careers.

Chapter Seven

Les Jeunes and 'the Lust of Possession'

Through the art dealer Robert Ross of the Carfax Gallery Marsh had begun to make friends with a handful of young artists, 'boys as they were then',[1] all of whom were students of the Slade School of Fine Art under the auspices of Henry Tonks. This group included Stanley Spencer, John Currie and Mark Gertler. These Slade artists, like many of their friends and contemporaries, rebelled against the conservatism and ideology of the Victorian and Edwardian eras. Leading Bohemian lives – a euphemism for poverty in most cases – they embraced new movements in art: they associated with the Bloomsbury Group, became Neo-Primitives, Neo-Pagans, Futurists or Vorticists. The avant-garde confronted societal norms and social order. Marsh, the monocle-wearing, responsible civil servant and the ultimate establishment figure, seems an unlikely ambassador of these artistic movements; but he had found an attractive incentive for wanting to engage with contemporary art in the new age.

Marsh had met John Currie at one of the occasional *Rhythm* magazine dinners hosted by John Middleton Murry. Currie, a boy from the Staffordshire Potteries, had attended the Hanley School of Art and been employed painting ceramics, when his fellow 'Potteries' man, the celebrated novelist Arnold Bennett, encouraged him to go to London, where in 1905 he attended the Royal College of Art. Bennett had bought Currie's work; Currie's painting *Penkhull* used to hang in the dining room in his country house, 'Comarques'. After time spent in Bristol and Dublin Currie moved to London, where in the summer of 1910 he briefly attended the Slade School of Art. There he became firm friends with Mark Gertler, who was seven years his junior.

Gertler was the youngest son of a Jewish immigrant family living shoulder to shoulder in poverty in London's East End. His father, Louis, was a furrier by trade, and his mother, Golda, was the lynchpin of the family. Like the relationships Marsh and Rupert Brooke had with their mothers, Mark was Golda's darling boy. He had shown an aptitude for drawing at an early age, and after leaving school at fourteen obtained a place at the Regent Street Polytechnic where he began his formal training as an artist. He was later taken under the wing of the prominent Jewish artist William Rothenstein, who recommended him to the Slade School where he himself had been a student. Gertler's fees were paid by the Jewish Education Aid Society, and on 13 October 1908 he enrolled at the Slade – 'the first working-class Jewish student of his generation to do so'.[2] Gertler's life would be transformed by his experience at the Slade and the changes taking place in the British contemporary art scene.

In 1910 Roger Fry's exhibition *Manet and the Post-Impressionists* had caused a furore. The critical response ranged from outrage to ridicule. However for Gertler and his Slade contemporaries it was a revelation. These young artists became conscious of 'a sudden liberation and encouragement to feel for oneself'.[3] The democratisation of art had begun in earnest.

Marsh was introduced to Gertler in 1913 by Currie and Gaudier-Brzeska at an Allied Artists' Association exhibition in the Royal Albert Hall.[4] The Association had been formed in 1908 as a platform for modernist art to 'enable artists to submit their work freely to the judgement of the public without the intervention of any middleman, be he dealer or artist also'.[5] It was based on cooperation between artists rather than competition, and each artist was permitted to exhibit three works.

Marsh was very taken with Gertler on their first encounter, describing him as 'a beautiful little Jew like a Lippo Lippi cherub'.[6] Not for the first time, he was bowled over by youthful masculine beauty. Shortly afterwards he hosted a 'delightful' dinner at his home to which Gertler and Currie, and Currie's mistress, 'an extremely pretty Irish girl with red hair called Dolly Henry', were invited.[7] A few weeks later Marsh again wrote in effusive terms to Rupert Brooke:

> I have conceived a passion for both him [Currie] and Gertler,
> they are decidedly two of the most interesting of *les jeunes*, and I

can hardly wait till you come back to make their acquaintance. Gertler is by birth an absolute little East End Jew. […] I am going to see him in Bishopsgate and be initiated into the Ghetto. He is rather beautiful, and has a funny little shiny black fringe, his mind is deep and simple, and I think he's got the *feu sacré*. He's only 22 – Currie I think a little older, and his pictures proportionately better, he can do what he wants, which Gertler can't quite yet, I think – but he will.[8]

Marsh was impressed not only by Gertler's good looks but also by his potential as an artist. At this time in his life Marsh himself was deemed to be an attractive man. Paul Nash, another of Marsh's young protégé painters, observed,

there was something equine about Eddie in a mettlesome sort of way. Not that he was the least horse-like in features, but he had a certain way of rearing his handsome head, up and across to one side, that was reminiscent. He had very fine eyes crowned by remarkable branching eyebrows, one of which curled round a bright monocle. It was the best combination of eye-brow and eye-glass I had seen. His other most eloquent feature were his hands. Unlike the average Englishman he used his hands in conversation.[9]

At first Gertler was apprehensive about his budding friendship with Marsh, and in a letter to his friend and fellow Slade student Dorothy Brett he wrote, 'He is a very nice man, but I am afraid he likes me, more than my work.'[10] Gertler's instinct was not wrong. Marsh the 'unobtrusive homosexual'[11] could not resist a pretty face; but Marsh was content to be in the company of these men without the need of a sexual relationship. Perhaps Marsh agreed with his friend T. E. Lawrence, who told him after reading D. H. Lawrence's *Lady Chatterley's Lover* which had been lent to him by Eddie that 'the sex business isn't worth all this damned fuss? […] I've only met a handful of people who care a biscuit for it.'[12] But it was common knowledge that Marsh did 'care a biscuit' for the companionship of beautiful young men. Dora Carrington, referring to her younger brother, Noel, told Gertler, 'It's a good thing Eddie doesn't know him, for he's almost as beautiful as Rupert Brooke.'[13] Carrington's remark leaves little doubt that Marsh was susceptible and even predatory; however Gertler, like Brooke, was interested in relationships with women, or rather one woman – Carrington. He became obsessed with her and was relentless in his pursuit of her, exclaiming, 'I could easily worship you'; she was 'the only thing outside painting worth living for'.[14] He was frustrated in every sense by her disinclination to engage in a sexual relationship and by her refusal of his marriage proposal. Instead he was obliged to settle for an unsatisfactory platonic friendship.

Putting aside his apprehensions concerning Marsh's sexuality, Gertler pursued his friendship to the advantage of his purse and Marsh's picture collection. Gertler realised that his artistic freedom and independence would not easily be achieved without financial assistance. He had been the recipient of grants, scholarships and several cash prizes. He had also received commissions for portraits from wealthy Jewish patrons, although he came to resent these patrons and rebelled against their interference in his work. Echoing Brooke's Fabian sentiments, Gertler wrote to Marsh in September 1913, 'I think poverty is a terrible tragedy. A modern artist must have an income.'[15] Fortunately for Gertler, Marsh was an enlightened patron. As with his beloved Brooke, the patronage Marsh extended to Gertler included breakfast, lunch and dinner parties at his home; trips to the theatre and opera; dinner at the Moulin d'Or and Eiffel Tower restaurants; nights at the Café Royal; and weekends in Cambridge with friends.[16] Gertler was also given a key to Marsh's lodgings.

In spite of his strongly held opinion that artists were beyond class distinction 'equal to the highest and lowest' in society,[17] Gertler was very conscious of the disparity between his family background and the sophisticated company he now kept. He was extremely sensitive to any perceived prejudice, and, coupled with his propensity to depression (not least due to his unrequited passion for Carrington), he often felt self-conscious in Marsh's company. After seeing George Bernard Shaw's play *The Doctor's Dilemma*, Gertler wrote to Carrington:

I have just had a depressing night with Marsh at the theatre. […]
the play […] disgusted me. […] I couldn't stand that terrible
middle-class audience […] I wanted to scream, but I only got a
terrible headache instead. I feel that I should like to excite all the
working class to, one night, break into these theatres and destroy
all those rich pleasure seekers![18]

For Gertler, weekends spent away with Marsh and his intellectual
Cambridge friends were not especially enjoyable either:

I haven't had a grand education and I don't understand all this
abstract intellectual nonsense! […] They seem to be clever –
very clever. They talk well, argue masterly, and yet, and yet there
is something – something – that makes me dislike them. Some
moments I hate them! […] I will triumph over those learned
Cambridge youths. One of them argued *down* at me about
painting![19]

Gertler often felt out of his depth; he felt unwashed and awkward
in evening dress; he was a cuckoo in Marsh's milieu. He got involved
in brawls and could be truculent and argumentative – a stark contrast
to the easy companionship that Marsh had enjoyed with Brooke. The
inevitable tension caused by Gertler's sense of alienation contributed
to his mood swings and volatile temper. However, Gertler's gift for
mimicry must have served him well in Marsh's lofty circles as his faux
Oxbridge accent 'was one of the best of his clever repertoire'.[20]

The immaculately attired Marsh reciprocated by venturing forth
into Gertler's world when he visited him at his studio in Whitechapel.
On his first foray he found Gertler working on *The Jewish Family*; he
was sufficiently impressed to ask the price. The surprised Gertler told
Dorothy Brett, 'Unfortunately I was so overwhelmed when he asked
me the price that I only asked £35.'[21] Marsh purchased the painting at
the bargain price. He later recalled,

I started my collection on no plan, […] I made up my mind
which of the painters were good judges of pictures; next I
picked their brains to find out which artists they thought well
of; and then I waited till I saw a work by one of those artists

which aroused in me what I can only call the Lust of Possession – a curious and very pleasant sensation of tingling, or perhaps gooseflesh.[22]

His 'good judges of pictures' were Currie and Gertler.

Eager to promote his fellow Whitechapel boys, on 10 November 1913 Gertler took his friend Isaac Rosenberg, who was both a poet and painter, to the Café Royal to meet Marsh. A few months later, on 8 May 1914, Rosenberg visited Marsh at his home. Aware of Marsh's involvement in *Georgian Poetry*, he took examples of his poems as well as his paintings. His poems were later published in *Georgian Poetry*, and Marsh purchased his small oil painting, *Sacred Love*. Gertler also recommended the work of another impoverished artist, David Bomberg, and Marsh obligingly purchased one of his drawings.

Marsh's picture collection grew exponentially, crammed into his small flat where the 'walls were compacted tight with drawings […] Everywhere pictures even on the doors. […] The paintings in oils crowded the green-carpeted steps and spilled into the hall and the sitting-room.'[23] This melange included one of Marsh's most significant early acquisitions – an occasion when he was most certainly taken with 'the Lust of Possession': a large oil painting, *Apple Gatherers*, by Stanley Spencer. The purchase proved to be a convoluted and argumentative business.

Spencer, nicknamed 'Cookham' after the village in Berkshire where he lived (he was the only Slade student of their group who lived at home and commuted every day from Cookham to Gower Street), was, of all their contemporaries, the most admired by Currie and Gertler.

Gertler had promised to take Marsh to meet him at his home in Cookham, but plans went awry. Spencer regularly corresponded with his friends from the Slade, Jacques and Gwen Raverat (also close friends of Rupert Brooke), and he wrote to tell them that

> Gertler is coming on Monday, it cannot be avoided. I want to see him but not in Cookham. He is bringing Edward Marsh you know. There's Gertler praising me to everybody, […] I wonder if he would if he knew what I thought of him. I must let him know.[24]

Later he related the argument that ensued:

> Gertler is not coming down on Monday: I wrote him a letter and
> in it I said this: 'I was sorry that you gave up painting in your old
> way, because while you did these things which were dull, you were
> in a fair way towards doing something good. Then you seemed
> to lose all faith and patience with your work and began trying to
> paint like Cézanne, and you were incapable of understanding
> him. […] you ought to be ashamed of yourself. […] My feelings
> towards Gertler are not malicious, and I did it intending to do
> him good.[25]

Gertler was deeply offended, and wrote to Marsh to say

> Cookham has written to me […] but in his letter he was so
> insultingly critical about my own work that I've done with him
> and could not think of going down to see him. You can go on
> Monday by yourself if you like.[26]

Gertler, according to Spencer, replied,

> Dear Spencer, I am not in the habit of being dictated to. I
> consider your letter was an outrageous insult. Remember you are
> not in the position to criticise other people's work and you have a
> long time to wait before you ever will be.[27]

The spat continued, with Spencer feeling aggrieved:

> Dear Gertler, I wrote that letter because I could not allow you
> to do me any favours without first letting you know my feelings
> towards you. If it was insulting, I apologise, but it was not
> insulting. You owe me an apology. Thank you for any kindness
> you have done me. Unless you regret sending me that letter, I
> forbid you to write to me again.[28]

Obviously Gertler failed to see the compliment that Spencer was
trying to pay him, albeit in a somewhat tactless manner. Their quarrel
had reached a stalemate, and Marsh was in the unenviable position of
trying to bridge the rift between them. He tried to placate Gertler, and
was moved by his plaintive lament, 'Remember that I am absolutely

alone and that I have loved without the slightest success'.[29] But he had seen Spencer's *The Apple Gatherers* at a recent Contemporary Art Society show and was terribly keen to purchase it. The painter Henry Lamb had already bought the picture for £30 in order to act as an agent for Spencer, and had received an offer of £50 from the Leeds academic and collector of avant-garde art Michael Sadler. However Spencer, who had visited Marsh for the first time in London, wrote to Lamb saying 'I like him very much', and gave instructions that 'if you cannot raise more money than Marsh has offered and cannot manage to keep it yourself, let Marsh have it.'[30] The deal was finally sealed in Marsh's favour when Spencer told Lamb:

> Marsh says that he has had a letter from you to say that Professor
> Sadler offered £50; he also says if there is such a difference
> made between his offer and Professor Sadler's, such as £50 or 50
> guineas, that he would also offer 50 guineas. […] If you must part
> with it I want Marsh to have it because he was first to make the
> offer and kept it open for a good time.[31]

Much to the consternation of Rupert Brooke, Spencer's painting hung over the bed in Marsh's spare room, 'Rupert's room'. Brooke disparagingly christened it 'The Bogeys';[32] furthermore, he was unhappy about the investment that Marsh was making in contemporary art, and wrote churlishly, 'I hate you lavishing all your mad aunt's money on those artists.'[33] Despite Brooke's obvious irritation with Marsh's painters, he and Stanley Spencer became friends. After meeting Brooke for the first time Spencer wrote to the Raverats, 'I like Rupert Brooke. He is a good man and I think he must be an Englishman – must be, you can't get away from it.'[34]

Undeterred by Brooke's protest, Marsh continued to spend his Perceval 'murder money' on his growing coterie of young artists. In December 1913 Spencer went to meet Marsh in London. On this occasion he was rather confused and disconcerted as he had expected to go to a house named Trevelier, not a restaurant of that name; nor was he expecting Marsh to turn up at their meeting wearing his monocle and looking 'exactly like a Private Secretary'. The conversation turned to the subject of the argument with Gertler, who, according to Marsh, was particularly angry that Spencer had said he did not understand Cézanne. Their lunch date must have progressed well, as afterwards Spencer went back to Raymond Buildings to see Marsh's picture collection; 'there I saw a Seabrooke that I actually liked and one thing by Currie that I liked.' He went on to tell the Raverats: 'I should like to see the Seabrooke again. Marsh has a nice photo of him and he has a big photo of Rupert Brooke. Marsh has given me his Georgian poetry book and in it there are some things by Brooke and I liked them. I drove from Marsh's to the Admiralty in a taxicab.'[35]

By the spring of 1914 Gertler and Spencer seemed to have put their differences aside, as Gertler explained to Carrington: 'The evening with Cookham was most successful and inspiring. We got on very well together and had a long talk on art. He talks remarkably well about it. Paul Nash was there too. […] He was very glad to make it up again with me. He wrote and told Marsh so.'[36] Marsh had obviously helped to broker the peace, as Spencer explained to the Raverats: 'I have also spent a weekend with Eddie Marsh. I had Currie and Gaudier for dinner one day, and Gertler and a man named Nash the next. I am glad that Gertler has agreed to be friends again. We agreed unconditionally.'[37]

It was at one of Marsh's many artists' evenings that Spencer conceived the idea for a *Georgian Drawings* volume as a companion to *Georgian Poetry*. It was to comprise of fifty drawings by relatively unknown artists, namely Marsh's Slade group, which also included Paul Nash who had been introduced to Marsh by his brother and fellow artist, John Nash, early in 1914.

Like Brooke and Gertler, 'My little Paul',[38] as Marsh referred to him, also had a key to Raymond Buildings. Paul Nash was intrigued by Marsh's expanding art collection which covered 'every available inch of wall space'; it was exclusively English artists, but, as he observed, no Pre-Raphaelites. Nash said, 'I found the work of my Slade colleagues, Gertler and Spencer, and a painting by Duncan Grant. What surprised me most, was the number of examples representing the younger men.'[39] It was due to Marsh's hospitality that Nash was able to visit

London more frequently. He stayed in the spare room where 'Groups of dwarfs by Gertler and Spencer seemed to menace me from every wall'[40] – the 'Bogeys' that Brooke had complained about.

It was at the instigation of Gertler that Marsh purchased a piece of Nash's work, 'a delicious water-colour tree-scape'.[41] In addition to his purchases Marsh would often be given work – usually drawings – in return for his generosity. Henri Gaudier-Brzeska in a letter asked Sophie Brzeska, 'Marsh has written to me again, asking me to dinner at the Moulin d'Or next Wednesday. Shall I square that by giving him 2 or 3 drawings or not?'[42] Gaudier-Brzeska did indeed give him the drawings, but Marsh was unable to afford to buy his sculptures, as Jim Ede recounts:

> Mr Edward Marsh says that when he went to Henri's studio, he
> never saw any drawings, that at that time he did not even know
> that Gaudier did drawings save for two or three slight ones which
> Gaudier had once sent him in a letter. All that was on view was a
> series of rather large pieces of sculpture, each costing about fifty
> pounds, quite a formidable sum in pre-war money.[43]

Marsh was not simply a collector of contemporary art: he was a collector of artists too. In spite of the vagaries of artistic temperaments (as is evident in Gertler's letters to Marsh) he was irresistibly drawn into the personal lives of his protégés. Gertler wrote to Marsh in an attempt to explain his unpredictable nature: 'I value your friendship. Don't be offended with me – never be offended with me – for with my friends I must be frank. Frankness walks arm-in-arm with rudeness […] Now we are friends, aren't we?'[44] Later, still anxious to affirm their friendship, Gertler wrote,

> You must forgive these curious ways of mine – I can't help it.
> […] I am your friend and yet I do not want to come down to the
> Admiralty to see what you are doing! Please excuse this long and
> serious letter. I know you prefer funny ones. P.S. Please may I
> have eggs and bacon for my breakfast on Wednesday?![45]

No doubt Gertler's polite child-like request for 'eggs and bacon' was granted.

The emotional ups and downs of Marsh's painters were everyday occurrences, but the drama involving John Currie was to eclipse them all. Currie's relationship with Dolly Henry was, by all accounts, a passionate one, often bordering on violence; Gertler, who spent a lot of time with them, often felt exhausted by its tempestuous nature. Dolly, who had also modelled for the painter Laura Knight, was described by Marsh as 'an exceedingly beautiful red-haired white-skinned Irish girl, who was the very worst kind of mate for an artist, for she was jealous of his work, and seasonally unfaithful into the bargain'.[46] Their relationship, which nowadays might be described as co-dependent, was a constant round of break-ups followed by passionate reunions. Currie painted her several times, and in one picture portrayed her as *The Witch*, having been driven to distraction by what he considered her flirtatious behaviour.

Marsh had written to Gertler expressing his concern for Currie: 'I think he will be done for if he doesn't get Dolly out of his head.'[47] On returning from a trip to France Currie discovered that she was living with another man. Marsh referred to this as Currie's 'breaking point': 'I remember his voice as he sat relaxed in a comfortable chair; "Oh Eddie, the peace of being here!" At an ordinary time I could have kept him with me, and perhaps seen him through.'[48] Due to the pressure of work at the Admiralty Marsh did not invite Currie to stay at Raymond Buildings that evening. Currie left, and one week later, on 8 October 1914, Marsh was called by the police who had found his name and address in Currie's pocket book. Currie, consumed with jealous rage, had shot Dolly dead and then turned the gun on himself. On hearing the news Gertler rushed to his bedside at the Chelsea Infirmary. Marsh went to the hospital too, where he found Currie dying. Currie simply told Marsh, 'It was all so ugly.'[49] Dolly was only twenty years old and Currie was just thirty. The date was 11 October 1914 and Britain was already at war with Germany.

Chapter Eight

Artists at War

In response to the news of Currie's death Gaudier-Brzeska wrote:

> I learnt of Currie's death while in the trenches near Rheims some
> time in November, I believe, and of course I was not surprised;
> he had tried once when I was at his place. He was a great painter,
> and a magnificent fellow; in ordinary times, I should naturally
> have been more afflicted, but as you may imagine, death is here a
> daily happening and one is expecting it every minute.[1]

The advent of the First World War shattered Marsh's group of painters as it did his Georgian poets. It was increasingly difficult for Marsh to
manage his personal, social and cultural interests with the demands of
his post at the Admiralty. D. H. Lawrence summed it up well when he
wrote to him in December 1913: 'Lord, you're a bit of a jigsaw puzzle
to start with, mixing poets and pictures, the Admiralty, and what-not,
like somebody shuffling cards.'[2]

However there were times when the worlds of art and work con-
flated, as in February 1914 when Marsh introduced the artist Eric Gill
to his chief. Churchill was keen for Gill to design a badge for his newly
formed Flying Corps. Gill was less than positive after the meeting, and
told Marsh, 'I'm not the least bit confident that I can perpetrate such
a badge as Mr. Churchill desires and suggests, […] he seems to me to
want a blooming picture.'[3]

At the outset of the war Paul Nash initially enlisted for Home Service
as a private in the 2nd Battalion Artists' Rifles, but in February 1917
he arrived in France as a second lieutenant in the Hampshire Regiment. Both he and his brother John saw active service on the Western
Front before being commissioned as Official War Artists. Paul pleaded
with Marsh, 'Can you by any fair or foul means help Jack home for
a commission?' Eventually Marsh was able to exert his influence to

bring John home on leave and hasten his appointment as an Official War Artist.[4] The Nash brothers were responsible for creating some of the most iconic images of the First World War. Their landscapes of war were a stark and brutal contrast to their former pastoral landscapes which had been acquired by Marsh, such as Paul Nash's *Elms* and John Nash's *The Cornfield*.

As with his Georgian poets, Marsh did his best to maintain the financial support of his group of painters throughout the war. Paul Nash was in no doubt as to the value of Marsh's patronage: writing to him after he had bought one of his drawings, he said, 'You are one of the very few men who collects honestly and about the only one who is going on collecting during the war. You are a valuable man, but at the moment your money is more valuable – since you can't keep artists going by any other means.'[5]

In fact Marsh's appetite for picture-collecting was unstinted. Early in May 1915 Spencer told the Raverats, 'I have just sold my big head painting to Eddie Marsh for £20, also a landscape for £15.'[6] (A total of around £3,000 in today's money.)

Stanley Spencer followed his brother Gilbert's example and in July 1915 enlisted as a private in the Royal Army Medical Corps working at the Beaufort War Hospital during his basic training. He wrote to Marsh of his experience: 'Nothing but drudgery & patients & lunatics [...] all very loathsome [...] I should like to hear from you or Gertler any time you can write.'[7] Spencer and Marsh corresponded regularly throughout the war; Spencer reported to the Raverats in July 1917, 'I have had a nice letter from Eddie Marsh, bless him.'[8] Writing at the same time to his sister Florence, 'Flongy', from the 143rd Field Hospital in Salonica, he again spoke of Marsh:

> I had a nice letter from Eddie Marsh. He is now in the Colonial Office. He is doing another 'Georgian Poetry' book. But I think he is too ready to recognise a man as a poet. However, it is better to have someone ready to publish almost anything, as Eddie seems to be, as there are plenty of critics about, writing like hungry wolves for their prey.[9]

Spencer's perceptive comment about Marsh's eagerness to find poetic talent in a man was not dissimilar to Marsh's willingness to see merit in a painting without any concern for the critics.

Marsh had left the Admiralty and was back at the Colonial Office as a consequence of Churchill's political fall following the disastrous Gallipoli campaign where Rupert Brooke had died. Marsh, though grieving for Brooke, was resolute in his effort to keep alive their joint enterprise of Georgian poetry, as well as trying to keep alive his poets and painters at war.

Gaudier-Brzeska wrote to Marsh from the Front in October 1914, 'Here I am face to the foe. I have been fighting at the Front for the last fortnight'. He goes on to describe a skirmish where seven out of the twelve men in his company are killed, but ends his letter on an optimistic note: 'Confident in ultimate success, I remain, Yours ever'.[10] He was killed in action on 5 June 1915.

Marsh's friendship with Isaac Rosenberg had developed to the extent that during the last few weeks prior to the declaration of war on Germany he had been in constant touch with him. Marsh helped him to refine the manuscript of a collection of poems, much to Rosenberg's amazement that anyone should take his work this seriously. Marsh also paid for the collection, *Youth*, to be privately printed. Rosenberg was delighted, and in return told Marsh, 'If you like you can have my three drawings for the money if you think they're worth it. You don't know how happy you have made me by giving me this chance to print.'[11]

Furthermore, Marsh used his influence with the Emigration Office to enable Rosenberg to visit his sister-in-law in South Africa. Rosenberg had been advised by his doctor, who suspected tuberculosis, to spend time in a warm climate for the sake of his health.

Following the outbreak of war Rosenberg returned to England in 1915, and despite the fact that he wrote to Marsh declaring 'I despise war and hate war'[12] he enlisted in the Suffolk Regiment. He explained to Marsh that he had not told his mother where he was going as he did not wish to distress her. He asked Marsh to help him out with the gift of £1 (about £130 today) in order to buy boots and to get back to London for Christmas, once again offering the pick of any subsequent drawings in return for the favour. Rosenberg assumed that Marsh 'must now be the busiest man in England'.[13] Nonetheless Marsh never failed to write to him, and tried to improve Rosenberg's situation whenever possible. At the beginning of 1917 Rosenberg became ill. Despite Marsh having written to Rosenberg's Commanding Officer expressing his concern, Rosenberg was deemed fit for active service. The war was seriously affecting Rosenberg's physical and mental health; back in the trenches, he told Marsh that most of the time was spent pulling one another out of the mud with the men suffering from diarrhoea and continually plagued by rats. Ill health and over-tiredness were affecting his memory and mental faculties; nevertheless he penned what is considered to be one of the greatest poems of the war, *Dead Man's Dump*. Rosenberg's sister pleaded with Marsh to try to get him home on sick leave or transferred to a Jewish battalion, but before that could be arranged on 1 April 1918 Rosenberg was killed in night combat on the front line. He had written, 'I never joined the army for patriotic reasons. Nothing can justify war. I suppose we must all fight to get the trouble over.'[14] Marsh's help had been crucial to Rosenberg from the Slade years to the end of his short life, from purchasing his pictures to critiquing and publishing his poems, or simply sending him chocolates when he was in a military hospital with both his hands badly cut. Marsh was upset that his advocacy had failed on Rosenberg's behalf, and his tragic death was yet another blow.

Years later, in June 1937, Marsh gave the opening speech at a retrospective exhibition of Rosenberg's work at the Whitechapel Gallery in London. In his memoir he said of 'poor little Isaac Rosenberg', 'surely one of the most futile of all the futile sacrifices of the War, for except courage he had no quality of the soldier, and if he had lived he must have done great things.'[15]

Mark Gertler, unlike his fellow Whitechapel boys Rosenberg and Bomberg, did not see active service in the war and created a different kind of problem for Marsh. Noel Carrington believed that the First World War had a negligible effect on Gertler's work,[16] and although he was appalled by the 'butchery'[17] of war he was not an active pacifist. As a result of Marsh's introductions Gertler had become closely

associated with John Middleton Murry, Katherine Mansfield, Gilbert
Cannan and D. H. Lawrence, who were all intense pacifists, and they
exerted a huge influence on him. He had also become 'great friends
with Lytton Strachey',[18] another pacifist, who had been declared unfit
for service. During the war Gertler's chosen milieu was that of intel-
lectuals and writers rather than painters; he was also taken under the
wing of Lady Ottoline Morrell and regularly attended her salons. Eventually this shift in Gertler's social scene would contribute to a schism
between Marsh and his erstwhile 'cherub'.

Marsh was inundated with war work; D. H. Lawrence wrote to him
on 13 September 1914 saying, 'I knew from Mark Gertler how busy you
are.'[19] Gertler spent increasing amounts of time away from Marsh with
his writer friends, the Cholesbury circle, in Buckinghamshire; even so,
he continued to be supported financially by Marsh. Gertler had chosen
to remain at home while the other Slade artists had signed up to fight,
and he was justifiably appreciative of Marsh's kindness towards him:

> My dear Eddie, I can't tell you how thankful I feel to you. It isn't
> the actual money that pleases me, but the generous and friendly
> feelings that prompted you to help me. I feel that you are a real
> friend and that makes me very happy. I do hope that someday
> I shall be able in some way to help you. I hope also to do such
> good work that you will feel that I was worthy of your help.[20]

The closest that Gertler came within the sphere of Marsh's work at
this time was a chance meeting with Churchill: 'This morning Eddie
introduced me to Winston Churchill. He was coming out of St Paul's as
we were going in. […] In the church we met Mrs Churchill.'[21] In spite
of his pacifist leanings being at odds with Marsh's wartime responsibil-
ities, Gertler was confident that he could rely on Marsh's backing: 'My
two great friends are Eddie Marsh and [Dorothy] Brett – they are both
godsends. Eddie offers me as much as £10 a month during war-time!!
He is also giving me a bedroom in his flat and a latchkey so I can always
sleep there!'[22] Gertler had been searching for a studio; having found
suitable premises in Hampstead, he nonetheless wrote to Marsh with a
request for continuing access to overnight accommodation: 'I should

want your bedroom pretty often, so may I have a key in any case?'[23] This turned out to be a good interim move for Gertler, who wrote to Carrington from Raymond Buildings, delighted with his current situation: 'For the present and until I am settled I am staying with Eddie. I have never been so comfortable before in my life and never before had a bath every morning, for over a week. Every morning at 9 o'clock Eddie comes and says, "Mark! Bath ready!" and helps me into a PURPLE SILK DRESSING-GOWN!'[24]

This account prompted Carrington to tease Gertler about his friendship with Marsh, to which Gertler retorted: 'No Eddie does not admire my legs. My legs are far too thin and hairy! He is used to legs of Jim Barnes and Rupert Brooke, whose legs are as pink and plump as yours! I cut a very sorry figure after those people. However Eddie is very kind to me in spite of my figure.'[25]

Marsh was probably as delighted with the circumstances as Gertler was, being happy to tend to his protégé's personal needs and ablutions. In exchange for Marsh's generosity Gertler gave him first refusal on his work, an arrangement which suited Marsh perfectly. He was thrilled with his purchase of Gertler's *Daffodils*, as he extolled in a letter to Denis Browne: 'Mark has painted *the* most lovely picture that I ever saw, of 2 bunches of daffodils against a blue background – it's a real inspiration I think, and convinces me of his genius more than anything he has done – and it's wonderfully painted – It will be nice to show it you after the war – (it's mine).'[26] Browne would not survive the war to see it.

Gertler wrote to Marsh concerning another of his paintings and his growing debt:

> I shall be very glad to let you have my interior as part payment
> of what I owe you. But I should be very thankful to you if you
> would let me keep it after it comes back [from an exhibition at
> the NEAC], as I may be able to sell it. This may sound horrid to
> you, but I know you will understand when I tell you that I am at
> this moment penniless! [...] The picture comes back today and if
> I don't sell it by next Saturday you will have it then. According to
> my accounts I owe you £64 and not £70 as you say.[27]

(£64 in 1915 would be worth around £5,300 in today's money.) Gertler was certainly racking up his debt to Marsh, but Marsh was clearly taking advantage by acquiring Gertler's paintings at less than the commercial rate.

By May 1915 Marsh was still embroiled in the business of war, devastated by the death of Rupert Brooke and the repercussions of the disastrous Dardanelles campaign. Gertler, who had little interest in politics, summed up the situation from his self-centred point view in a letter to Lytton Strachey:

> This coalition business in Parliament had caused me great anxiety. Never was I so feverishly interested in a political move, simply because it was the only one that stood any chance of directly affecting me. What affects Churchill, affects Eddie Marsh and what affects Eddie Marsh affects me!
>
> However, although they have both been driven out like Adam and Eve from the Garden of Eden, all is not black yet. Anyhow it is not going to affect me, but poor Eddie is rather unhappy and I am sorry for him as his goodness to me has really made me love him. He hates Lord Fisher now and has burnt his photograph! He seems to think that the other post they will get will be so dull; whilst at the Admiralty 'he did feel he was doing something for his country but now ...' Poor dear Eddie!!![28]

Whether Marsh actually burned Fisher's photograph is debatable; it may be dramatic licence on Gertler's part. Marsh's version of events was that he

> was so worked-up against 'Jackie' Fisher by what I then looked on as his falseness that I tore up his photograph, on which he had written 'Yours till Hell freezes' – it seemed that Hell had definitely frozen; but when after a decent interval the ever-placable Winston made it up with him, I regretted my sentimental act.[29]

Gertler's evident selfishness is only partly countered by his sympathy for Marsh, which is born out of a sense of indebtedness. It was a deeply unhappy time for Marsh both personally and professionally, and yet in the same letter Gertler, who had been suffering from a cold, mentions how Marsh 'was alarmed this morning at my appearance and has written to Winston Churchill's doctor for an appointment for me!'[30] Marsh typically thinking not of himself and anxious to care for his young artist friend would also have picked up the doctor's bill. Perhaps Gertler felt a pang of conscience at his flippant remarks to Strachey, as, after having been to see the doctor who found nothing much the matter, he wrote to Marsh to express his thanks in a more heartfelt manner:

> I feel extremely grateful to you for all this. I really cannot express my thanks to you for your extraordinary goodness. I must tell you that I feel that what you are doing for me is *far* more valuable to me than anybody else has ever done. […] if you find that you are hard up or that you do not feel inclined to continue your help during the war you must *immediately* tell me. I mean, supposing my work disappoints you or you get hard up or supposing the war lasts too long! Anyway you must not let me be a weight on you.[31]

Marsh's reply was reassuringly warm, indicating his strength of feeling for Gertler and his work:

> My Dear Mark, I am so glad to have your charming letter, first because it is a great relief to hear that there is nothing really wrong with you, and also because of course it is a pleasure to know that you think I am of use to you.
>
> Of course you know that I am very fond of you, and that I have a strong belief in your genius – and for both these reasons I couldn't make a better use of my resources than to help you along as much as I can.[32]

Gertler felt happy and comforted both by Marsh's faith in his ability and by his willingness to maintain his financial support. By return letter he arranged to stay overnight again. Unfortunately the domestic bliss was short-lived. By July 1915 Gertler found his financial dependence on Marsh was becoming a strain, and he complained to Carrington:

> Last night I stayed at Marsh's. Every time I see him I get depressed. I hate having to take this money from him. Today he

didn't give me the cheque – this was a great blow to me as I was waiting for it. I don't know whether he merely forgot or whether he doesn't intend giving it me because I sold a picture.[33]

Gertler need not have worried, as Marsh had duly sent him the cheque to Cholesbury, where he was staying. Whether Marsh had asked for an account, or whether Gertler simply felt he needed to work out the balance he owed, he wrote to him: 'You bought the "Agapanthus" for £25, "Drawing of Old Jew" £6, "Daffodils" for £20. That makes £51 – £51 away from £85 leaves £34. Therefore I owe you £34.'[34] He closed his letter with a request for Mrs Elgy to send his slippers.

Always ready with a sympathetic ear, Marsh placated Gertler:

My dear Mark, Your birth-pains over your pictures are quite torture enough for you. Don't worry yourself additionally about how you are to live, so long as you can manage on what I can do for you, and the extras that are quite certain to come in.

He continued,

Since the war, and still more since my friends died, I don't care to spend money on myself, beyond just keeping up my life here. You know I believe you were born to be a great painter, and if that is true it will have been a proud thing in my life to have been able to help you, and leave you more or less free to develop yourself unhampered – I can't imagine a worthier use of my money – and even suppose we were wrong about your painting! you are still my friend, and I should hate to be 'rolling' while you were in straits. I should be ashamed of being comparatively well-off, if I don't take advantage of it to help my friends who are younger, and poorer and cleverer and better than I am.[35]

Gertler received another cheque from Marsh in August, at which time he had been asked by Mr Edmund Harvey MP to paint a portrait of Marsh's acquaintance, Professor Michael Sadler, for the sum of £50. This would require Gertler travelling from Cholesbury to Leeds in order to fulfil the commission, and naturally he planned to stop for one night with Marsh en route. As with the commissions early in his career, Gertler found it an onerous task. He wrote to Marsh in typically dramatic fashion: 'Really commissioned portrait painting is a dreadful occupation. You can't think how this portrait is depressing me! […] Never again will I accept a portrait unless the sitter interests or inspires me to paint him or her. I would rather starve.' Of course Gertler could afford to be petulant about it in the knowledge that Marsh would never let him starve, and like a rather needy child closed his ranting letter with, 'Do please write to me very soon. I would like to get a letter from you here.'[36] He finished the portrait quickly, and his dislike of the whole process reaffirmed his appreciation of the artistic freedom that Marsh's support afforded him. He acknowledged this in a letter to Marsh: 'Your help is invaluable to me – you just let me paint that which I want to paint.' He planned to visit Marsh again on his return to Cholesbury from Leeds, and also implored him not to mention to Professor Sadler how much he had 'suffered in painting his portrait'.[37]

In his letter of 8 August to Gertler Marsh had set out the guiding principles by which he lived his life. Some of his contemporaries might have accused him of being generous to a fault, but, as he acknowledged, he received Gertler's pictures in return. What is most revealing is Marsh's similarity to Rupert Brooke in the value he placed on friendship, particularly the importance of friendship between men. He was a true philanthropist and an enlightened patron with an innate desire to nurture creative talent. Given his outpouring of reassurance to Gertler, how shocked he must have been when a couple of months later he received the following:

Dear Eddie, 'I have come to the conclusion that we two are too fundamentally different to continue to be friends. Since the war, you have gone in one direction and I in another. All the time I have been stifling my feelings. Firstly because of your kindness to me and secondly I did not want to hurt you. I am I believe what you call a 'Passivist' [*sic*]. I don't know exactly what that means, but I just hate this War and should really loathe to help in it. […] Of course from this you will understand that we had not better meet any more and that I cannot any longer accept your help. […] Your kindness has been an extraordinary help to me. Since your help I have done work far, far better than before. I shall therefore never cease to be thankful to you. Also if I ever earn any money by painting I shall return you what I owe you. I shall send you the latchkey and please would you get Mrs Elgy to send me my pyjamas and slippers.[38]

The combined persuasive influence of Ottoline Morrell's Garsington circle, the Lawrences and Gilbert Cannan had caused this crisis of conscience in Gertler. Ironically it was Marsh who had first introduced Gertler to Cannan, who, according to Gertler's biographer Sarah MacDougall had, 'despite military exemption, carried on an acrimonious correspondence about pacifism with Eddie'.[39] Even though Gertler was not quite sure what it meant to be a pacifist, he was certain that he hated the war. Marsh was immersed in the politics of it all, hence Gertler felt their friendship was untenable – though at least he had the grace to acknowledge what he owed Marsh, not just in pecuniary terms. It must have felt like a slap in the face for Marsh, although as he had confessed to Gertler earlier in 1915, the death of Brooke, his 'great sorrow', had '[so] completely absorbed all my power of feeling for the present that I really have nothing left over'.[40]

It was not long before Gertler's money started to run out, and he discovered that independence, and the lifestyle of a pacifist painter, was not all that he had hoped it might be: 'What frightens me most is the possibility of having to give up my studio. […] I feel *almost* sorry that I gave up Eddie Marsh! for after all his money was such a help. And isn't it after all worth undergoing any trouble and humiliation to be enabled to paint?'[41]

It was apparent that he had begun to regret being so hasty to cut the ties with Marsh, and even D. H. Lawrence enquired whether he was 'reconciled to Eddie?'[42] Money troubles were Gertler's biggest worry, and he resented the fact that money was necessary in order to have the freedom to paint. The ambiguous nature of patronage tormented him; he felt the obvious benefits were outweighed by dependence and obligation. This problem was elucidated by Montague Shearman, another picture collector who had befriended Gertler:

> Money is a horrible thing. I should like you to feel however
> that you can always have what you want from me if you like. But
> it must be as between friends and there must be no feeling of
> patronage or obligation whatever. I don't want to be a Conway
> or an Eddie Marsh – not that I am saying a word against Eddie
> Marsh, who I am sure meant to be kind. But I am not, as you
> know, the sort of person who would give money and expect to
> take pictures instead. If I want a picture I would buy it outright.[43]

Shearman's veiled criticism of Marsh juxtaposed with his own view
which allowed for independence on the part of the artist would have
coincided with Gertler's thinking. Indeed Marsh had 'meant to be
kind', but patronage was also a way in which he could keep his young
men tied closer to him.

By the end of 1916 Gertler had completed his painting *The Merry-
Go-Round*, which is probably regarded as his greatest work. D. H. Lawrence described it as 'the best modern picture I have seen: I think it is
great and true.'[44]

In April 1917, despite his artistic success and his friendship with
the wealthy Shearman, Gertler was once again impoverished. Out of
necessity he put aside his moral objections, and Marsh restored his
financial support. Marsh also interceded on Gertler's behalf: when the
sale of his painting *Eve* to Lady Cunard did not materialise, Marsh used
his influence to persuade Jasper Ridley to purchase it instead. However
this reunion of patron and painter was relatively short-lived, as a letter
from Ottoline Morrell to Gertler in June 1919 implies: 'I am so thankful that you kicked off from him [Eddie]. It was a good thing.'[45]

While poetry and painting were passionate interests for Marsh, his
work was also a consuming aspect of his life. Early on he had decided to
align his Civil Service career to Churchill's political one; it was a recurring motif in all areas of Marsh's life to play the supporting role rather
than the lead. Pinning his fate to his friend and chief was wonderful
when Churchill's star was in the ascendancy, but detrimental to Marsh
when it fell to earth as it did after the Dardanelles campaign. Following this disaster Churchill left office and returned to arms as Major
Churchill of the Oxfordshire Yeomanry and set off for France to fight.

Churchill had asked Asquith to take Marsh on; Marsh explained to his friend Lance Sieveking in November 1915: 'The P.M. is taking me on as extra Private Secretary, which I consider as falling as nearly as possible on my feet, after the shock of breaking my 10 years' association with Winston.'[46] Marsh worked at 10 Downing Street and was responsible for Civil List Pensions, which Asquith 'hoped would make him feel a little less of a motherless child'.[47] Marsh had bid a tearful farewell to Churchill and was in constant touch with him while he was in France. When Asquith was defeated in late 1916, Lloyd George formed a coalition government and Marsh was unhappy to find himself virtually back where he had started his career in the West African Department of the Colonial Office. In an effort to bolster his morale Marsh's friend Lady Juliet Duff wrote to him:

> The things that matter in *your* life are your unselfishness
> to Winston, your countless kindnesses to and sacrifices for
> struggling people; your encouragement of Art; your marvellous
> gift of friendship and never failing sympathy, never 'put on' but
> coming straight from your heart. I *know*, dear Eddie, that those
> are the things which count; in fact they are the only ones that
> matter at all. All the rest is dross.[48]

After almost a year a call came from Churchill who had been appointed Minister of Munitions and invited Marsh to join him. As Marsh recalled, 'It was delightful to be with him again, and from that moment to the end of the war I lived once more at high pressure.'[49]

Marsh lived his life to the full; being busy at work and play helped him to come to terms with not only his profound sorrow at losing Rupert Brooke but also the loss of many other young men in his circle. Reflecting on the end of the war, he said, 'nearly every one of the closest among my younger friends had been killed – I had to begin all over again.'[50] Marsh was not alone in mourning a lost generation of youth.

Chapter Nine

The Collector and the Contemporary Art Society

In 1916 Marsh was encouraged by Robbie Ross and Professor Michael Sadler to show his picture collection at the Burlington Fine Arts Club. According to Sadler, Marsh's collection reflected 'a love for the great past and a faith in the future'; furthermore, 'To have brought these together, out of so many things seen, is itself a creative act like painting a great picture.'[1] Although it was his collection of old English drawings and watercolours that proved to be the most popular with the public audience, Marsh nonetheless continued to devote his attention to the work of contemporary artists.

In 1923 Marsh was elected by the Contemporary Art Society as its 'buyer of the year'. This required official visits to exhibitions to purchase on behalf of the Society and increased his contact with artists, one of whom was the painter Christopher Wood. He, like so many before him, was invited to see Marsh's collection at Raymond Buildings. Marsh purchased Wood's paintings for his own collection as well as on behalf of the Society. Wood was thrilled, and hoped that Marsh's influence would encourage others to follow his example. In May 1927 Wood wrote to him from France, 'You are the only person who takes true interest in the painters of your own country […] Wish you were here to drive me on.'[2] Christopher Wood was a troubled soul, prone to depression; he drank heavily and was addicted to opium. Marsh visited him in the South of France later that summer and returned with a few canvases with the hope of interesting London dealers in Wood's work. He had also helped Wood financially. Wood wrote to him, 'Thanks so much for the enormous cheque, it gave me quite a shock, as I really didn't expect to be heavily paid for paintings by you.'[3]

Although Marsh and others endeavoured to help Wood's career, his mental health problems worsened, descending into episodes of paranoia. On 21 August 1930, just three years after Marsh had visited him in Cannes, Christopher Wood was killed when he fell in front of a train pulling into Salisbury station at the age of twenty-nine.

Marsh also bought a number of paintings by Wood's friend Cedric Morris, including *Breton Landscape* painted during his time in Tréboul with Wood. Eager to promote Morris to potential buyers, Marsh introduced him to Winston Churchill, who also purchased his paintings. Marsh habitually brought artists together too, and he introduced the sculptor John Skeaping to Morris; the pair became great friends, and Morris was particularly supportive of Skeaping when his marriage to Barbara Hepworth broke down.

From 10 to 11 July 1927 Marsh opened his rooms at Raymond Buildings to show his art collection to the public. He charged an entrance fee of 2s 6d (around £6 in today's money), which was to go in support of the YWCA, the Young Women's Christian Association. In October 1929 much of Marsh's collection (270 pictures in total) was on show again to the general public, this time at the Whitechapel Gallery.

Marsh had also lent several paintings (and books) to Ivor Novello, who furnished his home, Redroofs, with them. But this was not simply generosity on Marsh's part, for as he confessed 'I am like the Old Woman who lived in a Shoe – I have so many pictures that unless at least twenty are boarded-out, I don't know what to do.'[4] He was not exaggerating.

Following his retirement from the Civil Service and the award of his knighthood, on 17 March 1937 a celebratory dinner at the Mayfair Hotel was hosted by Sir William Rothenstein in Marsh's honour. It had a glittering guest list made up of former colleagues, personal friends, and representatives from the arts, all of whom had been asked to contribute towards the purchase of a work of art for Marsh. Ivor Novello responded in typical comic form:

> Of course I am only too delighted to subscribe, and enclose a cheque for £5 5s., thus setting aside the insulting suggestion that One Guinea is enough. I shall unfortunately be unable to attend the dinner as I am playing the leading part at Drury Lane in a play called *Turgid Rancour* (limericks by Christopher Hassall).

As Sir Edward has been a close friend of mine for many years, in fact, for almost too long, I am sure neither he nor the Committee would object to a shower of leaflets advertising the above play being let down from the ceiling just at that moment when Sir Edward gets up to respond to any good wishes that may be handed out. I have chosen this moment as the most romantic of the evening.

Novello signed off as 'Ivor Novello, President of the S.P.C.E.' – the Society for the Prevention of Cruelty to Eddie.[5]

Duncan Grant was rather more circumspect. He was keen to contribute, but said he would 'like to be able to subscribe a little towards giving him something which I myself would like'.[6] Marsh was delighted when Winston Churchill presented him with two Augustus John drawings (*Seated Woman* and *Draped Standing Woman*) to add to his already bursting collection. I hope and think that Duncan Grant would have been happy with the choice of work too.

Although he was pleased about becoming 'Sir Edward', and would be taken aback by anyone who henceforth lapsed and referred to him as plain Mr Marsh, he had mixed feelings about his retirement. Following the celebration, which he thought was 'a really wonderful affair', he complained bitterly, 'The rest of my life will be one long anti-climax. I ought to have jumped into the Thames.'[7] It was just as well that he did not consign himself to a watery grave: on 16 February 1937 he was elected as a Trustee of the Tate Gallery, and subsequently devoted much of his time working to promote the Tate and the Contemporary Art Society. Ever keen to evangelise and encourage others to follow his example by supporting contemporary artists, he wrote an article, 'Patronage in Art To-day', which appeared in the *Listener* magazine in 1935. He was a devotee of contemporary art, but he drew the line at abstract art, maintaining 'I am anxious to be stigmatised as a consistent and brazen upholder of "representational" art.'[8]

Marsh continued to be immersed in the artistic social scene. He recalled one particular dinner at the Café Royal in 1937 which had been hosted by an art dealer, deploring 'the spirit in which people come to such dinners'. Marsh disliked the fact that many guests came for social reasons, wanting to be present at a fashionable party, rather than possessing a genuine enthusiasm for art. He concluded that on this occasion 'The best thing was Alfred Munnings who got up and recited two Norfolk ballads of his own writing which were remarkably racy and spirited. I had no idea he had this talent; two or three people said how much better they were than his pictures. He promised to send me one. I hope he will.'[9]

Munnings was acknowledged as a fine painter of horses, and in the First World War had served as a War Artist attached to the Canadian Cavalry Brigade. In 1944 he was elected as President of the Royal Academy (Marsh was 'amused at his prompt insertion of "P" before his R.A.'),[10] and Winston Churchill was awarded the status of an Honorary Royal Academician during Munnings' presidency. Munnings was a notable and vociferous critic of Modernism in painting, which may well have provoked the disparaging comments made by the 'two or three people' whom Marsh met that evening. A few years later Munnings gave Marsh a lift home from yet another dinner and Marsh invited him in to look at his collection. Munnings was suitably impressed: 'You're a damned good buyer' he said, but what pleased Marsh the most was his admiration for his paintings by Leonard Appelbee: Munnings placed them on his knee and 'communed with them as if they had been lovely children'[11] – a moment of uncharacteristic tenderness from the curmudgeonly Munnings.

Sadly the breach between Marsh and Mark Gertler continued after the end of the First World War until 1933, when the publication of Marsh's translation of *The Fables of La Fontaine* prompted Gertler to write to him. By this time Gertler's health was deteriorating; he was suffering from tuberculosis which involved frequent stays in sanatoriums, and he was laid low with increasing bouts of depression. In May 1939 he wrote to Marsh about his latest exhibition at the Lefèvre Gallery, London:

> I'm afraid I am very depressed about my show. I've sold only
> one so far! […] That show represents two years' hard work and

there is all the expense, frames, etc., attached to it. It's very disheartening. I was pleased to see you last Thursday and shall look forward to reading your book. Ever yours, Mark.[12]

Marsh took it upon himself to respond to Gertler with a negative appraisal of his recent work; but Gertler was consistent in his rebuttal that he never set out to paint in order to please other people:

My dear Eddie of course I'm not angry with you for writing what you think – you are much too old a friend and have done so much for me in the past that you have a *right* to say what you think. Besides what you say is, I suppose, true in a sense, as obviously a number of people feel as you do about my recent works. [...] Of course I love it when people like my pictures. But to *set out* to please would ruin my process [...] In very friendly spirit, I am yours ever, Mark.[13]

The renewal of their friendship was to be cut short when a few weeks later, on 23 June 1939, Gertler took his own life. The post-mortem concluded that the cause of death was 'coal-gas poisoning'.[14] There was no suicide note, but perhaps in the depths of his depression he truly felt unappreciated as an artist; as he had said to Marsh, 'many works by artists of the past were considered unattractive during their life time. My works may be more appreciated in the future.'[15] In contrast to his outpouring of grief following Brooke's death, there is no record of how Marsh responded to the news of Gertler's suicide, nor is there any reference to his attending the funeral. There is no evidence of him speaking of Gertler in a personal way again, until he wrote to Christopher Hassall in 1944: 'You may not have noticed Eric Newton's review of Mark Gertler's exhibition, which seems to me sadly truthful. I've lent 10 pictures to the show. I'm glad to see that Newton picks out the one of Mark's studio [...] I've always thought it was his best.'[16]

The exhibition took place at the Ben Uri Gallery from 16 November to 17 December 1944. Eric Newton wrote: 'Looking at his collected work in this exhibition is like looking at a nearly completed jig-saw puzzle from which the key pieces are missing.'[17] Newton's review is critical, and he asserts that Gertler failed to create masterpieces because rather than sincerity of approach he tried too hard to invoke the greatness of other painters like Renoir or Cézanne. However Marsh was gratified when Newton praised his picture of the artist's studio: 'One is suddenly in a place that he knew and understood, with no attempt at greatness interfering between artist and spectator. The effect is as of a live thrush breaking into song in the impressive but mute company of stuffed eagles.'[18] Marsh was quick to concur with Newton's judgment and quick to forget his own effusive praise of Gertler's talent when he had first discovered him. Perhaps it is no coincidence that Marsh's diminished opinion of Gertler's painting reflected the many fractures in their relationship over the years.

Following the outbreak of the Second World War in 1939, Marsh was eventually obliged to leave his beloved Raymond Buildings where so many encounters with painters and poets had taken place. The regular bombing raids meant it was too hazardous to remain in London. In January 1941 Raymond Buildings was seriously damaged by a bomb blast. Fortunately Marsh was not in residence at the time, but he had to take steps to protect his collection.

His pictures were stored at the Tate and his furniture and books were deposited at Compton Place near Eastbourne, a property belonging to the Duke and Duchess of Devonshire. As well as storing his property, the Devonshires took Marsh in as their guest at Churchdale on the Chatsworth Estate in Derbyshire. Their daughter-in-law, Deborah – Debo Mitford – recalled how Marsh had been knocked over by a London cab during the blackout: although he was not badly hurt the Duke had taken pity on him and invited him to stay in order to recuperate from the shock. Most people gave fond descriptions of Marsh, who was usually deemed to be the perfect house guest, but upon his arrival at Churchdale Debo was immediately irritated by him and 'his boring tales of his old boss [Churchill] and the stage folk he knew'. She complained to her sister, Diana Mosley, that he was 'such a silly old man and eats a terrible lot'.[19] She gives a very disparaging but amusing account of him in her memoir:

He insisted on listening to the nine o'clock news, which interrupted our records of Harry Roy and the like, but as soon as Alvar Liddell's soothing voice came over the wireless telling of the latest disaster, Eddie fell asleep. The little click when we turned off the wireless to go back to our favourite dance bands woke him with a start, and it was back to Alvar Liddell. [...] For exercise, Eddie tossed a pack of playing cards on the floor and picked them up one by one. I often wondered why he could not do something more useful – dig the garden for instance – but no, he was too special for that. After he had been with us for about a month, a van arrived at Churchdale with his cellar (many cases of Drambuie) and we realized that he was in for a long stay. He was so dug in, and I suppose thought himself part of the family, that whenever the Devonshires moved from Compton Place to Churchdale and back, Eddie Marsh went too. [...] After fourteen and a half months, Eddie finally left. He would have stayed longer but Edward, the butler, and my sisters-in-law formed up to his hosts and said enough was enough. He arrived in November 1940 and left in January 1942. Talk about the man who came to dinner ...[20]

Sir Alan (Tommy) Lascelles also recalled how Marsh had billeted himself at Chatsworth and the difficulty the family had in getting him to leave:

they couldn't get rid of him nohow. At last they told him he simply must go because Lady Hartington was going to have a baby. Shortly afterwards I met him in St James's Street, and he said ecstatically, 'Isn't it splendid – she's had a miscarriage, and I can stay.' I, who didn't know the background, thought he'd gone mad.[21]

Marsh's usual empathy seemed to have deserted him on this occasion. He eventually left Churchdale (much to Debo's relief) to stay with friends near Tunbridge Wells. That sojourn was short-lived. Ivor Novello expressed his concern: 'Darling Eddie, [...] I was very distressed that you had to make another move so soon – I hate you being hounded, and pillaried [*sic*] and posted! – You must tell me how it is with you when you are here […] don't stay out of inertia – find somewhere else.'[22]

Marsh did find somewhere else. In April 1942, following the death of his sister, Marsh went to Cambridge to live with his brother-in-law, Sir Frederick Maurice. He eventually left Cambridge for a stay in Oxford in 1944 before finally returning to London. Throughout the war, wherever he was staying, he continued to travel to London in order to attend regular meetings at the Tate. In 1944, at the end of his seven-year term, Marsh retired from the Board of Trustees of the Tate. Jasper Ridley, Chairman of the Trustees, described him as 'the ideal 20th-century patron of art'.[23] Towards the end of the war Marsh had a financial imperative to sell one of his treasured pictures. He sold *The Vale of Aylesbury* by John Nash, and generously sent half the proceeds to the artist; the balance paid for his own somewhat costly and luxurious accommodation at the prestigious Goring Hotel.

Marsh's nomadic lifestyle continued after the war. He either stayed with friends in the country or in London hotels and clubs, until finally he moved into 86 Walton Street in 1946. To make him feel more settled in his new home, the Cornfords organised for a wireless to be purchased and installed. But Marsh was worried about the move. He was pleased to have a home of his own again, but limited space necessitated his selling many of his books and leaving several of his pictures deposited in the Tate vaults or lent out to friends. He surrounded himself with the remainder of his collection, filling all the available wall space or stacking pictures on the floor. Interspersed with the art were copious invitations to private views saved as mementoes of exhibitions he had attended. Speaking about his collection as early as 1939 he had described it as 'a continual joy in the making, and in the end a source of pride and enduring content'.[24] Marsh's picture collection was a reflection of his life in art. Each one a contained a story and was part of him.

Marsh was a seminal figure in the history of the Contemporary Art Society. He influenced acquisitions through his role as a collector, and when he became Chairman in 1936 he determined its policy and direction and membership grew exponentially. He remains one of its greatest benefactors. Furthermore, in his role as a vice-president of the Empire Art Council

> [he] manifested particular interest in art students of the Empire and Commonwealth who visited this country to further their studies. He conceived it to be his duty not only to allow them access to his rare collection of works of art but was at some pains personally to explain their technique. He made himself a friend of a vast circle of youthful enthusiasts.[25]

To the end of his days, although on a relatively modest budget, Marsh never ceased to support emerging artistic talent with unquestioning generosity. Christopher Hassall recalled visiting him in his flat one day where 'a funny little painter' had spread paintings all over the floor and Marsh 'out of pure kindness' was buying one. Hassall felt obliged to join Marsh in his praise of the paintings, but privately thought they were 'frightful'. [26]

Marsh was delighted when Ivon Hitchens (whom Marsh had first spotted in 1925), wrote to thank him: 'I expect you don't realize the affectionate respect we probably all feel – & certainly I do, & always have – for the first patron whose encouragement helped me to keep the flame alight in the days when no one knew or cared about such an unknown painter.'[27] Marsh thought it 'a wonderful thing to be told',[28] and was happy in the knowledge that his support had made such an impact.

In November 1952, in order to celebrate his eightieth birthday, the Contemporary Art Society commissioned the artist Graham Sutherland (who had also benefited from Marsh's patronage early in his career) to paint Marsh's portrait. Marsh's portrait was never painted, as he died two months after his birthday, long before Sutherland could start work. (In 1954 Sutherland was again commissioned, this time by Lord Beaverbrook, to paint Sir Winston Churchill's portrait to celebrate his eightieth birthday.)

In the last years of his life he was sought out by another young painter, Harry Drury. Marsh had met Drury informally at the Burlington Galleries and took up his cause, supporting him by paying the rent on a studio for him in Paris. Drury had returned to London from Paris armed with three paintings which Marsh thought 'a good start'. He invited Robin Darwin, then Rector of the Royal College of Art, to lunch in order to meet Drury, hoping Darwin would be of use to him – 'a great name for my purpose'.[29] Marsh was also a sitter for Drury. After Marsh's death, Drury, in expectation of a bequest from his will, called on Marsh's friend, the biographer James Pope-Hennessy, who had witnessed a codicil to Marsh's will which had promised to provide something for Drury. Pope-Hennessy was disparaging about Drury. Writing to Christopher Hassall, he said:

> Harry Drury suddenly turned up. He was half-drunk but quite intelligible. I gather that he has found his level in Saint-Germain-des-Prés and the phony world that gathers there, and that he only wishes to be able to live in Paris and paint. […] I strongly urged Drury to go to America, a place he longs to visit, and if possible stay there. I slightly incline to think him mad. Sordid he undeniably seems.[30]

Pope-Hennessy was no stranger to the sordid side of life himself: a heavy drinker, he was also a homosexual who frequented shady Soho nightclubs and made use of 'Dilly' (Piccadilly) rent boys who were controlled and manipulated by criminal gangs. It is not clear exactly when he and Marsh had first met, but they had mutual friends who included Harold Nicolson and the spy Guy Burgess. Marsh had first met Burgess at a dinner in 1940: 'I sat next to a very attractive youth called Guy Burgess, working in M.I.6, most intelligent, & "live-wire" […] I think I established relations with him & he promised to ring up & come here [Raymond Buildings], I hope he will.'[31]

Marsh's impressive political and social contacts as well as his penchant for high society gossip would probably have been of interest to Burgess. Burgess defected to the USSR in 1951, so it is not surprising that he is not mentioned in Hassall's biography of Marsh published in 1959, or that the letter referring to him is absent from the volume of their correspondence published in 1964. In 1945 Pope-Hennessy, on his return to London from Washington where he had risen through the ranks of the British Army working in military intelligence, shared a flat in London with Burgess. They had much in common, not least their homosexuality and propensity for alcohol.

Pope-Hennessy had become close to Marsh in his later years. He helped to organise Marsh's eightieth birthday celebratory dinner at the Travellers Club and commemorated the occasion by writing an affectionate piece about him for *The Spectator*.[32] He was very upset at the news of Marsh's death: 'No more generous or painstaking friend could one have had. I was devoted to him, and I shall miss him all my life.'[33] (Tragically his own life was cut short on 25 January 1974, when he was brutally murdered in his flat by three young men after money – Pope-Hennessy had been given a lucrative advance to write a biography of Noël Coward. One of the men, John O'Brien, had been living with him for months before.)

It is not clear whether Harry Drury ever received his bequest, but according to his biographical statement published online in 2000, 'His sojourn to London's bustling art scene of the 40's brought him an artist's grant from Sir Edward Marsh, [...] the Tate gallery exhibited Drury's work in 1950.'[34] It appears that Drury followed Pope-Hennessy's advice and settled in the USA.

Marsh was consistent in his support for British contemporary art until his death. He thought Lucien Freud's work was brilliant, but unable to resist a joke he wrote to Hassall after attending a private view of Freud's work describing one of the paintings:

> a portrait of his wife (Epstein's daughter) with a white fox-terrier in her lap, an agonized expression, & her dress in such sweet disorder that her right breast is completely exposed, with one very pronounced tit sticking up in the middle of it, 'Girl with a dog' was the title in the catalogue, but I think it must be a misprint & should be 'Girl with a dug'.[35]

Above all, it was the original group of Slade students – his 'Georgian painters' – whose work had inspired the strong visceral response he experienced when looking at paintings. As John Rothenstein Director of the Tate Gallery, confirmed in his tribute to Marsh, 'In his heart […] he remained faithful to the artists – the Spencer and the Nash brothers, Grant, Gertler, and their contemporaries – who had first aroused in him the lust of possession.'[36]

THE PLAYERS

Chapter Ten

'*All* plays are divine'

Diana Mosley, who had frequently encountered Marsh on her visits to Chartwell, acknowledged his great passion for art, but more memorable for her was his interest in the theatre: 'He fired us all with enthusiasm for various second-rate painters and some first-rate ones too, but his chief interest was the theatre. The Churchill children said that if he was asked what he thought of the play he would reply: "*All* plays are divine, but some are diviner than others."'[1]

Marsh was certainly an avid theatre-goer. His fervent enthusiasm earned him a reputation as 'the best known first-nighter in London'.[2] It was not unusual for him to see two plays in a day, as well as paying regular visits to the cinema to see the latest films. His letters contain effusive descriptions of plays, films, the writers, and the actors starring in them. Hugh Walpole remarked in his diary, 'He [Marsh] seems to do nothing but read novels and go to first nights, with intervals of doing some work for Winston.'[3] Walpole's subtle smirch could just as easily have applied to himself: he was as keen a theatre-goer as Marsh, and as his biographer Rupert Hart-Davis pointed out, 'All his life he went to every play he could, including revues, musical comedies, and, later on, films.'[4] Walpole and Marsh no doubt bumped into each other on countless first nights.

H. H. Asquith in a letter to Venetia Stanley mentioned attending a party at the Connaught Rooms to celebrate the 500th night of Arnold Bennett's play *The Great Adventure* where he encountered 'a lot of actors & actresses with Eddie Marsh'.[5] Marsh was in his element.

An article about Marsh in the *Leader Magazine* stated that 'Nowhere was he happier than at a theatrical first night. Since, at fourteen, he saw Henry Irving and Ellen Terry in the *Merchant of Venice* he has been faithful to this worship.'[6] An earlier feature in *The Bystander* described him as 'one of the most persistent first-nighters in the country';[7] and Noël Coward referred to him as 'dear Eddie Marsh, that Dean of first nighters'.[8] Even when Marsh had collapsed on his Corsican holiday, wondering whether or not he would survive, he had thought, 'If I survived, would Ivor Novello be able to arrange for me to attend the first night of his play *The Truth Game* as a stretcher case?'[9]

The theatre critic St John Ervine alleged, 'His devotion to the theatre was so deep he saw every sort of play, including many that would have seemed unlikely to interest a man of his quality.'[10] Marsh confessed, 'I enjoy the play like a child, and show it; which makes me popular with the players, but gets me into trouble with the critics.'[11] He was sentimental and easily moved by a play: Harold Nicolson recalled, 'How often, on emerging from some really horrible play, have we encountered Eddie Marsh with tears still wet upon his cheeks!'[12] Furthermore Ervine recalled how during one performance he was 'distracted by the sound of heavy sobs' only to discover that it was Marsh who was crying and 'uttering banshee sobs', much to the acute embarrassment of his companion, Ivor Novello.[13]

Diana Mosley remembered running into an animated Marsh at the premiere of Noël Coward's *Bitter Sweet*, on 18 July 1929 at Her Majesty's Theatre: '"What do you think of it? Isn't it divine?" he said, his monocle glittering with delight. "Well, not *very*," I said, "but I'm glad we came because it won't run will it?" I thought it was bound to flop. "My dear Artemis, it will run forever," said Eddie. He knew what was what.'[14] Its London run lasted for 697 performances at five different theatres.

Marsh's opinion of a play was not discriminating enough for some people; it was as if his usual critical powers had been diluted by his suspension of disbelief during a performance. Arnold Bennett, for one, would have disagreed that Marsh 'knew what was what' when it came to an appraisal of a play. Decrying Marsh's enjoyment of a new play that Bennett had not liked, he reportedly said, 'hang Eddie Marsh, he's a miserable fellow – he enjoys everything.' On another occasion, after the first act of a performance of Chekhov's *The Seagull*, Marsh had rushed across the theatre to speak to Bennett, convinced that they would agree the play was 'heaven', only to be reprimanded for getting so 'carried away' and told that it was a 'shocking production!' Their discord culminated at the first night performance of *Polly* (the sequel to John Gay's *The Beggar's Opera*), when Bennett accused Marsh of leading the encores and making the proceedings 'much too long'.[15] Marsh was oblivious to Bennett's criticisms.

Marsh was interested not only in plays but in the actors themselves. Somerset Maugham was disparaging about his 'spluttering admiration for actors' that Maugham regarded as 'over-estimated'.[16] Nonetheless, Marsh would count among his friends a stellar cast which included the luminaries John Gielgud, Ralph Richardson, Celia Johnson, Michael Redgrave, Sybil Thorndike, Vivien Leigh and Laurence Olivier. He adored the atmosphere of the theatre, and never missed an opportunity to go backstage after a performance to hobnob with the cast. As a young boy, long before he was permitted to go to a performance, he knew all the names of the stars of the day. Though lavish with his praise publicly, he would often criticise the performers in private. He said of one actress, '[she] sings like a cow with adenoids, besides which her head is too big for her body, which is saying A LOT', and of another, 'She smiles like Malvolio and can hardly finish a sentence in her impatience to get all her teeth on view again.'[17] He was also critical of Laurence Olivier's performance in the 1944 film of Shakespeare's *Henry V*. Despite thinking the film an 'extraordinary achievement', which it was by the technical standards of the day, he found it 'disappointing'; and he was 'disappointed in Larry too, he had come straight out of a bandbox – and his face off a chocolate box, and his voice seemed harsh and too high, and almost unmodulated – a great contrast with his stage Richard III'.[18] According to St John Ervine, Marsh was also 'sharply critical' of Olivier's performance as Romeo.[19] However, Marsh particularly admired Olivier's wife, Vivien Leigh, for her acting talent and her 'ravishing looks and exquisite movements'.[20] Flora Robson did not come off so well in his eyes: after watching her play Thérèse

Raquin in *Guilty* at the Old Vic in 1944, Marsh callously complained that 'Flora R[obson] has got really too ugly – she does nothing about it, & when the girl says how beautiful & like a fairy princess she looks in her wedding dress, it's quite embarrassing.'[21]

Marsh's interest in the theatre had been fostered by his disreputable Uncle Norman, but his father – who was nothing like Uncle Norman – had also taken the young Eddie to the theatre. His mother thoroughly disapproved, and soon put a stop to the father and son bonding after a trip to the Adelphi Theatre in 1887 to see the romantic drama *The Bells of Haslemere*, starring the ill-fated actor William Terriss (he was to be murdered ten years later). Marsh was only fourteen years old at the time, but despite her best efforts his mother was unable to destroy his fascination for the theatre. Moreover, once Marsh was firmly ensconced at Cambridge he found himself engaged as the theatre and music critic for Oswald Sickert's publishing venture the *Cambridge Observer*. He wrote a well-received piece on the first performance in England of Ibsen's *A Doll's House*, which Sickert sent to Oscar Wilde. Wilde, who was Sickert's family friend, responded with an invitation for Sickert and Marsh to visit him. Regrettably for Marsh the meeting never took place, but he did attend the opening night of Wilde's *The Importance of Being Earnest*, and declared it 'the greatest thing since Sheridan'.[22]

Marsh's appetite for the theatre was all-embracing. A convert to Ibsen, he was a frequent attendee at the Independent Theatre, which was set up as a subscription-only theatre in order to put on plays which had literary and artistic merit over commercial value. Here he saw Ibsen's *Rosmersholm* and *The Master Builder*. He found himself in good literary company, as Thomas Hardy and Henry James were also members. He enjoyed the plays, but was frustrated by the management of the place: he bemoaned the ineptitude of the Acting Manager and complained that 'The performances generally begin 20 minutes late [...] You're never safe from the irruption of a cat in the most moving scenes, the actors aren't ready to come on at their cues, or the curtain stays up at the end of the act.'[23] Given Marsh's account it is not surprising that the theatre was wound up after only six years, its ambition thwarted by lack of financial success.

The *Cambridge Observer* was also short-lived, but its failure did not dampen Marsh's love of the theatre. On his initial visit home after his first term at Cambridge his mother noted in her journal, 'Of course theatre is the thing he looks forward to most.'[24] During his vacations from Cambridge on his travels abroad Marsh would frequently attend the theatre: in Berlin he saw plays by Hauptmann and Wagner's opera *Lohengrin*.

Marsh liked to share his passion for the stage with his young friends, notably Rupert Brooke (several of his letters to Brooke include effusive descriptions of the latest plays). Determined to introduce Brooke to the theatrical delights of London, Marsh invited him to the opening of Henry Hamilton's *The Whip* at Drury Lane in 1909 as well as a performance of Oscar Wilde's *The Importance of Being Earnest* at the St James's Theatre. Thereafter Brooke was a regular theatre-goer, albeit mainly due to Marsh's largesse. One play in particular had captured Marsh's interest, John Galworthy's *Justice*. The play, which opened in 1910 at the Duke of York's Theatre, contributed to the widespread debate around the campaign to reform conditions in prisons. Marsh was 'tremendously for it', and thought it 'an exceedingly able play and the acting and production [...] beyond praise'.[25]

In the course of his youthful forays into high society, at a private party hosted by the Duke and Duchess of Rutland at Belvoir Castle Marsh met the opera singer Dame Nellie Melba. She had refused to sing at the party, he said, so he 'sang to her instead, and had a great success with her'.[26]

Also at the party was Diana Manners, the daughter of Violet, Duchess of Rutland, and a society beauty. From the time she was a debutante Diana was rarely out of the newspapers and gossip columns. Like so many men, Marsh admired Diana's good looks; on this occasion he described her as being 'more beautiful than ever, her complexion is easily the most wonderful I've ever seen'.[27] Marsh may have admired Diana's appearance, but her behaviour was risqué by Edwardian standards – although those standards often simply meant preserving appearances: as long as people were discreet they could behave in immoral ways. Diana wanted to be seen as avant-garde, and she thrived on her hedonistic notoriety: smoking, alcohol and drugs were de rigueur. Speaking of her friendship with Marsh, Diana recalled, 'I knew him best when I was 14.'[28] Diana was precocious, and mixed with a much older set – the same Oxford friends that Marsh spent time with – which included her future husband, Duff Cooper. It was a small world of a privileged elite which shared not only interests and friendships but also lovers.

Like Marsh, Diana Manners was enthralled with the theatre. Her friends Iris and Viola Tree were the daughters of the actor Sir Herbert Beerbohm Tree, who was an intimate friend of her mother. From an early age she accompanied her mother to the theatre, and amateur performances were a regular occurrence at Belvoir. She was especially inspired by Diaghilev's Russian Ballet, which took London by storm when the company appeared at Covent Garden in the summer of 1911. Marsh too was 'enraptured from the moment the curtain went up. It's a Post-Impressionist picture put in motion' he said.[29] Marsh followed this experience a few years later with the debut performance of Nijinsky's own company on 2 March 1914 at the Palace Theatre. The Russian Ballet was a phenomenal success that signalled the dawn of a new artistic sensibility in the early twentieth century.

Diana Manners was unconcerned that actresses were deemed to have a somewhat colourful reputation. After her marriage to Duff Cooper in 1919 she went on to pursue a short-lived but relatively successful acting career, starring in films and on the stage in London and the USA.

Marsh's circle of thespian friends was growing exponentially; he had become intimate friends with Cathleen Nesbitt through her relationship with Rupert Brooke, but he also counted Viola Tree and the *grande dame* of the theatre, Mrs Patrick Campbell, among his close friends. The latter was one of the most successful actresses of her day and was the object of George Bernard Shaw's long-lasting infatuation.

Marsh's persistent passion for plays – and players – was to find its apotheosis in 1916 when he met a handsome young composer from Wales: David Ivor Davies, better known as Ivor Novello.

Chapter Eleven

Ivor Novello: 'A genius for happiness'

Ivor Novello was born David Ivor Davies in Cardiff on 15 January 1893 to Clara Novello Davies and David Davies. His family always referred to him as Ivor and later he adopted his mother's name 'Novello' as his stage name. In 1927 he formally changed his name to Ivor Novello by deed poll. His mother (simply referred to as 'Mam' by Novello and his circle) was the most important influence in his life. Clara Novello Davies was destined for a musical career. She had been named after the famous soprano Clara Novello and was initially taught music by her father, Jacob Davies, a miner and leader of the local church choir. Later on she was taught by Charles Williams, the organist at Llandaff Cathedral, and while still a young woman she accompanied the prize-winning Cardiff United Choir and Cardiff Blue Ribbon Choir. Clara was very ambitious, and in 1883 she founded and conducted the Welsh Ladies Choir which went on to win prizes at the Chicago World Fair in 1893 and the Paris Exposition in 1900. The choir was also invited to perform for Queen Victoria, and henceforth she was given permission to call her choir the Royal Welsh Ladies Choir. She also taught piano and gave singing lessons. Her fame grew rapidly and she regularly travelled to London to teach, eventually renting a house in Maida Vale and another studio near Hanover Square, where actresses and chorus girls would come for singing lessons. She was a *tour de force*, and ambitious not only for herself but also for her son, to whom she was devoted.

Ivor Novello was an adored child, bright, funny and imaginative. Encouraged by Mam, he demonstrated a precocious musical talent, both in singing and in playing the piano. He loved trips to the theatre and was thrilled by the illusion, extravagance and gaiety of Edwardian musicals. However Mam was keen that her son should have a serious musical education, and her persistence paid off when she entered him for a scholarship at Magdalen College Choir School, Oxford, at the age of ten. Novello was awarded the Soprano Scholarship and he spent five happy years there. He left abruptly at the age of sixteen, allegedly as a result of sexual improprieties. It has been suggested that Novello seduced most, if not all, the members of the choir, but there is no evidence to support these rumours. But certainly by the age of sixteen his voice had broken.

After Oxford he returned to London and worked with Mam accompanying singers on the piano and giving piano lessons, but that soon gave way to composing music and popular songs. This was the beginning of what was to become an illustrious career. His songs were published and performed by the stars of the day. Novello also harboured dreams of performing on the stage, but Mam thwarted his early attempts at that and insisted he focus on composing. In 1913 they moved to a flat (simply referred to thereafter as 'The Flat') above the Strand Theatre at 11 Aldwych, where Mam 'gave interminable singing lessons to small Welsh women in grey clothes'.[1] That was to be Novello's London residence for the rest of his life.

Meanwhile Mam's talent for self-promotion continued unabated. In the summer of 1914 she decided to take her singing school pupils from the polluted air of London to a campsite in Biggin Hill, Kent. With Novello in tow, they hired a gypsy caravan and emulated a rustic, bohemian lifestyle; the endeavour was recorded in a photo-shoot by the popular *Tatler* magazine and brought much welcome publicity. It was a fleeting adventure, as the prospect of war brought them back to London. The country was gripped by war fever, and, not one to miss an opportunity, Mam tried to convince Novello to capitalise on this impassioned patriotism and compose a war song along the lines of the popular tune *It's a Long Way to Tipperary*. He was reluctant to do so, but was finally persuaded when he heard Mam's own attempt, *Keep the Flag a' Flying*, which he thought appalling. Novello collaborated with an American friend and lyricist, Lena Guilbert Ford, and together they came up with the legendary song *Keep the Home Fires Burning*. It was a favourite with the troops and public alike and became an anthem of the First World War, as much a part of British cultural history as Rupert

Brooke's poem *The Soldier*. There was however one famous soldier poet, Siegfried Sassoon, who dissented and made no secret of disliking the song and despising its composer.

Novello, whose good looks and innate charm made him generally popular, had acquired a large circle of theatrical friends, one of whom was Viola Tree. In December 1915 Marsh had been invited by Viola Tree to see *Mavoureen*, starring Lily Elsie as Nell Gwynn, at Her Majesty's Theatre. Unusually Marsh was sent his ticket beforehand: Viola explained that on this occasion they would not be sitting together. During the performance Marsh noticed her sitting with 'a remarkably good-looking young man';[2] after the first act Marsh was invited to meet her handsome companion, Ivor Novello. On being asked by Novello what he thought of Lily Elsie, Marsh replied with rapturous enthusiasm, which was absolutely the right response, as Novello was a devotee: the walls of his room in the Aldwych flat were covered with photographs of her in *The Merry Widow*. Having ingratiated himself with Novello, Marsh joined them in their box for the remainder of the play. This event was the beginning of a significant friendship for both men; several years later Christopher Hassall mused, 'I have often reflected on the strange devices of Destiny, and on this meeting at His Majesty's, so important to the lives of all three of us, which occurred while I was asleep in my cot, not far away at Notting Hill Gate, an infant three years old.'[3]

While Marsh thought Novello 'a remarkably good-looking young man', what might Novello have made of Marsh? He would have observed

> a dapper man of about forty, in an elegant grey suit, with a
> grey silk tie of a slightly lighter shade. He held himself upright,
> making quick movements like a bird. And when he spoke, it was
> with a bird's voice. The pitch was high, and very slightly nasal.
> When he was excited or amused, he twittered like a bird. His eyes
> were bright, and his bushy eyebrows swept upwards into points,
> like a genial Mephistopheles. His ears […] were perfectly flat,
> having no curl on the outward edge.[4]

On 1 January 1916 Marsh went to visit the Aldwych flat for the first time. It was also his first encounter with the antiquated and temperamental lift that frequently got stuck between floors and in which on one occasion he was trapped for hours. He met Mam and Mr Davies, Novello's father, who had retired from his job with Cardiff Council and, according to Marsh, was a 'dear pathetic old thing',[5] as well as 'the laziest man I've ever known'.[6] Marsh was not overly impressed with Mam either; he observed, 'She accounts for a good deal of Ivor but he's still a freak of heredity. She has a bracelet with a photograph of him on each arm.'[7]

Marsh took it upon himself, not for the first time in his life, to supervise, broaden and refine Novello's education. He began by giving him a copy of Rupert Brooke's *Letters from America*. He also had a piano installed in his flat in Raymond Buildings so that Novello could work away from the distraction of Mam and her pupils. This was not a purely altruistic move on Marsh's part, as he was extremely happy to have Novello spend time under his roof. They quickly became inseparable. Marsh's morning drop-in visits to see Novello were augmented by regular theatre trips, which included far more musical comedy than the urbane Marsh had previously enjoyed, followed by late-night parties back at The Flat. As well as a hectic social life with Marsh Novello was kept busy with theatrical obligations, one of which he had taken on to please Marsh. Novello wrote the music of two songs sung by Viola Tree in Gordon Bottomley's play *King Lear's Wife*. Bottomley was one of the many Georgian poets that Marsh was anxious for Novello to meet.

Notwithstanding his burgeoning theatrical career, Novello was keen to join the ongoing war effort, and enlisted Marsh's help with an application to join the Royal Naval Air Service (RNAS). Marsh had already helped another young man, Lance Sieveking, to join the RNAS. Sieveking had enlisted with the Artists Rifles, where he had met Marsh's young artist friend Paul Nash: feeling that Sieveking was 'inconveniently tall for the trenches'[8] Nash encouraged him to contact Marsh. As a result he was fast-tracked to a commission in the RNAS. Sieveking and Marsh became lifelong friends and their paths were to cross many times, especially when Sieveking later became a renowned producer at the BBC. Sieveking recalled in his memoir:

> I have sometimes felt, looking back, that he was already looking for someone to fill the place in his life left suddenly empty by the loss of his great friend Rupert Brooke, and that he greeted each new man he came across hopefully. If so, he was, in my case, very completely disappointed. But our friendship was wonderful for me.[9]

Marsh's efforts on Novello's behalf were equally successful: on 25 June 1916 he reported for training as 'D. Davies, Probationary Flight Sub-Lieutenant RNAS'. Novello was most pleased with his appearance in his uniform and happily surprised by his ability to understand the lectures. Marsh had exerted his influence behind the scenes for Rupert Brooke with tragic consequences, but as Sieveking intuited, though still mourning the death of Brooke Marsh felt he had found in Novello, with his musical talent and ravishing good looks, a perfect successor on which to bestow his interest and affection. Novello was the perfect antidote to grief.

Through Marsh and the RNAS Sieveking naturally made the acquaintance of Novello, who he found 'one of the most spontaneously warm-hearted people I ever met. It was wonderful to be with him for even an hour. However tired or depressed one might have been, one always left him feeling happy and well and ready for anything.'[10]

No wonder Marsh found Novello irresistible. He had an appealing *joie de vivre*: even Mrs Elgy observed 'How Mr. Novello does enjoy fun, it fairly beams out of him!'[11] As a great mimic he managed to entertain and endear himself to people as opposed to offending them. Marsh described how on Ivor's first meeting with Mrs Patrick Campbell 'he had the impudence to mimic her to her face. When she told him she didn't talk like that, he said: "You're *doo*ing it *naawh.*" She adored him for it.'[12]

Marsh was determined to broaden Novello's artistic horizons: he criticised him for 'turning out catchy tunes which are very pretty and great fun, but not so good as he ought to do'.[13] He decided to introduce

Novello to Robert Graves (who had been sent home from the Front after sustaining a serious injury) in an attempt to encourage him to compose settings for a selection of Graves's poems. Graves wrote to Marsh while recuperating: 'I'm longing to see you on Sat. Try to bring Ivor Novello with you. I'd love to meet him if he wouldn't be bored.'[14]

Marsh also set about making introductions to polite society for Novello as he had for Rupert Brooke. They attended soirées hosted by the great and the good, and were invited to dine at home with Lady Randolph Churchill and her son, Winston (waited on by female footmen in pale blue tailcoats).[15] Winston Churchill's extensive repertoire of music hall numbers was sung over port with Novello accompanying on the piano; there was an anxious moment for Novello when Churchill said, 'Do you know you'd be far better off in a home?' Fortunately it was the title of an obscure music hall ditty, not an exclamation on Novello's sanity. Marsh topped this with an introduction to Novello's heroine, Lily Elsie, at 10 Downing Street at a tea arranged by Elizabeth Asquith, the Prime Minister's daughter.

A particularly significant introduction that Marsh made for Novello during this time was to another attractive and witty young man of his acquaintance, the actor Robert Andrews. Bobbie Andrews, whose older sister was an actress, had begun his stage career as a child and was a contemporary of Noël Coward, who had also begun his career as a child actor. Novello and Andrews were instantly attracted to each other, and quickly became friends and lovers. Andrews provided stability in Novello's life, and although they both had sexual relationships with other men, their personal and professional partnership endured until Novello's death. While Novello's stage career was to reach meteoric heights, Andrews' acting career remained low-key, but he was always in work, often appearing in parts written for him by Novello. Marsh and Andrews inevitably became close friends through their mutual affection for Novello.

Novello's military career took a different turn: he made as many solo flights as crash landings, two in all, but emerged from the wreckage nonplussed. As a result Marsh organised a safer option, a job in the Air Ministry, based at the Hotel Cecil in London, in front of a typewriter. Novello found time between his official duties to compose for the theatre: his reputation as an accomplished composer of light music and popular songs was growing apace. During the war musical theatre prospered; British soldiers home on leave wanted to be entertained rather than educated. Initially Marsh was determined to elevate Novello to a higher intellectual level, but eventually it was Marsh who succumbed to Novello's irrepressible talent to provide joy and entertainment. Novello was capricious, eccentric, utterly charming, and irresistible to the cultured civil servant. Nonetheless Marsh was concerned about Novello's lack of purpose and drive. But that was about to change.

In January 1919, approaching his twenty-sixth birthday, Novello, accompanied by Bobbie Andrews, crossed the Atlantic to New York. Mam had already established herself there, where she had rented a studio and was giving singing lessons. Immediately Novello immersed himself in the vibrant atmosphere of the city: he wrote to Marsh telling him that he had seen '26 plays, 6 operas and been to 18 parties'.[16] Novello's missives to Marsh were very different from Brooke's letters from America. Busy enjoying himself, he was in any case an unreliable correspondent, as Marsh later complained: 'Ivor is the only person I love enough to write to without getting proper answers – he always says he adores my letters, but he hardly ever replies, and when he does he never takes the slightest notice of anything I've said (which is always so disappointing).'[17]

After a five month stay Novello was on his way back to Britain when he received a cable from a London theatrical agent asking him whether he would like to appear in a film. The Swiss film director Louis Mercanton had seen a photograph of the handsome Novello, sporting a Latin-lover look reminiscent of the exotic Rudolph Valentino, and decided that he would be the perfect romantic lead in his next film, *The Call of the Blood*. Without any formal training, but as an inveterate observer of actors, Novello instinctively flourished as a performer in front of the camera, not least due to his powerful physical presence. The filming took place in Sicily and Rome. Eager to assist, Marsh contacted the British Embassy in Rome on his behalf, and Novello was royally entertained during his stay there. He was in high spirits, and wrote to Marsh: 'I can't tell you what fun I'm having – the best for ages'; as for the film work, 'Apparently I'm thought to have a marvellous flair, and a great future and fortune, and really Eddie, it does seem to come so easy.'[18] Novello worked on several films, including two by Alfred Hitchcock, *The Lodger* (1926) and *Downhill* (1927). He soon became one of the most popular film stars of the 1920s – a matinee idol in Britain, and, following his appearance in *The White Rose* (1923), described by the American press as 'the most handsome man in England'.

Notwithstanding Novello's film success Marsh continued to press him to write; he had managed to get a short story that Novello had penned, *Red Buttons*, published in the *Westminster Gazette*. They even wrote a song together, *The Land of Might Have Been*, with Marsh's lyrics (albeit written under the pseudonym of Edward Moore) set to Novello's melody; it became a popular classic of the time and featured in *Our Nell* at the Gaiety Theatre. Their friendship blossomed, as did Novello's career, in tandem with the inevitable social round of parties, the epicentre of which was the Aldwych flat. Marsh was in the habit of calling on Novello each morning, no matter whether Novello was in bed or not. After shows there would be supper and songs back at The Flat with a cornucopia of friends, many of whom comprised the cream of London's West End. Noël Coward was a frequent visitor. He recalled: 'I saw a lot of Ivor and Bobbie […] In his flat there was a delicious atmosphere of slight quarrels and gossiping. Everyone drank a lot of tea and discussed what [André] Charlot had said and what Fay [Compton] had said and how Eddie thought it was marvellous anyway.'[19]

Novello had been introduced to Noël Coward by Bobbie Andrews in 1917 in Manchester, where the musical comedy *Arlette* for which Novello had written seven songs was playing. Novello invited Coward to tea and Coward recalled how he had 'envied thoroughly everything about him. His looks, his personality, his assured position, his dinner clothes […] I didn't begrudge him his glamorous life. Nobody who knew Ivor for five minutes could ever begrudge him anything.'[20] In turn, Novello introduced Noël Coward to Marsh. He had asked Marsh for his thoughts on the manuscript of a play that Coward had just written, *The Rat Trap*, his 'first serious attempt at psychological conflict'.[21] Like so many writers before and after him Coward was immensely grateful for Marsh's '*brilliant* criticism'.[22] Coward found Marsh's 'passionate interest in the theatre, painting and everything to do with the Arts [...] immensely stimulating'.[23] He was however no doubt relieved when Marsh's negative critique following the first night of his *Hayfever* at the Ambassadors Theatre on 8 June 1925 was proved wrong. 'Not this time Noël',[24] Marsh had pronounced, but *Hayfever*, which starred Bobbie Andrews, ran for 337 performances in London and has been revived many times since. Although Marsh was dismissive of *Hayfever*, he spoke highly of the man himself: 'Noël Coward who for a boy of 26 is really miraculous – I don't mean to put him too high, but he has a sense of the theatre and a sense of style which might carry him anywhere.'[25] In this instance Marsh's judgement was spot on.

Throughout their careers Novello and Coward were both friends and rivals. In 1941 Novello's play *Breakaway* was produced at the Windsor Repertory Theatre; neither Bobbie Andrews nor Marsh thought it was very good, but Novello thought it had been 'rapturously received at Windsor' and was 'convinced of its Entertainment Value'. One member of the audience had written to tell her mother:

> We were given 4 tickets by the manager of the Windsor Repertory theatre to see the 1st night of Ivor Novello's new play 'Breakaway' last night [...] I didn't think it a particularly good play but it was very amusing and well done. Afterwards Novello made his usual gushing speech – then we went to the bar where we saw a very motley crew of actors.[26]

Marsh was particularly concerned with how *Breakaway* would compare to Coward's latest production: 'I actually dared to tell Ivor that I should be sorry if he were represented by it in London just when *Blithe Spirit* was showing Noël at his cleverest.'[27] *Blithe Spirit* was a notable success, but according to Marsh Coward did not like Margaret Rutherford's performance in the play; Novello reportedly said, 'it's an odd thing, N. [Noël] never likes anyone who makes a success in a play of his.'[28]

The only time Novello and Coward collaborated on a production it was a fiasco. In 1927 Basil Dean produced Coward's play *Sirocco*, and Novello played the leading man. Coward recalled, 'Although his looks were marvellous for the part, and his name, owing to film successes, was a big draw, his acting experience in those days was negligible.'[29] According to Coward, in Act II 'the storm broke during Ivor's love scene', when the hostile audience shrieked with laughter and yelled abuse at the actors, and 'the last act was chaos from beginning to end'.[30] In his autobiography, *Present Indicative* (which Novello thought should have been entitled *Past Provocative*) Coward gave a glowing tribute to Novello's spirit:

> Ivor's behaviour all through was remarkable. He had played a
> long and strenuous part in the face of dreadful odds without
> betraying for an instant that he was even conscious of them, and
> at the end, with full realisation that all his trouble and hard work
> had gone for less than nothing, his sense of humour was still clear
> and strong enough to enable him to make a joke of the whole
> thing. Nor was he apparently in the least ruffled by the inevitable
> Press blast the next day. He made no complaints, attached no
> blame or responsibilities to anyone, and accepted failure with the
> same grace with which he has always accepted success.[31]

Novello was a life-enhancing presence. After the disastrous performance Marsh accompanied them both back to The Flat for a post-mortem on the proceedings. He was impressed by their courage and lack of self-pity, and especially by Novello's modesty and ability to laugh at himself. The next day Coward and his party met Novello and his coterie for lunch at the Ivy 'and discussed the miseries of the night before with growing hilarity'.[32] *Sirocco*, which had opened on 24 November 1927, closed after twenty-eight performances.

Marsh was a sympathetic friend and theatre-goer. When Dodie Smith's first play, *Autumn Crocus*, which she had written under the alias of C. L. Anthony, was staged in 1931 it too did not go down well with the audience. There were heckling and boos from the crowd in the gallery; in response, the audience in the stalls (which comprised a large contingent of Miss Smith's friends and colleagues from Heal's (the furniture store where she worked) started to boo the hecklers, and Marsh 'stood up and shook his fist at the mob'.[33] Fortunately the critics were more enthusiastic than the gallery audience, and when her real identity was disclosed the popular headlines read 'Shopgirl writes play'.

Novello and Coward now moved in the same elevated social circles as Marsh and attended fashionable parties hosted by two of the best known hostesses in London, Lady (Emerald) Cunard and Lady Sibyl Colefax. In 1925 they were invited as special guests to judge the fancy dresses at the Carnival Ball in the Hammersmith Palais de Danse, which was a fundraising event for the British Fascists (a precursor to Oswald Mosley's British Union of Fascists). This was hardly what Philip Hoare in 2014 described as a 'flirtation with fascism' on their part,[34] but Marsh could be said to have had a 'flirtation with fascism' by way of his association with Diana Mosley (wife of Oswald Mosley) and James 'Jim' Strachey Barnes.

Barnes had been one of Marsh's great friends before becoming a right-wing radical and an apologist for fascism. He resided in Italy during the Second World War and was an outspoken champion of Benito Mussolini. The friendship between Marsh and Barnes had been forged while they were undergraduates at Cambridge through their connections with the Bloomsbury Group. As young men they went on walking holidays in Spain and Italy together; Marsh never forgot how Barnes had forced him to walk across the Roman aqueduct at Tarragona, known as the Devil's Bridge. On one of their trips to Italy in January 1914 Marsh had introduced Barnes to D. H. Lawrence and his wife, Frieda, who were living in Lerici. He described how the three men 'walked by moonlight through the olives up the stony hillside path to the little house where the genial Frieda was waiting to welcome us'.[35] Barnes was an admirer of Lawrence, not least as they shared a love of Italy, and Lawrence also had a leaning towards fascism. George Barnes recalled his brother's friendship with Marsh: 'He was certainly a great friend and as a child I remember Jim talking more about Eddie Marsh than about anyone.'[36] In his youth Jim Barnes had been a member of the Fabian Society, but given his political views in later life it is not surprising that Marsh distanced himself from him, describing him as an 'ex-friend' and 'the Italian Haw-Haw'.[37]

Novello, whose penchant was for celebratory parties rather than political parties, did not always enjoy the parties he attended. Marsh gave an account of a disappointing celebrity party hosted by the *Daily Mirror* at which they were both guests: 'Ivor thought the party sadly squalid & vulgar, as indeed it was – & Ivor took me off to the flat, where I assisted at his couchee – & got home about 2.30.'[38] By way of contrast, both men enjoyed the sophisticated parties hosted by Somerset Maugham and his wife, the interior designer Syrie Maugham. Literary young men tended to gravitate around Maugham, while Syrie attracted artistic types like Oliver Messel and Cecil Beaton. Beaton's early ambition was to design theatrical scenery, and he was encouraged by his tutor, Billie Bullivant, to meet Noël Coward and Ivor Novello as Bullivant thought they could help him. Beaton was apprehensive: 'I just half wondered later if I wanted to get into the Ivor, Noel naughty set. They're rather cheap and horrid and yet sometimes very nice. If I got my start through them I should soon give them up and get on myself.'[39] Naughty or not, Beaton and Novello became friends. Beaton photographed Novello in the late 1940s; though Novello was still a handsome man, Beaton reported him as saying: 'I used to be considered a beauty. The only thing left is for me to become a genius.'[40]

The 'naughty set' to which Beaton referred also included Somerset Maugham, who, like Marsh, enjoyed being surrounded by attractive young men. Both would happily use their influence to help a youth with whom they were taken; however, the similarity between them ended there. Maugham was a promiscuous homosexual with a voracious sexual appetite, whereas Marsh was seemingly homosexual but celibate. Henry 'Chips' Channon described Marsh (and Marsh's friend Edward Knoblock) in his diary as 'fat and eunuchy and middle-aged'[41] – an unflattering portrayal, but Marsh was sexually ineffectual, not a player in this milieu, or a rival to Maugham as a sexual predator. Young ambitious men, like the writer and journalist Beverley Nichols, were happy to oblige Maugham's sexual proclivities, especially as he was known to entertain generously, shower his lovers with expensive gifts, and use his influence whenever he could. Nichols shocked Cecil Beaton with explicit tales of his visits to male brothels, sexual affairs with men, and his first-hand knowledge of the homosexual activity of Maugham and his set. Marsh was fond of Nichols and would socialise with him from time to time, but these were platonic encounters. Marsh's friend Lance Sieveking observed, 'I have sometimes wondered about Eddie and sex. He was nearly forty-three when I met him, and it seemed to have no place in his life.'[42]

At one party Maugham was introduced to an attractive young man, Alan Searle, whom Lytton Strachey called his 'Bronzino Boy'.[43] Maugham was immediately smitten, and learning that Searle yearned to travel invited him to leave the party to discuss plans for a Continental tour. Maugham was peeved to discover that Searle had already made arrangements with Novello that evening.[44] Searle eventually became Maugham's long-term companion, and between them they were responsible for spreading a titillating story concerning Winston Churchill. According to Maugham, during a lunch with Churchill he alleged that Churchill's mother had often implied that in his youth he had engaged in affairs with men. Maugham said that Churchill emphatically denied this, but said that he had once been to bed with a man to see what it was like. When asked with whom, he had replied 'Ivor Novello', and punned that the experience had been 'musical' – a euphemism for homosexual. As Novello's biographer James Harding rightly points out, since both Maugham and Searle were 'skilled raconteurs given to embroidering their tales for artistic effect, it may not be taken too seriously, if only because it would cast the highly respectable Eddie Marsh, then Winston's secretary, in the role of pimp'.[45] Marsh may have been obliging in many ways and adept at connecting people, but that would be taking it too far.

Novello enjoyed throwing parties as much as the Maughams did. After he purchased Redroofs, near Maidenhead in Berkshire, in 1927 a group of house guests would arrive most weekends, much to the amusement of the local residents of Littlewick Green who remarked upon the fancy cars and cloud of fragrance that accompanied them. The guests were usually famous, glamorous, bohemian and frequently homosexual, but while Mam was in residence Novello was on his best behaviour. Marsh used to spend many Sundays at Redroofs (usually travelling from London by bus), as well as most Christmas holidays. In 1936 a photo-feature appeared in *The Bystander*, 'Careless Country Rapture, Ivor Novello Entertains at Maidenhead': the photograph of a smiling Novello with his arm around his beloved Mam stands out from the page. Marsh described one such weekend party to Christopher Hassall:

> I had a lovely Sunday at Redroofs, a party of nine boys (even Mam didn't appear, as she has 'something bronchial') [...] most of the boys you can guess; the additions were Keneth [the actor Keneth Kent] (whom I like and you don't), Kenneth (whom neither of us likes very much, but he's rather appealing now, you know his father died suddenly & left him & Audrey literally penniless), and Barry Sinclair, who has great charm – but not very much to say for himself![46]

The weekend set was usually comprised of Novello's theatrical friends – writers, librettists, producers and actors – with the addition of Marsh, who was content to remain on the periphery of this glittering scene, taking his respectable place alongside Mam. The common ground between Marsh and Mam was their love for Novello, but Marsh's irritation at her behaviour was often barely concealed. Novello was Mam's 'precious angel', and when she was apart from him she relied on Marsh to ensure that all was well. She was keen to remind Marsh of his place in the hierarchy of Novello's affections and asked him to 'Tell Ivor I've got an Eddie too', but was quick to add, 'but, of course not like his Eddie'. In her absence she exhorted Marsh to 'Hug my precious one for me.'[47] What Marsh was blissfully unaware of was that Mam, despite considering him one of her dearest friends, had never understood a word he had said in the thirty years she had known him.

As her own fame and popularity dwindled Mam took on the mantle of pseudo-royalty; a veritable queen mother, she attended her son's first night performances and graced the Royal Box with great splendour. Mam was an emotional and financial drain on Novello, which was a cause of concern for Marsh and Bobbie Andrews. On one occasion while staying at Redroofs Marsh remarked, 'Mam is also here, in very high spirits & full flow, with new dresses […]. Ivor was deploring that the rent of her London flat has to be paid till March, but she took this very airily, saying "Nobody bothers about rent nowadays" – what could she mean by this?'[48]

Marsh was extremely irritated by Mam's profligacy. He composed an ode, *Mater pauperis Ivori* (Mother makes Ivor a pauper), to protest: 'How long, old Madam, will you carry on / This monstrous racket, which your patient *son* / So obviously can't afford?'[49] But Novello would not tolerate any overt criticism of his mother, so his partner, Bobbie Andrews, would vent his frustration and confide in Marsh when Mam was 'being troublesome about money'.[50]

Marsh was no more sympathetic towards Mam's health problems than her financial predicament. He firmly believed that her various illnesses were a device for commanding Novello's attention. On one occasion she had woken up in the middle of the night with a swollen tongue, 'too big for her mouth – it was most alarming', but Marsh quickly dismissed it with 'she seems all right again today'.[51] Much to Marsh's annoyance, Mam's persistent ailments disrupted Novello during a tour. While performing in Edinburgh Novello had been obliged to travel back to Redroofs as Mam was suffering from bronchitis. According to Marsh, 'The nurse had said she wouldn't live through the night, but when Ivor got there she seemed quite all right, & B. [Bobbie Andrews] is of course convinced that it's all some plot to get money out of him! Bobbie is lunching with me tomorrow, & I shall hear more.'[52] Marsh would have been delighted to join Andrews in carping complaints about Mam.

One evening Marsh and Mam, accompanied by Lily Elsie, were watching a performance of Novello's show *The Dancing Years* when 'Mam went away after the first act saying she was too ill to stay'; Marsh admits that he was anxious about her, but he 'learnt later that she was better than she had been for days, but was having a tantrum because

Ivor had put an end to her negotiations for a new flat at the cost of £675 [around £25,000 in today's money]!'[53]

Novello adored his mother. Marsh, who had experienced a powerful bond with his own mother, recognised the strength of the attachment between them and was jealous of their closeness. He seems to have been more sympathetic towards her when she became seriously ill: 'Poor old Mam is in rather a bad way, suffering great pain from sclerosis of the liver – the doctors say it won't kill her, but it seems to be incurable, & Ivor thinks there is nothing before her but gradual deterioration.'[54]

Less than a year after her diagnosis of sclerosis Mam passed away in her sleep on 7 February 1943. Novello was deeply upset, and felt as if he had been 'knocked sideways'. Marsh's attitude was hard-nosed: 'he was a good son, & really loved her; but it's in the natural course of things – & really, let's face it, a millstone off his neck.'[55] With Mam out of the way, Marsh could now assume what he believed was his rightful place as Novello's ersatz guardian. On the morning of Mam's funeral he had a pragmatic heart-to-heart with Novello which he related to Christopher Hassall: 'He is very sad, but realizes that it was for the best, & I admire the way he is taking it. He said that he wanted his memory of Mam to be just as she was, not idealized, but remembering her with character, with all her "naughtiness" as well as her qualities.'[56]

Marsh's reiteration of how Novello wanted to remember Mam is somewhat ironic, given the criticism levelled at his own idealised memoir of Rupert Brooke. Mam's funeral took place at Golders Green, her send-off aptly accompanied by a Welsh choir. Although Marsh claimed to have become fond of her, neither he nor Bobbie Andrews shed tears. Marsh remarked, 'It's such a good thing that Bobbie has been away all through this, there was such bitter hatred between him & Mam that it would have been a very difficult situation.'[57]

Mam had been the most important woman in Novello's life, but he had many close female friends. Although he was sexually attracted to men, he adored women and they adored him back. The renowned actress Gladys Cooper was said to have been in love with Novello even 'to the extent of contemplating marriage', imagining it would 'cure him of his bisexuality'.[58] Most of Novello's fans were women, which meant that throughout his career he had to achieve a balance between his public persona and his private life. In order to protect his reputation and stage career his homosexuality was largely concealed from his fans. Those in Novello's inner circle were aware of his sexual behaviour, which some considered notorious. While Marsh may not have been privy to all his antics he could not have been oblivious to what went on, but neither rumours nor disapproval of Novello could dispel his deep affection for him, so he was content to preserve the façade. Phyllis Bottome, also a close friend of Novello, observed that Marsh 'had a strange power of identifying himself with his friends while keeping his intellect objectively clear in their service'.[59]

Marsh's association with Novello may have been one of the reasons why his once warm friendship with Neville Lytton was never rekindled. Lytton's son recalled, 'Neville considered Novello an obstacle because he once said so and looking back long afterwards with an air of regret that the break should have been so complete – it was clear that he did not approve of Novello or his ring.'[60] He went on to say, 'I think Eddie's exceptional interest in Ivor Novello was of an intensity which drove out the earlier affection between Neville and Eddie.' In addition to their polarised views on art (Neville Lytton believed that Eddie had done 'incalculable harm to British art' during his time at the Tate Gallery) it was clear that Lytton greatly disapproved of Marsh's involvement with the theatrical set and the homosexual Novello. Noel Anthony Lytton, who remembered Marsh as 'Uncle Eddie' who had played bears with him under the schoolroom table, obviously regretted the rift with his father, and lamented: 'Dear Uncle Eddie – would that we could drop 50 years and go back to the pre-tulip age'[61] – a reference to Marsh's purchase of Duncan Grant's painting *Parrot Tulips*, and the beginning of the end of his friendship with Lytton. The break in their friendship had caused Marsh some concern when drafting his memoir, *A Number of People*. 'I *must* put in something about the Neville Ls, as they *were* such terrific friends – and now they've lapsed, which makes it difficult.'[62]

Marsh may have lost Neville Lytton's amity, but in Novello he had a warm and generous friend. In addition to providing a second home for Marsh at Redroofs, Novello also arranged countless complimentary tickets to his shows for Marsh and his various acquaintances; even Mrs Elgy, Marsh's housekeeper, regularly received tickets for first-night performances. He gave Marsh many presents too. The writer Dorothy Colston-Baynes described how she had bumped into Marsh in London 'looking very beaming in his great-coat with a really remarkably beautiful silk scarf tucked under his chin. [...] "Given me by Ivor Novello!" he cried with a note of triumph in his little, high voice, and his eyes gleamed'.[63] Marsh thought this 'the most beautiful Sulka scarf I ever saw'.[64] Other presents from Novello included an expensive set of brandy glasses that Marsh had admired, and he was 'deeply pleased and touched'[65] when Novello presented him with the gold watch that had once belonged to his father – a gift which demonstrated his affection for Marsh who was like a father to him. However the greatest gift that Novello bestowed on Marsh was an introduction to a young actor in his company, Christopher Vernon Hassall, who was to become a 'landmark'[66] in his friendships.

Chapter Twelve

'My beloved Chris'

Early in December 1933 Christopher Hassall, a young actor playing a small role in *Henry VIII* at the Old Vic, wrote to Ivor Novello asking whether he would be prepared to take him on as his understudy for a planned production of *Romeo and Juliet*. Hassall had played the part of Romeo in John Gielgud's production for the Oxford University Dramatic Society (OUDS), and enclosed with his speculative letter a note of introduction from Novello's friend Athene Seyler, who was also appearing in *Henry VIII*. On receipt of the letter Novello telephoned Hassall, inviting him to a matinee of his play *Proscenium* in which he was starring, with firm instructions to present himself at his dressing-room after the performance. Hassall duly arrived, and was impressed by Novello's good looks. His effusive description of him is reminiscent of Marsh's reaction on first setting eyes on Rupert Brooke:

> I was surprised afresh at the narrowness of him, and the deep-
> set small brown eyes that had an eager smile of their own, the
> delicate face wistful in repose, a physical presence that was now
> in its prime and disconcertingly radiant, so troublesomely perfect
> was that narrow head with all its long, black, orderly hair.[1]

Novello was obviously enthusiastic about Hassall, as he offered him the role of his understudy in the forthcoming touring production of *Proscenium*. This proved to be not entirely successful for Hassall. During one performance in Liverpool Novello had been hit in the groin during a scene change by the iron handle used to revolve the scenery. Hassall was ordered to stand by, but in spite of his injury Novello decided to soldier on with the performance, not least as the stage manager made it clear to him that his understudy was hardly word perfect. Hassall feared that he would be asked to leave the company, and his financial prospects, having no private resources, were bleak. Instead, after the show, he was invited by Novello to a champagne dinner à deux. Hassall described Novello's attitude as 'magnanimous';[2] their discussion veered towards what other occupations Hassall might consider, as Novello thought he was not really cut out to be an actor. Nonetheless, during the course of the tour, Novello took Hassall under his wing. He gave him clothes – his cast-offs – which included a winter coat and garish shirts purchased in Hollywood but deemed too flashy for touring the provinces, and he frequently invited Hassall to dine with him. Their friendship developed through their love of music: as Hassall recalled, 'for the next seventeen years our talks on music and our work together on his own compositions was only interrupted by the war.'[3] Hassall was honest about his ambition to be a writer and a poet, and Novello knew exactly the man to introduce him to. Marsh had announced that he intended to catch up with the tour in Oxford, and Novello took this opportunity to bring Marsh and Hassall together over supper. Their meeting took place at the Clarendon Hotel on 9 March 1934.

Marsh was sixty-one years old, forty years older than Hassall, and on the brink of retirement. Many years of fine dining – all those luncheons and dinners – had taken its toll on his dapper appearance and he was by now quite a 'portly gentleman'.[4] The journalist Charles Graves – brother of the poet Robert Graves – gave a wonderful pen portrait of Marsh around this time. He describes Marsh's distinctive eyebrows as 'satanic', and goes on to say:

> Eddie Marsh speaks quickly, nervously and almost anxiously. He is fond of saying 'Yes, yes,' a trifle querulously, while his left elbow fidgets and his right hand rattles the coins in his trousers' pocket. He wears an eyeglass, plays a keen game of tennis, looks rather quaint in the water, [...]. In a morning coat he provides a bland, slightly plump exterior and a certain knowledge that he must be the perfect house guest – witty, fastidious, kindly, unruffled, easily interested, interesting, quiet and exceedingly patient. [...] When selfconscious for a moment he will put out his right hand, palm facing down and slightly behind him. [...] You will notice, too,

how his hand is poised, all stiff, when he is about to say goodbye, while his eyebrows rise still higher up his forehead.[5]

Hassall's first impression of Marsh was of a man 'square-shouldered and robust, scrupulously well-groomed in his dinner jacket with stiff butterfly collar and monocle dangling at the ready'.[6] The evening did not get off to a good start, as supper was delayed until midnight. Hassall and Novello had been diverted after the show by a private OUDS event – Hassall was keen to show Novello his old haunts – and Marsh was disgruntled having been kept waiting so long. He was soon mollified by the arrival of food, wine, Novello and his young companion. The evening ended better than it had begun, as Marsh invited Hassall to join him for lunch at the hotel the following day and to Raymond Buildings four days later so Hassall could show him his poems. Hassall was somewhat diffident, but under the table Novello pressed his foot on Hassall's, exerting more pressure as he whispered, 'Don't you dare refuse.'[7]

Their friendship blossomed very quickly, with Marsh as usual being the driving force and a fervent letter writer. On 14 March 1934, less than a week after their first meeting, he put pen to paper, telling Hassall, 'I am so glad we have met, I enjoyed our evening enormously.'[8] He included a sheaf of detailed criticisms of Hassall's poems and extended an invitation to meet Gordon Bottomley, one of Marsh's Georgian poets. At the time Hassall was renting an attic room in Church Street Kensington, rehearsing frantically for a Novello play, *Fresh Fields*, and about to embark on a tour opening in Edinburgh. Undeterred, Marsh insisted that he send him more poems, and asked him not to be discouraged by his criticisms; Marsh said that 'he was a vigilant and careful writer, so that perhaps I might be a good example to you in the matter of style', although he confessed to having 'no creative power whatever'.[9]

Hassall was an impressionable youth, and although initially in awe of Marsh he was grateful to have such a sympathetic ear. He soon realised that he could pour out his woes and frustrations to Marsh, who was eager to help him. Hassall had quickly become disillusioned with

Paul Nash, *Elms*, 1914

Paul Nash, *Wire*, 1918

Sir Stanley Spencer, *Self-portrait*, 1913

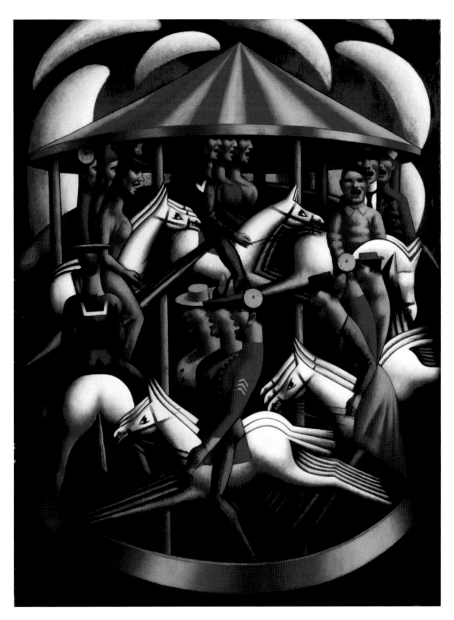

Mark Gertler, *The Merry-Go-Round*, oil painting, 1916

Eddie Marsh at
Gray's Inn, 1938

Edward Marsh's living room, Raymond Buildings, *c.*1934

Ivor Novello

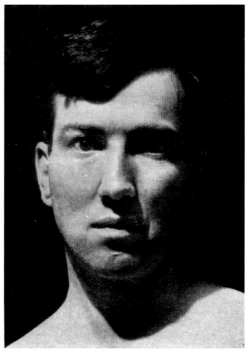

Robert Graves, 1929

M

Careless Country Rapture

Ivor Novello Entertains at Maidenhead

"A Scarf Like That Goes Like This"

To "make a photograph" Ivor Novello acted dresser to Dorothy Dickson who was one of his week-end guests. She and Zena Dare are his two leading ladies at Drury Lane, where "Careless Rapture" has already fixed itself as one of his greatest successes

Mme. Novello Davies and Ivor Novello

Ivor Novello has an attractive house at Maidenhead where he spends some of his week-ends. He had a party there just after "Careless Rapture" opened at Drury Lane, with his mother, Mme. Novello Davies, to do hostess for him

Photographs by Swaebe

September Sunday Morning by the Swimming Pool

Here is the rest of Ivor Novello's week-end party—standing on the left are Richard Rose and Keneth ("Napoleon") Kent; sitting are Peter Graves, Dorothy Dickson, the host, Zena Dare, Fobia Drake and Christopher Hassall who has written the lyrics for "Careless Rapture." He was also responsible for the "Glamorous Night" ones

The Bystander, 30 December 1936

Christopher Vernon Hassall
by Joan Hassall, oil painting,
c.1930–31

Sir Edward Howard Marsh by
Bassano Ltd, 11 December 1935

Eddie Marsh, photo by Lady
Ottoline Morrell, *c*.1935

Stephen Haggard by Bassano
Ltd, June 1938

acting and the relentless drudgery of being on tour. In a matter of weeks after their first meeting he confessed, 'I get so fed up with the stage at times. I ought to be in business. One does meet the most loathsome people in this profession.' He went on to say, 'It's so lovely to have someone to write to when one is in a depressed mood, I'm so grateful to you.'[10] Marsh was elated to have a young man in tow once more, especially one who seemed content to depend on him. Marsh needed to be needed. He reassured Hassall, 'It's an untold joy to me that you should find it a comfort to write to me when you are feeling "depressed"; […] so I expect you and I are a mutual godsend.'[11] He started sending Hassall gifts: a copy of his *Fables of La Fontaine*, followed by a scarf, and a copy of John Donne's collected poems. Hassall had spilt ink over his copy of Donne, and Marsh was keen to replace it, but he asked Hassall to give him the damaged copy in exchange. He explained, 'I possess Rupert's copy of Donne, and it would be delightful to have side by side with it the one you spilt the ink over at Glasgow.'[12] Marsh had very quickly contrived an emotional link between his beloved Brooke and his latest protégé. Hassall was very responsive to Marsh's care and attention; he explained, 'while I write to you, I look upon you more as an abstract kindred spirit, […] as it were a projection of myself, a brother (or shall we say *uncle*) in art and interests.'[13] Furthermore, he exclaimed, 'I wish you could realize what *tremendous* happiness your letters have given me […] I'm so grateful. Love Chris.'[14] Marsh's devotion encouraged Hassall to treat him as a confidant. While still a jobbing actor Hassall's propensity to melancholy persisted. In January 1935, after attending a party by the actor Robert Donat, Hassall wrote to Marsh lamenting, 'The Spleen is upon me again! The most awful melancholy!'[15] This was followed three days later by another letter: 'O Eddie, if only I could become a major poet! I'm in high spirits tonight. So looking forward to seeing you. Best love, Chris.'[16] Hassall's fluctuating moods, his desire to become a poet, and his trust and dependence on Marsh formed the incentive that Marsh needed to extend his help. Hassall was frequently unwell, with a succession of colds and bilious attacks and painful eczema, but it was for relief from his depressive moods that he was most grateful to Marsh: 'It is the feeling of your confidence in me & your interest, that on so many occasions has saved me from complete and black despair.'[17]

Hassall was young, but not such an innocent; he quickly realised that Marsh was the conduit to further his ambition, and he found that he could easily manipulate his good nature.

Shortly after meeting Hassall Marsh met another young actor, Stephen Haggard, who was to become a significant figure in both their lives. Haggard was playing the part of Henri Gaudier-Brzeska in a new production of *The Laughing Woman*[18] and Marsh was ecstatic about his performance. He told Novello:

> it was the boy's evening, his spontaneity and his charm and the unity in variety of his mercurial temperament glued every eye and heart upon him. [...] He got an absolute ovation [...] I feel rather proud of having 'picked him out' in that tiny part, Silvius, in *As You Like It*, but I admit I had no idea *what* an actor he is![19]

He praised Haggard for 'the most convincing embodiment of creative genius that I have seen on the stage'.[20] Marsh had been so impressed that he had gone backstage to introduce himself to Haggard, and afterwards promptly sent an invitation to lunch. Haggard responded:

> It was kind of you to write and to come round after the first night. If you knew Gaudier it was so very nice of you to be forebearing [*sic*] about my performance which must have seemed to you in some ways impudent and in bad taste. You were kind enough to say it wasn't, and I'm hoping that it's true.[21]

Haggard declined Marsh's invitation on this occasion, but Marsh was persistent, and two weeks later Haggard wrote to Marsh again, to thank him not only for lunch but also for a rather special gift: 'I really cannot thank you enough for my beautiful Gaudier, it was so very nice of you to give it to me.' A Gaudier drawing was a very considerable gift to someone that Marsh barely knew, but his romantic sentiment and enthusiasm tended to get the better of him. Their friendship continued, and although a recipient of Marsh's high praise Haggard, like so many others, found him somewhat indiscriminate when it came to his appraisal of theatrical productions: 'You're a good friend but a bad critic', he told him.[22]

One of Marsh's greatest pleasures was to bring like-minded people together, and he very quickly introduced Haggard to Hassall, inviting them both to one of his famed luncheon parties 'justly renowned for good talk and haddock done in cream'.[23] Subsequently Haggard and Hassall, who were contemporaries, became very close friends. Around this time Marsh also introduced Hassall to the young writer Noel Langley, who was also to become a close friend. Hassall did not warm to him instantly, but persuaded by Marsh to spend time with Langley in Cornwall Hassall wrote effusively:

> First let me say all along you have been so right about Noel, and I have been so wrong. He has become one of my closest friends […] Noel said such lovely things about you, […] I nearly cried. If ever you have done a really wise and profitable act, it was your persuading me to go to Fowey. It did us both no end of good. Both Noel and I have found a new and genuine friend, and I sincerely believe, on Noel's side, a little faith in human nature, – and that is entirely your doing Eddie.[24]

Langley was a prolific writer, enjoying success in Britain and Hollywood as a screenwriter.

Hassall was soon able to give up his mediocre acting career, as Ivor Novello had recruited him as his lyricist. This role was far better suited to Hassall's talents, and they were a phenomenally successful songwriting duo. Novello, like Marsh, wanted Hassall close to him; consequently Hassall spent many enjoyable weekends with Novello and his friends at Redroofs. Although Hassall was in showbusiness himself he was often star-struck, and he relished weekends spent in the company of the likes of Angela Baddeley, Lawrence Olivier and Vivien Leigh. There were often occasions when Hassall was invited to spend time at Redroofs when Marsh had not been invited, much to Marsh's pique. On one such occasion Marsh assumed the role of martyr; he was checking the proofs of Hassall's latest poems, and said peevishly: 'they will be something to do on Sunday when you are gallivanting at Redroofs (I suppose I'm the only person who sees how odd it is that Ivor doesn't invite me!).'[25] Hassall accused Marsh of being over-sensitive, and retorted: 'Only recently you were staying in Southport, seeing Ivor a great deal, whereas it's only natural he should ask me down this week-end having omitted to invite me during *the last four months almost*!'[26] For Marsh an idyllic weekend would be spent in the company of both men, as his New Year greetings reveal: 'I wish you *such* a Happy NY dear Chris – I am to see it in with Ivor & I shall think of you! Wishing you were there too.'[27]

Notwithstanding his successful partnership with Novello, Hassall was frustrated by being perceived simply as a lyricist for popular songs: he also wanted to be well regarded as a poet. Marsh was delighted by the friendship and professional partnership that had been forged between Novello and Hassall, but he too was keen that Hassall should concentrate his energies on his poetry. Marsh had transposed his former ambitions and hopes for Brooke to Hassall, who in turn responded to his unequivocal encouragement by taking this lofty aim (and himself) very seriously. Marsh began a relentless round of introductions to useful contacts, such as Eddy Sackville-West, whom he invited to lunch and insisted that Hassall put the date 'in his little black book'.[28] He also wrote to Vita Sackville-West who replied, 'I should love to come to luncheon with you and meet your new discovery.'[29] Marsh also took Hassall to stay at Holker Hall, home of Lord and Lady Cavendish, and to Knebworth to stay with Lord and Lady Lytton. He was especially pleased that Hassall was a great success with his old friend Lady Lytton. Another important connection was Lady Ottoline Morrell, who seemed to have put aside her apparent dislike of Marsh and said, 'I should like to meet him [Hassall]. If he would care to come and see me.'[30] Hassall did care to see her: he told his mother, 'I went to tea with Lady Ottoline Morrell, where I sat with Sturge Moore on my right, James Stephens on my left, André Maurois opposite me, and T. S. Eliot at the head of the table.'[31] Hassall reported to Marsh that he felt 'like Marlowe coming face to face with Queen Elizabeth'.[32] It was through Lady Ottoline Morrell and her salon that Hassall met

Laurence Whistler. He enthused, 'I made a life-long friendship with Laurence Whistler who won the King's Poetry prize this year. Last Saturday I had lunch with him & Eddie. He is exactly my own age, and a friendly person.'[33] Hassall and Whistler were indeed to become 'life-long' friends.

Marsh and Hassall had a mutual friend in the poet Edmund Blunden, who was a Fellow of Merton College while Hassall was an undergraduate. At Oxford Hassall had also made the acquaintance of Michael Sadler and David Cecil, both of whom Marsh counted as part of his circle. Very soon most of Marsh's Georgian poets had been introduced to Hassall, and some, like Siegfried Sassoon, actively befriended the young poet. Marsh and Hassall's separate social circles were overlapping, largely to Hassall's advantage. The *quid pro quo* for Marsh's efforts on Hassall's behalf was an unremitting expectation of his time and company. They attended many society functions together, as is evident in *The Times* Court Circular listings of the mid to late 1930s. Marsh was quite bereft when Hassall was away from London. His only compensation was copious correspondence; as he put it, 'I miss you very much, but on the other hand, as you see, I enjoy corresponding with you, which I couldn't do if you were in London – it's a good instance of my philosophy.'[34] His letters were increasingly affectionate, usually signed off with 'Best love, E' but by 1937 he was writing 'Goodnight my beloved Chris, Eddie'.[35] Despite Marsh's professed joy in their correspondence he frequently wrote that he longed to see him, and urged him to 'Tell me when you will be back in London, & keep me your first evening.' This was followed by 'Do come on Tuesday [...] "Your" new blue bedroom will await you, I hope you can stay the night!'[36]

Marsh also told him that he was 'meditating making a Will' and expressed his intention to give Hassall 'the little MS book in which the poets have written their poems'.[37] It is clear from their correspondence that Marsh gave Hassall not only moral support but generous financial assistance too. His letters contain many references to his 'Rupert money', of which Hassall was frequently the beneficiary. Hassall would protest, but Marsh was insistent: 'I hear from the publishers that they have a "Rupert" cheque for me, so I shall be able to make up to you for what you sent to your sister. *Please* Chris don't object to this, as I couldn't bear that your *entire* first earnings from D. D. [*Devil's Dyke*] should be snatched away from you.'[38]

Despite his protestations, Hassall was grateful for Marsh's 'lovely Rupert money'[39] and always thanked him profusely: 'so many lasting and deep thank-yous, not only for this last, but for your continual kindnesses, dear Eddie!'[40]

Marsh's efforts to improve and promote Hassall's poetry bore fruit when *Poems of Two Years* was published in 1935 and *Devil's Dyke* in 1936. The frontispiece of *Devil's Dyke* is a woodcut by Joan Hassall, the poet's sister, whom Marsh also befriended. One of the poems is dedicated to Marsh; it is a reflection on life, death, chance and the Muse, inspired by Marsh's Corsican misadventure, and includes the lines:

Dear Friend, had you not liv'd to guide my pen,
I should have met you on the lips of men,
Found you in many books, in quiet hearts
Where smoke the blood-red altars of the Arts.
It was our joy in knowing you to-day.[41]

Hassall was pleased with his literary progress but frustrated by his mother's negative response to his poems. He complained to Marsh, 'I am being continually mortified and discouraged by the one person who has dedicated all her resources to making me happy. But it is a stifling, deadening sort of mother love that is more dangerous than any man's downright enmity.'[42] Hassall's words convey a mother and son relationship that is strikingly similar to Rupert Brooke's relationship with his mother. A devout Christian, Constance Hassall was a loving mother, and if she did not always understand her son's poems she was nonetheless (along with Marsh) his greatest supporter. When Hassall was suffering another of his spells of self-doubt she was ready with words of encouragement: 'Dear Son, You must not for a moment think that your poems have not made a permanent contribution to the uplift & refreshment of the mind, how many people have already been inspired by them.'[43] When Hassall was awarded the Hawthornden

Prize in 1939 for *Penthesperon* she told him that it was a proud moment for her and that she hoped his work 'may always continue to be an inspiration to noble thought, & a refreshment to the minds of everyone'.[44]

Hassall's receipt of the Hawthornden Prize was achieved with some assistance from Marsh, who was a member of the prize committee. Marsh had also exerted his influence for his protégés in 1928, when Siegfried Sassoon had won the prize for *Memoirs of a Fox-Hunting Man*, and again in 1935 when Robert Graves was awarded the prize for *I, Claudius*.

Marsh was keen to meet Hassall's parents; he had taken the young Christopher Hassall under his wing and wanted their blessing to treat him as his unofficial adopted son. Over the course of their friendship Marsh helped the Hassall family financially, even to the extent that he secured a Civil List pension for Christopher's father, John Hassall, an impecunious but well-regarded artist.

In October 1938 Hassall announced that he was to be married to Eve Lynett (née Evelyn Chapman), a petite, beautiful and exotic young actress of Anglo-Indian heritage who had appeared on stage and screen in minor roles. Eve Lynett and Hassall enjoyed a whirl-wind romance, and there is no mention of their courtship in any of Hassall's early letters to Marsh. Given the frank and intimate nature of their correspondence, it is astonishing that there is no mention of Eve before this time. Hassall's mother wrote to her son on the morning of his wedding day expressing her joy that his love of home & family had never faltered, and she remarked on his union with Eve to whom he had 'been faithful for so long'.[45] Had Hassall kept his courtship with Eve a secret from Marsh? What pangs did Marsh suffer at the prospect of Hassall's affection being diverted from him? Both Marsh and Novello had become used to having first call on Hassall's time and attention. Marsh had not concealed his romantic feelings for Hassall, which he expressed by sending affectionate telegrams to mark the anniversary of their first meeting. Nevertheless, with seeming good spirit and echoes of his letter to Judith Blunt upon her marriage to Neville Lytton, Marsh wrote to Eve following her engagement to Christopher:

Christopher has told me the great news! You know my deep
affection for him & how important all his 'doings' are to me,
so I think you will be glad to hear that I am very happy about
it, & that I feel his marriage will bring him strength & peace as
well as joy. I hope you will take me into your friendship. Yours,
Eddie[46]

On 6 November 1938 Hassall brought Eve to lunch at Raymond
Buildings to meet his patron and mentor. Hassall and Eve were married
shortly afterwards, on 28 December 1938, at St Anne's church, High-
gate Hill. Hassall spent his last evening as a single man with Marsh at
Raymond Buildings, and remembered:

> next day he [Eddie] took his place between my parents at the
> ceremony conducted by the poet Andrew Young, and signed the
> register as witness. It must have been the only wedding service
> he had ever gone to (in company with the groom and best man)
> by tram. After the ceremony Stephen Haggard was his chauffeur
> for the day and he saw us off to Barbados. He turned back to
> Novello and his circle, where there was much to engage his
> interest.[47]

When Marsh saw them off on their honeymoon he had presented
Eve with three orchids, but in Hassall's absence there was not so much
to engage Marsh's interest as was implied. Despite being on his honeymoon with his new bride, Hassall continued to correspond with
Marsh. On 16 January he wrote, 'Dearest Eddie, It seems so strange to
have lived so long without an exchange of news with you.'[48] Just two
days later he sent Marsh a telegram: 'THANKS GORGEOUS LETTER
BOTH HAPPY. CHRIS.'[49] According to Hassall the honeymoon was cut
short as both he and Novello were already far advanced in the prep-
aration of the operetta *The Dancing Years*. Undoubtedly Marsh would
have been happy for Novello to put pressure on Hassall to return at
the earliest opportunity.

Hassall's bride was a woman of independent means. In 1938 she
had read about the impresario John Counsell and his bid to save
the Theatre Royal Windsor in the *Daily Express*, and telephoned him

stating her intention to help him financially. Counsell was at first exasperated, imagining she was an actress who would offer £50 in return for a part as a leading lady. When they met to discuss her proposal he was engaged by her prettiness and her 'piquant personality',[50] and offered her a part in his company, assuming he could get the theatre going again. Eve came to his rescue; she had planned to propose £500 but increased her offer to £1,000 (around £54,000 in today's money). Counsell responded with 'Will you please put that down in writing in front of my solicitor this afternoon?' Much to Counsell's relief, she wrote out a cheque and said that she was 'going to forget about it and asked [Counsell] to do the same'.[51] The Theatre Royal Windsor was back in business.

Marsh was a frequent visitor to the theatre in Windsor where Novello regularly toured his productions. When he accompanied Novello to see the Emlyn Williams play *A Murder has been Arranged* he met the Counsells. He wrote to Hassall afterwards, reporting that they had 'told Ivor and me how supreme Eve had been in *Dear Brutus*. There's such a pretty photograph of her – as herself – in the corridor.'[52] One can only surmise as to whether her generous patronage had influenced their good opinion and was the reason she was cast in the play. Counsell wrote that she had made the offer 'without strings',[53] but she was delighted and honoured to be part of his company, and insisted that the rest of the company should not know that she had been his benefactor.

Eve's acting career seems to have come to a halt after her marriage. Her fortune too seemed to dwindle considerably; fortunately for Hassall, Marsh could be relied upon as a financial backstop when his finances ebbed rather than flowed.

A year after the Hassalls' marriage the war cloud over Europe loomed once more. In the summer of 1939 Winston Churchill had told Marsh that war with Hitler and Germany was unavoidable. Marsh was preoccupied with his translation of the *Odes of Horace* at the time and paid little attention to world affairs. He did not own a wireless, and had not listened to Chamberlain's declaration of war with Germany broadcast by the BBC on 3 September 1939. Instead, Christopher

Hassall telephoned him with the news. Marsh promptly purchased a wireless, and, along with the rest of Britain, braced himself for the worst.

THE THEATRE OF WAR

Chapter Thirteen

Cambridge and Friends

When war broke out in 1939 Marsh had been determined to stay in London, ensconced in Raymond Buildings, but when part of the building was hit by a bomb during a Blitz raid he was forced to reconsider. Siegfried Sassoon wrote to console him:

> My dear Eddie, I am so sad to hear of the destruction of Raymond Buildings; it is a 'blessing' (!) anyhow that your belongings aren't damaged. But I know what it must mean to you; & your friends certainly owe that delightful interior a debt of gratitude, However, –
>
> > Cram the monocle into your eye;
> > Damn the bangs which descend from the sky;
> > And make the most, though horrors be harsh,
> > Of being that boon to the Muses – E. Marsh.[1]

Sassoon recognised the significance of place, and of Marsh's contribution to his poets and painters. Marsh reluctantly set forth on his exile from London. Christopher Hassall had made it clear that as his mother-in-law was a permanent guest at their house there would be no accommodation with them, so on 20 April 1942, having outstayed his welcome with the Duke and Duchess of Devonshire, Marsh returned to his alma mater and was happily lodged with his widowed brother-in-law, Sir Frederick Maurice, at King's College, Cambridge. He reported to Christopher Hassall:

> Just a line to report my safe arrival and I think promising installation here. I have a good bedroom, and F. L. Lucas's room entirely lined with books as my 'den'. Fred most welcoming and

agreeable. Dinner was very pleasant – and he goes to bed at 10. We shall dine at Kings on Saturdays, […] and twice a month at Trinity. I had quite forgotten the Master, my old friend George Trevelyan, as one of the attractions of Cambridge! We are going to tea at the Lodge on Saturday. The theatre is near the house and booming.[2]

Cambridge was a happy home-from-home for Marsh, not least as he had good friends, like Francis and Frances Cornford, who lived there. He enjoyed many Sundays at the Cornfords' home, contentedly dead-heading roses in their garden and playing with their grandson. Marsh seems to have been a frustrated gardener, as in addition to dead-heading the Cornfords' roses, on visits to Siegfried Sassoon's home at Heytesbury in Wiltshire he would weed the flowerbeds.

Marsh was surprised to discover that one of his Georgian poets, Robert Nichols, was also now living in Cambridge; however he found that he was 'living in rather dingy lodgings, where he can't write, and slaving away at things for the B.B.C. by which he hopes to make a little money'; Marsh claimed that Nichols had 'never learnt to manage his life', but took pity on him and gave him some 'Rupert money' 'to have the room done up more cheerfully'.[3]

In many ways Cambridge had not changed since his undergraduate days; Marsh enjoyed the familiar college tradition of dining in Hall, where Fellows mixed with distinguished guests as well as undergraduates. It was the ideal environment for the scholarly and sociable man who enjoyed attending the lectures as well as the frequent concerts, recitals and plays. He also made regular forays to Heffers Bookshop, not least in order to purchase a considerable number of books to dispatch to Christopher Hassall. It was as though the war had not affected his life and yet Cambridge was only an hour away from London by train. The proximity meant he could regularly visit his various clubs, galleries and theatres, and see his London friends. Although Marsh was seemingly content to be in Cambridge, the living arrangement with his brother-in-law was not always harmonious. After the initial euphoria at his welcome he became irked that he was obliged to share a copy of *The Times*, and he was exasperated when the housekeeper refused to sew on his pyjama buttons: it was certainly not the kind of service he had come to expect from his dear Mrs Elgy.

George 'Dadie' Rylands was another of Marsh's acquaintances that he was delighted to re-connect with in Cambridge. The name Dadie had been ascribed to him when he was a small child as he could not pronounce 'baby', and it stuck with him all his life. Rylands, an Eton schoolboy, went to Cambridge to read Classics, later switching to English. He was a contemporary of Cecil Beaton, with whom he was a member of the ADC (Amateur Dramatic Company), Footlights, and the Marlowe Society. Rylands was President of the ADC when Beaton first met him; he described Rylands as 'quite nice-looking' and thought that he 'spoke exactly like Bobbie Andrews'.[4] Rylands described Beaton as being 'clever as a monkey'.[5] Beaton was elected to the committee of the ADC in October 1923 and was put in charge of costume and scenery; being extravagant by nature, he had a great deal of trouble keeping within a modest budget. Rylands was especially engaged with the Marlowe Society, appearing in, and directing, many productions. According to Beaton's biographer, Hugo Vickers, when the Marlowe Society staged a production of Webster's *Duchess of Malfi* in 1924 Beaton had failed to get a part: the star part went to Rylands, whereupon 'Cecil took his revenge by publishing a mean caricature of him in *Granta*.'[6]

Rylands made his life in Cambridge. In 1927 he was awarded a Fellowship at King's College, where he went on successfully to combine both academic and theatrical careers as a renowned Shakespeare scholar and a director. Rylands exerted a considerable influence on English theatre, and was taken up by the Bloomsbury Group, in particular Lytton Strachey and Virginia Woolf. The doors and fireplaces of his rooms in King's College were embellished with paint by Dora Carrington. It was in his rooms that Rylands hosted the extravagant dinner that Virginia Woolf described in *A Room of One's Own* (1929). Rylands was close to Maynard Keynes too, and together they were instrumental in establishing the Cambridge Arts Theatre. During his career Rylands directed John Gielgud and Peggy Ashcroft and influenced the likes of Sir Peter Hall and Sir Trevor Nunn. On the occasion of his ninetieth birthday he was honoured by the Royal Shakespeare Company.

Marsh was impressed by the energetic and vivacious Rylands, whom he described as having 'a very good mind and much charm'. There was something reminiscent of Rupert Brooke about Rylands – young, blonde and handsome with a 'pussy-cat smile' – which would have appealed to Marsh. Like Brooke, Rylands was concerned about 'the horrors of life, and getting old […] and how the Cambridge undergraduates looked on him as an old fogey'.[7] Virginia Woolf had written to Jacques Raverat about him: 'At King's they are all reminded of Rupert – partly his yellow hair, partly his poetry, which is not so good as Rupert's […] at heart he is uncorrupted […] and all young and oldish men […] fall in love with him, and he dines out every night, and treats his lovers abominably.'[8] Woolf also admitted in her diary, 'For Dadie I feel considerable affection – so sensitive & tender is he.'[9]

One of the 'oldish men' who had ostensibly fallen in love with Rylands was Somerset Maugham. During the 1930s Rylands and his Cambridge friend Arthur Marshall frequently took holidays in Monte Carlo, tempted by casinos, tennis and sunshine. On one occasion Victor Rothschild joined them on a trip which included a visit to Somerset Maugham at his Villa Mauresque in Cap Ferrat. Rothschild thought that Maugham 'may have misunderstood the purpose of our visit, at least a stroll in the garden with Gerald Haxton [Maugham's partner] led me to that conclusion'.[10] However, Rylands had not misunderstood Maugham's intention. Homosexual and sexually uninhibited, he was propositioned by Maugham and quickly became part of Maugham's circle, as did Arthur Marshall.

Rothschild said, 'I never met anyone who did not admire and, indeed love Dadie.'[11] Maugham was no exception. He also appreciated the fact that Rylands had no ulterior motive beyond their friendship. Rylands said of him, 'he loved to make one laugh out loud' and 'he loved to *tease*'.[12] Marshall recalled, 'I had little of interest or profit to offer but Willie never let me feel out of things and he was unfailingly kind and thoughtful and benevolent.'[13] Among Rylands' many attributes Maugham appreciated his brilliant intellect. Like Marsh, he was sometimes prevailed upon to check Maugham's proofs.

Marsh and Hassall were invited too. Maugham obviously regarded them as a couple, and said 'should you & Christopher by any chance be looking for somewhere to go at Easter I should be delighted to put you both up. George Rylands & Arthur are coming on 4th April. Yours affectionately, Willie.'[14]

In 1954 Maugham was appointed Companion of Honour (at Winston Churchill's suggestion), and it was with Dadie Rylands and Arthur Marshall that he celebrated over lunch at the Garrick.[15] He was just one of many friends in common for Marsh and Rylands. Anthony Blunt, who later became Surveyor of the Queen's Pictures and was eventually exposed as a Russian spy, was also part of Rylands' coterie, like him and Marsh a member of the Apostles. Following Marsh's arrival in Cambridge, Rylands invited him to dine at High Table in King's College on several occasions, and Marsh took great pleasure in the introductions that Rylands made on his behalf, such as that as to Noel Annan, who flattered Marsh by saying that his translation of Horace was 'the joy of his life'.[16]

Marsh shared Rylands' enthusiasm for the Classics and the theatre. He had avidly read Rylands' Shakespeare anthology, *The Ages of Man*, which he carried about with him 'to read in the Tube' and on walks in the park.[17] He also greatly enjoyed watching Rylands in the Marlowe Society's production of Shakespeare's *King Lear*. Marsh thought his performance was 'remarkable', and claimed it was 'the best Lear I ever saw'[18] – high praise indeed, although, as ever, Marsh's enthusiasm was prone to be effusive for attractive young men with whom he had formed an attachment.

Another of Marsh's longstanding acquaintances who came to stay in Cambridge during the war was Eddie Knoblock. He was an American from a wealthy family of German extraction who had changed his name from Knoblauch to Knoblock when he became a naturalised British citizen in 1916. A gifted linguist, he worked with the British intelligence service (as did Somerset Maugham and Hugh Walpole) in the Mediterranean, Greece and Baltic regions during the First World War. Knoblock had enjoyed success in London and Hollywood as a playwright and screenwriter, most notably for *Kismet* (1911), and he had collaborated on two plays with Arnold Bennett, *Milestones* (1912) and *London Life* (1924). He also worked with another of Marsh's acquaintances, the ubiquitous Beverley Nichols, on the adaptation of his novel *Evensong* (1932).

Marsh would occasionally see Knoblock at Redroofs, as he was part of Novello's theatre crowd and both were friends with Somerset Maugham. They saw each other and corresponded regularly, and it was to Maugham, who was in a long-term relationship with Gerald Haxton, that Knoblock turned for advice about bringing his American boyfriend to live with him in London.

According to Maugham's biographer, Selina Hastings, Knoblock was 'very camp' and 'on at least one occasion turned up [at Maugham's house] dressed as a woman'.[19] Maugham refers to Knoblock's 'passion for the macabre',[20] but Hastings also describes him as 'sweet-natured and gregarious'. A generous man, Knoblock frequently supported worthy causes, from writing short plays for fundraising events to lending his beautifully restored Regency home, Beach House in Worthing, for local charity fetes. He also supported the Old Vic Theatre: writing to *The Times* on 7 September 1937 he claimed the Old Vic was England's 'National Theatre', so it was not necessary to build a new one.[21] Like Marsh he was an avid socialite, and his name frequently appears in *The Times* Court Circular. One event that Knoblock, Marsh, Novello, Maugham and Hugh Walpole all attended was a matinée performance on the occasion of the actress Marie Tempest's jubilee, organised by the *Daily Telegraph* in the presence of King George V and Queen Mary on 28 May 1935.

Although Knoblock enjoyed an active social life he did not enjoy good health. He recorded in his memoir that he was diagnosed with colitis in 1912, and he experienced regular flare-ups of what he called 'his infernal trouble' In 1923 *The Times* reported that he was 'lying seriously ill in a nursing home';[22] although no details are given as to the nature of his illness, it is likely that it was ulcerative colitis again. Following a visit to Redroofs in 1941, Marsh was concerned but vague about Knoblock's poor health: 'Eddie Knob[lock] went away yesterday, to stay with A. E. W. Mason – the doctor promises him complete recovery 6 weeks hence. He was wonderfully cheerful and serene.'[23] In 1944 Marsh reported on Knoblock's health again: 'Eddie Knoblock is staying in Cambridge. He dined with me in Trinity last night. Entirely worn out by his work for the French Committee, he slept for most of the first week he was here. I hope he's going to give it up, as it's nearly killing him.'[24] Knoblock died a year later, on 19 July 1945, at his sister's home in London, and it was not his work that had killed him. The obituary in *The Times* concluded: 'A bachelor, sociable, amusing, good company and warm hearted, Knoblock made and kept many firm friends among both men and women.'[25] Interestingly the friendship between Knoblock and Marsh is not mentioned in Hassall's biography of Marsh; perhaps Hassall thought him too overtly homosexual to be included. Knoblock states in his memoir: 'My sexual life I have purposely not touched on. I think far too much importance is given to it nowadays, thanks to the universal craze for psycho-analysis.'[26]

As well as renewing old acquaintances, Marsh also made new friends in Cambridge, one of whom was another exile from London, John Hayward. Hayward was a considerable man of letters. He was excited by the avant-garde as represented by Edith Sitwell and her circle, and yet was also fascinated by antiquarian bibliography, in particular seventeenth-century literature. He had undertaken to prepare an edition of the works of John Wilmot, Earl of Rochester, while still an undergraduate at King's College, Cambridge. During his undergraduate days he had met older members of the Bloomsbury Group and become friends with Dadie Rylands, who introduced him to the younger Bloomsbury set. Their shared love of acting, the Marlowe Society and parties cemented their friendship. Rylands also introduced Hayward to Victor Rothschild, and they became lifelong friends.

In 1939 Rothschild rented Merton Hall, an Elizabethan house overlooking the Backs, as a safe haven from the perils of London during the war, and he invited Hayward to stay for the duration of the war. In return Hayward helped to organise the running of the house and was also an acting librarian and archivist for Lord Rothschild's various acquisitions. Hayward was forever grateful to Rothschild for his kindness towards him, but he was disconcerted by the move from London, and complained to Graham Greene: 'Dragged out of my groove and separated from all the people and objects and activities that made up my old life, I feel horribly helpless and burdensome.'[27] But life in London during the Blitz would have been extremely difficult for him: as a child he had been diagnosed with incipient muscular dystrophy, and he had been mostly wheelchair-bound since graduation.

In 1942 Hayward welcomed the arrival of the erudite Marsh to the community of displaced Londoners living in Cambridge. Marsh was a regular visitor to Merton Hall, which Hayward had established as a *de facto* salon. He enjoyed Hayward's company enormously, and was impressed by the way in which Hayward had dealt with his 'cruel affliction': he thought it 'a great achievement to have lived it down'.[28] Although they had many mutual friends and shared interests, not least the theatre and dinner parties, their literary tastes were not always entirely compatible. Hayward had been openly critical of *Georgian Poetry*, albeit as a schoolboy he had been fond of the work of Walter de la Mare, James Elroy Flecker and John Masefield. He had written in his notebook 'I especially love Rupert Brooke's poems', and Brooke's influence is evident in his own adolescent poetry.[29]

Hayward set about trying to convert Marsh to the poetry of T. S. Eliot and modern verse (Eliot, like Hayward, had been critical of the *Georgian Poetry* anthologies). Marsh confessed, 'The trouble with me is, I *can't* give myself up to Eliot, can't let him carry me along with him, [...] I suppose it's stupid to say that he has no sense of humour; but he says things that I might enjoy if anybody else had written them.'[30] Marsh found Eliot's poetry, and modern verse in general, irritating and obscure. Writing to Hassall, he remarked, 'I've ordered the two new Eliots, I expect I shall pass on the poetry book pretty soon, as it sounds incomprehensible, but the critical one [*The Classics and the Man of Letters* (OUP, 1942)] will be interesting.'[31] Marsh's dismissive view of Eliot's poetry was fairly entrenched, and he even found Eliot's criticism of the Classics 'arid and clumsy'.[32]

But Hayward was rewarded when after reading the opening lines of Eliot's *Dry Salvages* to Marsh he saw that Marsh had been moved to tears. In spite of his reservations, Marsh had also been moved at the first night of Eliot's verse drama *Murder in the Cathedral* concerning the murder of Archbishop Thomas Becket in Canterbury Cathedral, which he had seen in 1935 and thought 'very impressive'.[33] Marsh's prejudice against Eliot's poetry was gradually dissolving – and on the occasion of his eightieth birthday celebration in 1952 his former antagonist was invited as a notable guest representing the world of poetry.

Conversely, Hayward and T. S. Eliot were intimate friends. They had first met at Cambridge in 1926, when Hayward as an undergraduate had attended Eliot's Clark Lectures on 'The Metaphysical Poets of the Seventeenth Century'. After graduation Hayward decide to pursue a career as an editor and writer and contacted Eliot, who invited him to contribute to *The Criterion*, a quarterly magazine that he had set up. Eliot was impressed with Hayward's work, and subsequently, despite the sixteen-year age gap, they formed a close and lasting friendship. Their association was consolidated in 1938 when Eliot asked Hayward to be his literary executor, professing, 'I don't know anyone else besides yourself whom I should altogether trust in that capacity.'[34]

The many conversations between Marsh and Hayward may have been mainly of a literary nature, but they were not all highbrow. As Marsh related,

> I had another very pleasant dinner on Thursday with John Hayward […] The talk fell on unconscious literary obscenities, of which you know I have a pretty little collection – John made a surprising addition to it from *Martin Chuzzlewit*, Chap XXIV: 'She touched his organ; and from that bright epoch it, the dear companion of his happiest hours, which he had thought incapable of elevation, received a new and deified existence.' Nobody before John seems to have noticed this.[35]

Marsh and Hayward shared a risqué sense of humour and delighted in a play on words. Another of Hayward's stories that Marsh found highly amusing concerned 'a French master at Eton who, after teaching there for 30 years, brought out a little book of instructional dialogues, the first of which began: "One of the boys in our house has three balls." "Has he? Hurrah!" The book had to be recalled, and another first page substituted.'[36]

Joking aside, Marsh was keen to assist Hayward in his work, and in the absence of typists wrote out by hand the poems for his anthology

Seventeenth Century Poetry. Marsh also had the tedious task of reading the proofs, that he found 'satisfactory except that there seemed to be an unnecessary number of double entries'.[37]

Marsh introduced Hayward to Frances Cornford and Robert Nichols too. Cornford and Hayward were on friendly terms and she valued his feedback on her work, but Hayward was not a fan of Nichols's work. Nonetheless he 'listened to the "effusions of Nichols, dressed in poetic garb in his yellow shirt and petunia velvet breeks", who spoke with pride of his contributions to "English Poesy."'[38]

Marsh's happy interlude in Cambridge came to an end in October 1944. His brother-in-law had given him notice, 'rather coolly' according to Marsh, as he was retiring and wanted to make use of his rooms to compensate for those he would no longer enjoy at King's College. Marsh complained that he would be 'turned loose on the world again'.[39] His next destination was Oxford. He was sad to leave Cambridge, and particularly Hayward. He said of his friend, 'I took a tender farewell of John Hayward yesterday, he has been a great resource, and I think he'll miss me.'[40] Hayward finally returned to London on 14 March 1946 from his 'exile' in Cambridge to a flat in Carlyle Mansions, Cheyne Walk, Chelsea, a location with a fine literary pedigree – Henry James had lived in the flat above – and Hayward was especially delighted that T. S. Eliot had agreed to be his lodger.

Chapter Fourteen

Love, Loss and Loneliness

Having lost so many of his young friends, Marsh was well aware of the wretchedness that war wreaks on lives. In 1940 Christopher Hassall joined the war effort; he felt like a fish out of water in the army, but having enlisted he did his best to be useful. Marsh, who saw him off, was bereft: 'This is the beginning of a new life, cut off from your delightful companionship by which I've lived through all these months – I must make the best of it!'[1] His greatest fear was that Christopher Hassall might be killed in action. They were in regular contact with each other. Marsh wrote almost daily missives to Hassall, and made sure that Hassall had a supply of postcards so he had no excuse not to reply. If Hassall did not reply as promptly as Marsh would have liked, he contacted Christopher's sister Joan for news. Marsh was saddened when he received a note from her explaining that the correspondence between him and Hassall would be 'even more one-sided' than he had anticipated.[2]

Marsh and Hassall spoke on the telephone from time to time, and Marsh was distraught if he missed Hassall's call: 'It gave me a pang to hear you had rung me up twice […] it would have been delicious to hear your actual voice.'[3] Marsh yearned for Hassall's physical presence, and whenever Hassall had leave from the army he was desperate to see him. He wrote plaintive letters: 'I'm longing to see you in your uniform.'[4] And although Marsh thought it was 'grand' to get a long letter from Hassall, and told him 'I love to be told that my existence is one of the things that keep you going', he still lamented, 'If only we could meet!'[5] They did meet on several occasions throughout the war, usually in London, while Marsh was staying at one of his clubs. Marsh would live off the joy of having seen Hassall in person for days on end: 'It was glorious seeing you in London, & you arranged your timetable so beautifully for my benefit.'[6] Hassall had little choice but to make meticulous arrangements if he was to meet Marsh's demands on his precious time. In addition to Marsh, his leave from the army had to be divided between his wife and children, his ageing parents, and Novello, who still expected Hassall to write lyrics for his musicals. Marsh had no compunction about soliciting invitations to Hassall's home or endeavouring to join him wherever he happened to be stationed. Fortunately for Hassall (and for Marsh) he did not see active service abroad, but instead – much to his disappointment – found himself based in Wakefield in Yorkshire. Throughout the war Hassall continued to pursue his ambition to be taken seriously as a poet and writer; he did not want to be remembered simply as a lyricist for Novello's operettas. Marsh was assiduous in his mission to support and promote him.

Hassall's health problems continued to plague him throughout the war, and he shared them in great detail with Marsh: 'my nose gives me local trouble, it keeps generating a mysterious discharge, which remits, without warning, at inconvenient intervals – very odd.'[7] The *quid pro quo* was that Marsh shared the minutiae of his visits to his doctor and dentist, which included detailed accounts of his prostate problems and the inconvenience of wearing false teeth. Hassall appeared to experience a relentless series of colds, flu and chest infections, all of which left him feeling run-down and dispirited. He also suffered with vertigo due to a mastoid, and in 1943 he had problems with his gall bladder and contracted jaundice. Eve Hassall wrote to Marsh describing the 'horrid disease' and the 'dark depression he suffers too'.[8]

Hassall's marriage, like so many, was tested by the war. Eve had suffered a miscarriage with their first baby, but their son, Nicholas, was born healthy, albeit during a Blitz raid on Chelsea Hospital. Hassall wrote to Marsh making it clear to him that his period of leave would be devoted to Eve and the baby: 'it's honestly no good our making a date in the normal sense of the word. I feel my glimpses of you would be a bit snatched here and there'; but as Marsh was very demanding, he did not rule out seeing him altogether: he offered some consolation with 'But surely a hasty meal is better than no bread in each other's company.'[9] Marsh was delighted when he was asked to be Nicholas's godparent. The Hassalls' second child, Jenny (Imogen), was born in 1942.

Hassall tried to keep his family close to him during the war and rented temporary accommodation for them at his various postings. However this was not entirely satisfactory. In 1941 the Hassalls had purchased (with Eve's money) Tonford Manor in Woking. Hassall explained to Marsh that Eve longed to buy it 'as an out of London refuge during the war & permanent residence afterwards'. He went on to placate Marsh, who was horrified that Hassall should consider living outside of London: 'it's hardly like living out of London – the bus stops twenty yards from the front garden gate – so there's no need to be appalled.'[10] Marsh hated queuing for buses.

To make matters worse, the purchase of Tonford Manor had a detrimental effect on Eve Hassall's finances:

> After paying off her overdraft of three thousand pounds [around £300,000 today]!! And two thousand for the Old Manor (which includes alterations) etc. she will have £3 a week for certain and for eight months £5. The Bank apart from the above large sums, is not going to honour any cheque of hers larger than £8. But after the War, her stocks may rise to at least £5 per week. That's the position. How *could* anyone owe the bank so much?[11]

Marsh was horrified by Hassall's account. He was incredulous at Eve's debt to the bank and anxious as to how they would manage to run the house; though he possessed nowhere near the sum of Eve's family wealth, he was always prepared to give money whenever Hassall's finances were shaky. In turn Hassall was extremely grateful for Marsh's regular interventions:

> I write within five minutes of getting your letter and cheque. The heart swells and then dissolves with the impact of such kindness. Your special reference to Eve makes it possible for me to accept it, though not easy. You give me figures to show you can spare the amount with ease; but they hardly do so. […] It's lovely and touching to think that you move among Prime Ministers, peers of the realm, and lords of the Theatre, but your pocket has always

remained among the poets, – not to mention your soul! Dearest Eddie, thank you. [...] I have long given up trying to keep account of all that I owe Providence for putting me in the way of your love.[12]

Nicholas Hassall recalled, 'Of all my father's friends he remains in my memory most clearly. I believe he may have contributed to the purchase of one of the houses that was bought.'[13]

Marsh was generous with gifts to the children too and was especially delighted when he was able to visit them at the family home. In July 1943 he wrote 'how deeply glad I am of my week-end at the Manor House. It was my first chance to get a real idea of the children & start a relation with them – they are both such darlings.'[14]

Life may have been inconvenient for Marsh as an evacuee from London, but his experience was nothing compared to the tragedies unfolding every day for so many people; everyone was affected in some way, great or small, by the Second World War. One tragic event that occurred during the war which affected Marsh and Hassall personally was the death of their friend Stephen Haggard in 1943. Haggard, whom Marsh had first met in 1934, had a flourishing acting career on stage and screen prior to the outbreak of war. Nevertheless, he was desperate to join the war effort and was recruited to the British Army Intelligence Corps. Captain Haggard was sent to Egypt where British troops on Allied operations in the Middle East were based. Also based in the region were the novelist Olivia Manning and her husband, Reggie Smith, whom she had accompanied while he was working with the British Council in Jerusalem. They befriended Haggard, and Smith enlisted him to play the leading roles in his productions of *Henry V* and *Hamlet* which were broadcast on local radio. Haggard worked hard and played hard. The mild Cairo winter quickly transitioned into a ferociously hot summer, and the British contingent (like Rupert Brooke on his brief stay in Egypt) was worn down by the relentless heat and gritty wind that blew through the city. Perhaps the extreme heat and overwork eventually took its toll on Haggard's health, as he appeared to be suffering from nervous exhaustion. On 25 February 1943 he committed suicide by shooting himself while travelling on a train between Jerusalem and Cairo. The manner of his death was not publicised at the time.

Marsh was distressed by the news and worried about its effect on Hassall: 'I'm so deeply grieved at Stephen Haggard's death, and I'm sure you are very unhappy about it – what a dismal, hateful waste. He might have done great things – and he was so devoted to you.'[15]

Hassall had received a long affectionate letter from Haggard in which he had written:

> I daresay my dear Christopher that we may not meet again,
> anyhow for some time. I should like to say […] that your
> friendship has been and is one of the things in my life that I value
> above all others: and I pray that we shall be allowed to develop
> our friendship and ourselves, side by side, for long lifetimes yet.
> If that is not to be […] I shall not die such a poor creature since I
> have been your friend.[16]

On reading this Marsh was swift to reply, 'He is not the only one to feel like that about you. It's a joy to remember that it was I who brought you and him together.'[17]

The letter seemed all the more poignant after Haggard's death. Hassall's sorrow at the loss of his friend spurred him on to write a biography of Haggard. Marsh was encouraging and sympathetic: 'how thrilling you are to write about Stephen, and how sad for you to get your last letter back – as I did mine to Rupert.'[18] Marsh was concerned by the extent of the project, but Hassall's response was simply 'my fate cries out that it's the right thing for me to persevere in; even though it takes me a year.'[19] With Marsh's editorial help, *The Timeless Quest: Stephen Haggard* was eventually published in 1948 and dedicated to Haggard's sons, Piers and Mark, the latter being Hassall's godson. Hassall is oblique in his account of Haggard's death, stating: 'No one came forward as an eye-witness, and therefore such evidence as there was must leave the manner of his death unproven.'[20] But a very different and clearer story emerges from the following correspondence between Hassall and Marsh which Hassall declined to publish in *Ambrosia and Small Beer*.

At the outset of his military service Haggard appeared to be happy; he had been promoted to the rank of captain and enjoyed his job. Hassall, who had met up with him in October 1941, described him as being 'well and full of life'.[21] A few months later Hassall had lunch with Haggard again and remarked, 'I liked Stephen even more than ever before, he was less of a clever young man, one of those whose glands has [*sic*] ceased to function, and more of a complete adult. His devotion to me is touching.'[22] Haggard and Hassall met for a farewell dinner in June 1942 after which Haggard set off for Egypt. What later came to light was that at the time of his death Haggard's exhaustion and deteriorating emotional state had been compounded by his distress over a failed love affair. This was confirmed in a letter that Hassall received from their friend, the actress Jill Whistler (wife of Laurence Whistler), the contents of which Hassall confided in a missive to Marsh:

> I beg you most earnestly not to breathe a word of this to anyone,
> for I'm really breaking my word by telling even you. Jill has had
> a letter from an Egyptian woman married to an Englishman,
> sent from Jerusalem. Stephen shot himself while travelling from
> Jerusalem to Cairo. He was violently in love with this Coptic lady
> – but what, I think, was by the way. I'll show you Jill's letter. Morna
> [Haggard's widow] it seems doesn't know: and indeed Eddie, no
> one must know but us.[23]

The mysterious Egyptian woman wrote more letters to Jill Whistler and it appeared that she had seen Haggard just prior to his suicide.[24] Hassall could count on Marsh's discretion, but Marsh was taken aback and deeply saddened by the revelation:

> What overwhelming news about Stephen! I'm glad you are able
> to take comfort that he went by his own desire – but without
> knowing more of the facts I can't take it like that. If he had been
> bombed, he might have known nothing about it & we might have
> thought he had been happy to the last – now I can only feel what
> misery he must have gone through before the end – also that if
> he had given himself the chance, he might have come out the

other side & been happy again. […] (Of course I won't breathe a word).[25]

Problems had arisen in Haggard's marriage long before he had left for Egypt, and Hassall had written to Marsh about it at the time, proclaiming: 'Now here's a fantastic piece of gossip about Stephen H.' The 'gossip' had come out of a conversation between Eve Hassall and Morna Haggard. Hassall listed 'the following utterly astonishing points' for Marsh's benefit in May 1942:

1. Stephen & Morna have been miserably unhappy for a long time.
2. They are going to separate.
3. Stephen has been looking out for another man for her.
4. He believes that he will be tender of his child if it is not 'attached' to him as legal father. He loves children, and *so,*
5. They intend to have another child before they part finally!!
6. This parting will be very soon, as Stephen has *volunteered* for the Middle East so as to make a break with the past.
7. The only person he loves & respects is 'yours truly', and
8. He has made his Will leaving *everything* to me, including responsibility for his published works!!!
9. I'm the only person he's going to say a proper goodbye to.
10. Morna herself is anxious to marry again, but the only person she considers suitable in all respects is not on the market, for it is – me.

   I entreat you to 'curb your magnanimity' and don't breathe a word of this should you meet a theatrical ear, or any other ear. But did you ever hear of such goings-on!![26]

Marsh was quick to respond:

I'm flabbergasted by Morna's revelations – Isn't it lucky you're married already? Apart from their several devotions to you, which show a gleam of reason, both she & S. must be raving lunatics. Do I gather that in order to achieve his ideal of fatherhood he is to get her with child which will pass for the offspring of the unfortunate man whom he hopes to find to marry her, & that he thinks he will then be allowed to cherish it with the paternal love which he will be freed to bestow on it by the absence of any legal tie? & is Morna prepared to lend herself to such a scheme? It's the most fantastic thing I ever heard of. And fancy her pouring it out to Eve, of all people.[27]

Not surprisingly none of these revelations appears in Hassall's biography of Haggard. Notwithstanding his own inclination for discretion, together with his desire to protect Haggard's reputation and the feelings of his widow, Hassall was frustrated by the limitations imposed on his manuscript by Stephen Haggard's parents. He complained about Godfrey Haggard, Stephen's father, to Marsh: 'He "anticipates difficulties"! Ominous. I can see I'm in for a trying time when I meet them. […] For if they try to impose a vast "Gosse" upon me (making all my "vociferous" into "kindliness") it will be more than my reputation's worth to publish so tame a thing.'[28]

As it turned out, the meeting with Godfrey Haggard and his wife was not as 'ominous' as Hassall feared: 'I had a most enjoyable tea with Godfrey & Georgette. The former allowed me to keep in the 'prayers' story about his father, and the latter approved of the new para about the death as revised by us, except for the last short sentence, which I don't mind cutting. *Immense* relief!'[29]

The Timeless Quest also included contributions from Haggard's friends and fellow actors – with the exception of John Gielgud, for although he was sympathetic he was not keen to write anything, as he 'hated' Stephen Haggard as an actor.[30] Hassall wrote to Marsh setting out the problem; 'It looks as though much diabolizing is needed if we are not to allow S's reputation to be injured.'[31] The biography was effectively bowdlerized by Hassall with Marsh's assistance (Hassall credits him for reading both the manuscript and the proofs). As far as Hassall was concerned the manner of Haggard's death had been successfully hushed up. However in the 1970s Olivia Manning had no scruple in making use of Haggard's tragic suicide in the creation of her character Aidan Sheridan, who appears in *The Levant Trilogy* and, having suffered unrequited love, 'shoots himself during an identical train journey'.[32]

Another casualty of war that affected Marsh was the death of his young friend, Tom Mitford. He lamented to Hassall:

There was such a sad piece of news this morning, the death of
Tom Mitford, he was a great friend of mine at one time, but I'd
hardly seen him since the war began, except for a brief meeting
just before he left England, looking so handsome & full of life.
He was the only son among those six daughters, only two of
whom are any good – three rotters, & one dull.[33]

Major Tom Mitford was killed while fighting in Burma with the Devonshire Regiment. Marsh was veiled as to which of the Mitford sisters fall
into which category, but one can be sure that his friend Diana Mosley
was one of the two whom he deemed were any good, despite her marriage to Oswald Mosley.

Further to his anxiety over Christopher Hassall during the war,
Marsh also fretted about Ivor Novello. His daily visits to the flat were no
longer possible but Marsh continued to meet up with him at Redroofs,
occasionally in London, or when Novello was on tour. When Marsh
was staying at Compton Place in Eastbourne as a guest of the Devonshires he contrived to see Novello's show in Brighton and arranged for
Novello to join them for tea. Debo Devonshire recalled: 'He [Marsh]
was head over heels in love with Ivor Novello (whose name he mad-
deningly pronounced "I-*vor*") and was in a state of high excitement the
day that Novello came to tea at Compton Place as Eddie's guest.' Unusually for Novello he was not a success with Debo, who complained,

Novello looked at my whippet, Studley, and said, his head to one
side, 'What an enchanting bit of beige.' Studley was a serious dog,
the hero of many hare-coursing days, and was not to be dismissed
as 'a bit of beige'. That was the end of the composer of *The
Dancing Years* as far as I was concerned.[34]

During his installation with the Devonshires at Churchdale Hall Marsh
went to see Novello on tour in Nottingham, but on this occasion an
invitation to tea was not forthcoming.

Despite the country being at war, Novello continued to enjoy great
success with his theatrical productions: his imagined world of Ruritania was the perfect antidote for the British public suffering the reality
of war. Marsh delighted in telling Hassall that Novello had 'played at

Nottingham to £2200 a week, £1700 being the previous record for the theatre [...] The D. Y. [*Dancing Years*] tour goes on to the end of July [...] He goes to Edinburgh on Tuesday for a fortnight, & then has a vacant week which I hope to spend with him at Reddas.'[35]

In June 1941 Marsh received a long letter from Novello, who was in very high spirits, because, as he explained, 'business is marvellous'. The stage production of *The Dancing Years* was a huge hit. According to Marsh, Novello was 'over the moon' and 'on the crest of a wave' about his success as *The Dancing Years* was 'going gloriously', playing to capacity at every performance at Drury Lane.[36] It was good news for Hassall too, who had written the lyrics for the songs in the show. Marsh was pleased for him: 'Your financial news is interesting, & I think reassuring, what pots of money you had made! [...] & if DY goes on as it's going now, there'll be quite a lot coming in.'[37] Marsh was equally flush having received £100 from Winston Churchill for his latest round of proofreading. Anxious that Hassall could always depend on him, Marsh volunteered, 'so there's always that to fall back on if you feel a sudden pinch! You would tell me wouldn't you?'[38] Hassall would certainly tell Marsh, albeit in a diffident manner, and was confident of receiving a handout.

There was also the prospect of *The Dancing Years* being made into a film. Novello had telegraphed Marsh to inform him that he had two imminent film-tests. Marsh was a little concerned: 'I do hope the camera won't show up his "Anno Domini," which is so imperceptible on the stage'; Marsh was encouraged however by 'a marvellous write-up in the Tatler' which said that 'Mr. N. had matured in his acting tho [*sic*] not in his appearance'[39] But whether or not it was down to his looks, Novello felt that the film test had been a failure.

Although Novello was in high spirits about the success of *The Dancing Years*, the strenuous effort required to keep the show on the road took its toll on his health. He suffered bouts of bronchitis, not helped by the fact that he smoked heavily. Marsh described him as being 'wretchedly ill', and made worse by the cure, 'a new fangled remedy [...] which makes one feel *far* worse at the time'. Ever compassionate where Novello was concerned, Marsh said 'I always feel, quite unreasonably, he's a person who ought not to be ill & unhappy!'[40] Marsh was anxious about him and felt that over-work was the reason why Novello 'never seems to get back to his robust health, & I don't see how he can, without a real rest, which how is he to get? The huge success of D. Y. Cuts both ways!'[41] Novello did bounce back, but his 'attempt to give up smoking only lasted two or three days'.[42]

Novello's erratic health suffered a serious setback when on 24 March 1944 he was charged with unlawful conspiracy to commit offences against the Motor Vehicles (Restriction of Use) Order 1942. Petrol had been strictly rationed during the war and the authorities had placed a ban on all private transport. Novello was desperate to be able to recuperate at Redroofs at weekends after a week performing in the West End. In 1942 he had tried to make a case for a special licence to allow him to drive his Rolls Royce from London to Maidenhead. He considered his stage work an important boost to public morale, but his application was denied. However he thought he had found a solution through the auspices of one of his ardent female fans, Grace Walton. She had been to watch him perform on several occasions while he was touring the country, and as he often did with fans he invited her to visit him (with his regular entourage) backstage in his dressing-room. Novello was intrigued to learn that her employer, a commercial company, was engaged on regular business travel which included visits to a branch in Reading not far from Redroofs. At her suggestion, Novello agreed that she should arrange for his car to be transferred to the company along with his chauffeur of twenty years. The plan was for him to have use of it on Saturdays and Mondays with it being at the disposal of the company the rest of the time. Novello naively thought this a grand scheme, and being used to having the practical administration of his daily life dealt with by others, thought no more of it. The happy arrangement came to an abrupt halt on 8 October 1943 when Grace Walton's employer contacted Novello informing him that they had been unaware of the arrangement; they did not have a Reading office; and furthermore Grace Walton was not a senior employee in the company as she had implied but rather a clerk whose name was Dora Grace Constable. She was simply an infatuated fan. Novello's solicitor informed the Petrol Board of the situation who decided to take the matter further, and Novello was summoned to appear at Bow Street Magistrates Court on 24 April 1944. Marsh thought it absurd that anyone would suppose Novello would have risked a scandal for a few gallons of petrol and that it was only his 'fatal good nature that made him come into the plan'.[43] Marsh was horrified when he learned the outcome of Novello's court appearance, and gave a fulsome account to Hassall:

> The sentence was the greatest possible shock, as I had never
> conceived it could be anything worse than a fine – I rushed up
> to London with visions of ruin & despair on my mind – & to my
> great relief found him chatting & laughing over the telephone.
> Of course he minds most terribly, but he's impeccably calm &
> courageous. [...] I do hope the public will rally round him, as his
> friends have.[44]

Novello was sentenced to eight weeks' imprisonment subject to appeal. In total sympathy with Novello, Marsh ranted against the presiding magistrate: 'It seems the magistrate, McKenna, has a reputation for capricious arbitrary & cruel sentences – his conduct of the case was extraordinary, paying no attention to Ivor's eminent counsel, & not allowing him to produce a letter from the woman confessing that she had lied.'[45]

Marsh was certain 'that in *intention*' Novello was 'entirely blameless'. He felt completely reassured when Novello had said to him, 'You know me well enough to know that if I were keeping anything back, I'd tell *you* so.'[46] Such was Marsh's confidence in the close nature of their relationship. He concluded, 'It seems clear that McKenna was determined to make him suffer because he's rich etc. – & made it prison because the maximum fine is £100, which he thought would be a flea bite.'[47] It may not have been simply Novello's apparent wealth that had stacked the odds against him, but also his star status and the perceived reputation of theatrical types for loose morals, let alone homosexuality.

Despite his bravado, Novello felt instinctively that he would lose his appeal against his prison sentence, which took place on 16 May 1944.

Marsh appeared fleetingly as one of his character witnesses, along with Sybil Thorndike and Lewis Casson. Marsh declared that his heart had been 'quite irrationally lightened since he [Novello] asked me to be his character witness – not of course from any idea that I shall turn the scale! but just from having a part to play'.[48] He was terribly anxious that he should discharge his duty effectively; he felt it was 'a great responsibility, but a great comfort to have something to do for him'.[49] Christopher Hassall was also aggrieved:

> I can't help but feel he has been hard done by to put it mildly, &
> yet it's awful to think thousands are about to die for the defence
> of impartial Justice – when it doesn't even exist in our capital city.
> I shall await anxiously the result of the appeal. What a despicable
> little cross-eyed bitch must that woman be![50]

It was a bad outcome for Novello: four weeks' imprisonment (reduced from eight) at Wormwood Scrubs. Marsh immediately put pen to paper: 'I write in such utter misery – having said goodbye to Ivor two hours ago. It's the most monstrous miscarriage of justice, and till it actually happened I could never believe that it would.' He went on to rail bitterly against 'the grotesque old judge, who looks as if he came out of Punch & Judy' and the other members of the Committee, whom he described as 'a sex-starved woman & four grocers, the sort of people no doubt who think of actors as rogues & vagabonds'.[51]

Novello's arrest and imprisonment brought Marsh and Bobbie Andrews closer together in their shared anguish. Andrews was in 'the most utter despair', and Marsh was 'profoundly moved by the depth of his selfless love for Ivor'.[52]

Adapting to prison life was difficult for Novello, who did not eat and could not sleep as he felt so cold. Marsh, desperate to alleviate his misery, rang the Home Office and arranged for Novello's doctor to meet the Head of the Prison Department. Marsh reported that 'The Home Office was quite as much concerned for its own sake […] because they thoroughly realized what a hot time they would have from the public if Ivor cracked-up under their charge.'[53] Marsh pressed for Novello's counsel to make an application to the Home

Secretary to exercise the King's Prerogative to release Novello, but to no avail. Novello was befriended by the prison chaplain and his wife (both of whom were Welsh), and he was given the task of cataloguing the books in the prison library; soon afterwards he had a piano at his disposal and was put in charge of the prison orchestra. Marsh was relieved to learn that Novello had 'made good friends among the prison authorities & tho' they aren't breaking any of the rules, they are stretching them in his favour as much as they can'.[54] He became more cheerful when he learned that Novello was playing the piano and appeared to be much more his old self and was 'actually laughing again'.

In anticipation of Novello's release Marsh booked a room at Brooks's 'so as to be on the spot when Ivor is let out. I don't suppose anything will be known of his plans till the last moment, but there might be a chance of seeing him.'[55] Marsh was delighted when he discovered that Novello had been released early. Novello, who had climbed into the car at midnight under the cloak of darkness, likened it to the escape of Marie Antoinette. Marsh hastened from Cambridge to Redroofs, stopping en route at the Tate where his pictures were being stored to pick out a painting as a gift for Novello. He was disconcerted to learn that the paintings he had in mind were either lost or out on loan, but eventually settled on a landscape painting of Arundel by the contemporary painter Ethelbert White. Novello was philosophical about his experience. He told Marsh that 'in the long-run his imprisonment, horrible tho' it was at the time, will have been better than a fine, which would have been regarded as a proper penalty for a real offence; whereas "jug" will be seen to have been an entirely disproportionate punishment for a peccadillo'.[56]

Following his prison experience Novello's return to the London stage was met with a rapturous response from the audience, and by September 1944 he was in Normandy with ENSA performing for the troops, having the time of his life and wishing he 'could follow the Army to Berlin'.[57]

By the end of the war Marsh was living at the Goring Hotel, Novello was back on stage with a new production, and Hassall had finished his tour of duty at the War Office in London. Marsh celebrated VE Day 'standing like a sardine on its tail' in front of Buckingham Palace, listening to the King and Churchill speak. He roamed to Trafalgar Square – 'everywhere such a happy, decent, orderly crowd' – and then to Piccadilly Circus, where even though 'the scene was rather more orgiastic with singing and dancing, there was no Excess'.[58]

Marsh was now seventy-two years old. He had to find a place to live, retrieve his books, paintings and furniture, and come to terms with a new way of living in post-war England.

LEGACY

Chapter Fifteen

'A master of literature and scholarship'

Eddie Marsh was never happier than in the company of writers, as his commitment to the Georgian poets demonstrated. His own literary output, beyond his contribution to *Georgian Poetry* consisted of *The Fables of Jean de la Fontaine* and *The Odes of Horace* which he translated into English verse, and a translation of Eugène Fromentin's novel *Dominique*. According to John Middleton Murry, Marsh considered La Fontaine the 'truest' of all French poets.[1] The *Fables* were first published in two volumes by Heinemann in 1924–5 as *Forty-two Fables of la Fontaine* and *More Fables of la Fontaine* respectively. The print run was limited to 165 copies, signed by the author. Marsh had undertaken this considerable task, which he described as 'two little volumes of experiments',[2] on a voyage to South Africa and back. Its publication caused quite a stir in Marsh's circle, as 'Chips' Channon recorded in his diary:

> Everyone is annoyed with Eddie Marsh. For forty years he has been a mild-mannered little man of charm and enthusiasm. [...]
> At last he has retaliated to all the good-natured chortles and jokes and fun London has had at his expense by publishing a brilliant translation of La Fontaine's *Fables*, the best English translation in existence. He has dedicated them to his friends – similarly. They are wild with rage, especially Lady Desborough – hers begins 'There was an old rat ...' – with delicate irony he has avenged himself on society, which really loves him![3]

Indeed, Marsh had dedicated each poem to one of his friends. 'There was some speculation as to why Mrs Patrick Campbell should grace a poem about a monkey'; Viola Tree was awarded a 'large elephant', and the Duke of Devonshire 'a singing cobbler'.[4] There was some embarrassment for Marsh from a few individuals who had construed spiteful innuendo in the attribution, but he insisted that he had intended 'nothing but compliment'[5] – and in any case the gossip that ensued was 'good for sales'.[6] Notwithstanding the veiled or unintended insults, his translation was favourably received by the critics. Marsh later revised the *Fables* and combined them into one complete volume which was published in 1933 and dedicated to the memory of Rupert Brooke.

Marsh's translation of the Odes of Horace was published by Macmillan in 1941, again to critical acclaim. L. P. Wilkinson, a Fellow of King's College, Cambridge, described it as 'a delightful book', praised Marsh's 'freedom from pedantry', and went on to say 'The first requisite for any translator of Horace is that he should have an ear for the beauty of words, and Sir Edward's rarely fails.'[7] Marsh was especially pleased to receive Somerset Maugham's comments:

> I've heard at last from Willie Maugham at Los Angeles – he says that tho' his memories of Horace are vague he has 'a feeling that my translations are brilliant. They are certainly very witty and easy; and they have a wonderfully epigrammatic savour. It really does one good in these times to read something so cultivated and urbane.'[8]

Marsh inscribed a presentation copy of *The Odes of Horace* to Christopher Hassall: 'The first copy for Christopher from Eddie. March 17th 1941'. Marsh had explained that the book was to be dedicated to 'The Three Ronalds, Knox, Storrs & Fuller who have helped & encouraged – (but the real dedication is to Christopher)'.[9] He also gave Hassall a presentation copy of the 1952 edition of *Fables*, inscribed 'For Christopher with all love from Eddie, May 24th 1952'.

Marsh's translation of *Dominique* was published by Cresset Press in 1948. Initially he had been hesitant to embark on another translation project, not least as he was by now seventy-four years old, but his friend John Hayward, who was General Editor of Cresset, had suggested the idea and so Marsh felt encouraged to take it on. Hayward had come across Marsh in the corner of the billiard room at Brooks's one evening listening to the radio and decided that Marsh was in need of a project. Marsh had already assisted Hayward in compiling his anthology of *Seventeenth Century Poetry* (1948), and Hayward had admired his translation of La Fontaine's *Fables*. According to Marsh, Hayward had 'positively *raved* about my La Fontaine – saying that he always disliked translations, and started reading mine with a strong prejudice against it, which changed into unlimited admiration.'[10]

In 1939 Marsh had published his memoir, *A Number of People*, which he dedicated to Christopher Hassall. It was greeted with positive reviews by Marsh's friends, but Geoffrey Grigson's comment was damning: 'There is no point in this book, [...] Every paragraph is impregnated with the gas of English mediocrity.'[11] Marsh was undeterred by Grigson's negative view, not least as he had several warm contacts in the publishing world. Roger Senhouse, 'a power in the firm of Martin Secker',[12] was a friend (he had been introduced to Senhouse at a dinner in Albany hosted by Cathleen Nesbitt), as was Charles Evans, Chairman and Managing Director of Heinemann. Literary, theatre and music critics such as Raymond Mortimer, James Pope-Hennessy, Desmond Shawe-Taylor and James Agate, all of whom were homosexual, also featured among his circle of friends and acquaintances.

Over the years Marsh was also a contributor (by invitation) to various publications. In addition to the articles for the *Manchester Guardian* that he wrote early in his Civil Service career, he occasionally contributed to the *Listener*. He also wrote about the London theatre (he was ably qualified) for *Harper's Bazaar*. Marsh's theatrical bent also helped when he deputised for Beverley Nichols as drama critic for the *Sunday Chronicle* while Nichols was on a six-week sojourn in France.

In 1944 Marsh was approached to write entries for the *Oxford Dictionary of National Biography* on his Georgian poetry associates John Drinkwater and Harold Monro, but he decided that he 'simply *couldn't*. [...] I'm not enthusiastic about either of them, & it would have meant reading all their works again, as I've almost completely forgotten them.'[13]

By way of contrast, one particular writing project that offered light relief and was very close to Marsh's heart was as a ghost-writer: 'a marvellous plan of Ivor's' was that Marsh should help him write his autobiography. Marsh was thrilled at the prospect of spending his month-long summer holiday at Redroofs with Novello. Writing to Christopher Hassall in confidence, he outlined the plan whereby 'He [Novello] would tell me what to say, & I would write it. He *most* generously proposes to give me half the profits, both serial & book of the book, which ought to come to something really considerable.' Marsh concluded, 'I expect I shall enjoy doing it enormously, […] I shall love working with & for him. Of course we shall neither of us want more people to know about it than necessary, but he wouldn't mind my telling you.'[14] Unfortunately for Marsh the project ever came to fruition.

A distinguished translator in his own right, it was however as a proofreader and textual editor that Marsh excelled. Walter de la Mare described him as a 'superb textual critic',[15] and many respected twentieth-century writers owed him a debt of thanks for his remarkable skill. It is impossible to know exactly how many venerated works of literature have been burnished by Marsh's invisible hand, but certainly the prodigious Somerset Maugham came to rely heavily on his editing talent. At one of the numerous parties they had attended Marsh happened to mention that he was correcting proofs of a book that Churchill was about to publish. Maugham could not believe that Marsh actually enjoyed what he considered to be a tiresome task. But Marsh was willing to help, and although Maugham offered to pay him he refused and insisted it was 'pure pleasure'. At least he said so to Maugham's face; in private he thought otherwise. Even with a writer of Maugham's stature, Marsh had his work cut out. He grumbled, 'Willie Maugham's proofs came this morning, so I have my Sunday task all right.'[16] Maugham, who was based in Hollywood for part of the war, would send Marsh packets of 'American delicacies', so he considered himself 'well-rewarded' for his labours.[17] Maugham confessed, 'I had forgotten how many corrections Eddie had to make in my prose; […] my only consolation is that Eddie told me that the corrections he had to make in my writings were nothing compared to what he had to make in those of a much more illustrious author than I.'[18] Maugham's slight was aimed at Winston Churchill, who was awarded the Nobel Prize for Literature in 1953 'for his mastery of historical and biographical description as well as for brilliant oratory in defending exalted human values'.[19]

It was for Churchill that Marsh proved his worth. He considered Churchill to be a remarkable man of letters; he not only regularly composed or corrected missives on his chief's behalf in his capacity as his Private Secretary, but also proofread the drafts of Churchill's great literary works, including his memoirs, *The Gathering Storm* and *Their Finest Hour,* which he checked for style and punctuation. Churchill was very grateful to his secretary: 'My dear Eddie you are always so kind in looking over my stuff and I have such confidence in your English and punctuation.'[20] However, Churchill was not always content to implement Marsh's emendations, and various arguments ensued about the use of commas: Churchill was adamant that a comma 'should only come in when it is absolutely necessary, to make b[loody] f[ool]s understand'. In contrast to the comma, he was 'very much in favour of the semi-colon', which he thought 'should have a good run for his money in the text'.[21]

Maugham shared Churchill's frustration about Marsh's 'mania for commas' which he liberally 'peppered' over the pages of his work, much to the irritation of the typesetters.[22] And Frances Cornford described watching Marsh 'give the whole of his formidable scrutiny to every misplaced comma' in the lines of her poetry.[23]

Another contentious issue between Marsh and Churchill was the use of hyphens. Churchill's exasperation is clear in this letter to Marsh:

My dear Eddie,
I am enormously obliged to you for the great pains you have
taken in correcting my proofs. I have adopted your punctuation
although I have been inclined to let 'and' play the part of a
coma as well as itself. I am really startled at your hyphens!
Parade-ground, riding-school, thorn-bushes etc. On these lines
you would write party politics with a hyphen. Surely nobody
does that. Could you let me know what is the rule about

hyphens, and whether there is not an option in a great many of these cases.[24]

Three years later the question of hyphens reared its head again, but Churchill told Marsh quite emphatically, 'Hyphens. I see Macauley [*sic*] writes "hotheaded" in one word. I am sure we ought not to have too many hyphens.'[25]

Aside from bickering about commas and hyphens, Churchill was extremely appreciative of Marsh's expertise, regarding him as a 'master of literature and scholarship',[26] and paid him well for his work.

Another of Maugham and Marsh's mutual acquaintances whom Marsh helped was the novelist Hugh Walpole. Maugham's liking of Walpole had waned from the early days of their friendship: he came to regard Walpole as a 'ridiculous creature',[27] and it was widely known that Maugham based the character Alroy Kear – a vain and humourless novelist with more ambition than literary talent – in his novel *Cakes and Ale* on Walpole. Marsh and Walpole, both Cambridge men, were acquainted for many years. Walpole often joined other writers, poets and painters at Marsh's late night supper parties. In 1931 Marsh holidayed at Walpole's home overlooking Derwentwater in the Lake District while Walpole was working on yet another novel, *The Fortress*. After his visit Marsh stated, 'I liked him very much, and shall never laugh at him again, at least I hope not.'[28] Marsh obviously felt some remorse for joining in with Maugham's ridicule of Walpole. They moved in the same close-knit literary milieu; Walpole and Marsh attended the *Rhythm* literary lunches (hosted by John Middleton Murry and paid for by Marsh) and Walpole entertained Marsh to tea along with Henry James. Walpole, like Marsh, had great admiration for the old guard of A. C. Benson, Edmund Gosse and Henry James. As a student he had experienced a crush on Benson. After Cambridge he enjoyed an intimate friendship with the older literary doyen, Henry James, who took him on as his protégé. The question of Henry James's sexuality has long been a matter of debate with his biographers; his affectionate and personal letters to Walpole certainly hint that he had indulged in homosexual intimacy of sorts. Maugham, who liked nothing better than spreading salacious stories, said that Walpole had sexually propositioned James, but James was far too reticent and inhibited to respond. Maugham's version of the story had James jumping out of bed in his nightshirt crying 'No it's impossible, it's impossible.'[29]

Marsh and Walpole had more in common than their homosexuality and shared friends: Marsh had also been parodied in a novel. H. G. Well's 1923 novel *Men Like Gods* features a utopian parallel universe where many of the characters are based on political figures of the 1920s. Winston Churchill, who was a great fan of Wells's books, was the inspiration for the character Rupert Catskill, the Secretary of State for War, and Marsh is barely concealed as the model for Catskill's secretary, 'the young gentleman with an eye-glass', Freddy Mush. Mush is described as having spoken in 'a kind of impotent falsetto',[30] and Wells elaborated: Mush had 'Taste. Good taste. He is awfully clever at finding out young poets and all that sort of literary thing. And he's Rupert's secretary. If there is a literary academy, they say, he's certain to be in it.' But Wells dealt a blow to Marsh with 'He's dreadfully critical and sarcastic.'[31] There are further jabs at Marsh through the character Freddy Mush with regard to religion, morals, and social organisations: Wells says, 'no gentleman of serious aesthetic pretensions betrays any interest whatever in such matters. [...] Under cross-examination Mr. Mush grew pink and restive and his eye-glass flashed defensively.'[32] Even Marsh's association with Georgian poetry came in for a swipe: 'And when Freddy Mush tried to interest them in Neo-Georgian poetry and the effect of the war upon literature, [...] they didn't even pretend to listen.'[33] This may have struck a particular chord with Marsh, who had once complained to the actress Joyce Grenfell that 'he didn't mind people looking at their watches when he was talking but he did object to them shaking them to make sure they were still going'.[34]

The portrayal prompted Churchill to write an article in response to Wells; as he explained to Marsh, 'I have also written an article answering Wells and giving him one or two wipes in the eye. I particularly want you to look through this for me, and I think you will like it in view of the impudent references to you in his book.'[35]

Marsh was deeply offended by Wells, and it was not until 1935 that they were reconciled at a weekend party hosted by Lady Wemyss. Marsh wrote to Wells beforehand, saying that given his depiction of Freddie Mush he must think him 'a very unpleasant character whom it could give you no satisfaction to know. But it's a very old story now. People say life is too short for quarrels. I would rather say it is too long.' Wells responded positively, stating that 'All quarrels are foolish.' He regretted their years of lost conversation, and admitted that 'I've been moved to speak to you on several occasions but you have a forbidding eye.'[36] They evidently buried the hatchet, as Wells was one of the notable guests at the celebratory dinner for Marsh's retirement in 1937.

A further similarity between Marsh and Walpole was their love of art. A prolific novelist, Walpole had amassed a substantial income which enabled him to buy paintings. In the *Times* obituary Sir Kenneth Clark thought him a discriminating collector and 'one of the three of four real patrons of art in this country'[37] (presumably Clark also regarded Marsh as one of that number). Walpole bequeathed several paintings, including works by Cézanne, Manet, Renoir and Tissot, to the Tate Gallery and the Fitzwilliam Museum.

Although Walpole's works have fallen out of fashion in recent years, he enjoyed great success as a writer. He spent time in Hollywood and wrote the screenplay for the film *David Copperfield* (and appeared in the film in a small cameo role as the Vicar of Blunderstone). Like so many others, he often relied on Marsh for his expert, if pedantic, editing skills.

Marsh congratulated Walpole on the publication in 1912 of *Prelude to Adventure*, but could not help saying, 'though you generally succeed in the difficult business of making it not a melodrama you do sometimes topple off the tightrope in a phrase.'[38] Walpole sent Marsh the manuscript of his 1914 novel *The Duchess of Wrexe*, and although Marsh thought Walpole had shown 'a great power of keeping up the interest' he felt that the main protagonist was 'a fine conception and admirably carried out in everything except her speech'. Marsh went on to point out other factual errors related to dance programmes and the playing of bridge. To counter his criticisms, he attempted to conciliate

Walpole with 'You know my morbid eye for detail.'[39] In *The Young Enchanted* Walpole had 'changed all the lunches into luncheons most meticulously', much to Marsh's satisfaction. Marsh wrote to him, 'it's admirable of you not to be faintly annoyed (or to conceal it if you are) at my shoals of little carps, which I should have thought would be like having one's hairs pulled out one by one.'[40] Marsh was precise and fastidious when it came to the written word. Harold Nicolson summed up the experience well after Marsh had checked the proofs of his book *Tennyson, Aspects of His Life Character and Poetry* (1923) when he said, 'It was a rewarding, but humiliating ordeal for any writer to submit his proofs to such implacable scrutiny.'[41] But he also acknowledged that Marsh's criticisms showed 'how wide a gulf is fixed between writing and good writing'.[42]

In addition to assisting established writers like Maugham and Walpole, Marsh was very keen to help young writers starting out on their careers. One of them, John Godley, Marsh mentored as a schoolboy. He was very proud when Godley was awarded a prize for his work: 'My Eton boy friend John Godley sends me a poem with which he has won the "Hervey Prize," he has come on enormously & I think it promising',[43] John Godley, later 3rd Baron Kilbracken, had come to know Marsh through his mother, Elizabeth (Betty) Kilbracken. Marsh was far less impressed by her poems than her son's, describing them as 'tripe'.[44] Godley went on to become a distinguished fighter pilot during the Second World War and enjoyed a successful career as a journalist and author.

George Mallory, another striking young man, also benefited from Marsh's critical attention. During his time as a schoolmaster at Charterhouse and long before he achieved fame for his ill-fated ascent on Mount Everest, he wrote a book on James Boswell, *Boswell the Biographer* (1912). Marsh, who had been introduced to Mallory by Neville Lytton, happily volunteered to check the proofs, which meant that he often visited him at Charterhouse, where they would read poetry to each other. Mallory frequently stayed at Raymond Buildings too. The two men also had a mutual friend in Duncan Grant, who may have been Mallory's lover and took a famous nude photograph of him.

It was Mallory who introduced Marsh to the poet Robert Graves when he was just sixteen years old. Mallory had befriended Graves, who was one of his pupils at Charterhouse. Graves described how Mallory treated him as an equal; he would spend his spare time with him reading in his rooms or accompanying him on country walks. Graves recalled meeting Marsh in Mallory's rooms. Marsh had liked his schoolboy poems, 'but pointed out that they were written in the poetic diction of fifty years ago',[45] and encouraged him to find his own voice. If Marsh's prowess for spotting young literary talent was exceptional, so was his appreciation of youthful good looks. Following a visit to Graves in Oxford he wrote: 'I was greatly struck with his beauty. Something has happened to his face which makes it, in spite of his crooked nose, one of the finest I've ever seen.'[46] In his autobiography *Goodbye to All That* (1929) Graves said of Marsh that he 'has always been a good friend to me, and with whom […] I have never quarrelled: in this he is almost unique among my pre-war friends.'[47] When Graves's *Collected Poems* (1938) was published he presented a copy to Marsh, inscribed 'Edward Marsh from Robert Graves, affectionately celebrating a quarter-century of uninterrupted friendship 1938'. Graves genuinely liked and respected Marsh. In 1918 Marsh attended Graves's wedding to Nancy Nicholson, along with Mallory, who was best man. Graves could always depend on Marsh, who gave him countless handouts when he found himself in debt or financial straits. Graves turned to Marsh for help in 1929 after Laura Riding, who had become his lover and partner when he was still married, attempted suicide by leaping out of the first floor window of their home. At the time suicide was a criminal offence; Marsh, as Churchill's Private Secretary, had political influence and could intercede on Graves's behalf. A case for extenuating circumstances was accepted, much to Graves's relief. Graves then moved with her to Mallorca, where they built a home, 'Ca n'Alluny', in Deià.

In 1935 Graves won two prestigious literary prizes for *I, Claudius*: the James Tait Black Memorial Prize and the Hawthornden Prize. Marsh delighted in Graves's Claudius novels (*I, Claudius*, and *Claudius the God*, both published in 1934); he remarked, 'I think the two together are an indubitable masterpiece.'[48]

Marsh was pleased when Graves returned to London from Mallorca following the outbreak of the Spanish Civil War in 1936 and attributed the longevity of their friendship to his 'good sense' in avoiding an introduction to Laura Riding, who had 'made him quarrel with *all* the others without exception'.[49] Marsh's dislike of Laura Riding is further apparent in a letter to Christopher Hassall:

> On Tuesday morning I expected a visit from Robert Graves and Laura Riding, for which I had been desperately preparing myself by a belated and unavailing attempt to read Laura's 'novel' about the Trojan War. The story is quite lost sight of in portentous conversations, mostly devoted to glorifying the female sex on grounds which are untenable. I was wondering what on earth I should say to Laura when she came [...] But all my anxieties were wasted because Robert came alone, Laura having been incapacitated by the malpractices of a Swiss dentist. *He* was charming, and the subject of the book didn't come up at all.[50]

Graves spent time in the USA with Riding until the breakup of their volatile relationship in 1939, after which he returned to Britain. He then lived with his new partner Beryl Hodge (they eventually married in 1950) in Devon until they moved back to Mallorca in 1946. Graves wrote to Marsh reiterating his appreciation for everything that Marsh had done for him: 'On the list of my benefactors in this life your name comes at the top, in gold letters; and I want you to realize this.' Typically self-deprecating, Marsh simply said, 'I really don't know what I ever did to deserve it.'[51]

Another young poet that Marsh had encouraged from the outset of his poetical career was Siegfried Sassoon. Edmund Gosse had first asked Marsh to look at Sassoon's early poems, and Marsh was impressed enough to encourage Sassoon to leave rural Kent and move to London. Sassoon took his advice, and, keen to be close to his new mentor, rented rooms at No. 1 Raymond Buildings; Marsh was his neighbour at No. 5. When Sassoon had achieved fame and recognition as a poet he still asked Marsh to cast his critical eye over his work.

Marsh was particularly pleased to be asked to read the proofs of Sassoon's memoir, *The Weald of Youth* (1942). He described reading them as his 'chief excitement and pleasure', not least as Sassoon had written 'the *most* delightful things' about him.[52] Sassoon thought Marsh 'the prince of proof-correctors'[53] – which was just as well since Marsh could be critical of his work, though always careful to be diplomatic. He found one of Sassoon's poems 'closely wrought and deeply felt', but queried that it 'should be addressed to the rain'. What he did not tell Sassoon was that he had been 'embarrassed by the poem'; he thought that 'poets are too apt to address sweeping questions to the elements – it's become almost a cliché'.[54] They remained good friends and in regular contact with each other.

The travel writer Patrick Leigh Fermor first met Marsh at a meeting of the Horatian Society in the summer of 1950 when he was thirty-five years old, at the outset of his most productive years as a writer. Fermor later told Christopher Hassall, 'He was always wonderfully kind and encouraging and helpful, and just when one needed those things the most.'[55]

The playwright and novelist Patrick Hamilton had been befriended by Marsh early on in his career, as he recalled:

> I met him first in 1929, when he at once began to help me on
> the struggle of my play *Rope* and a novel, *The Midnight Bell* – both
> of which were produced and published that year. I was 25 and
> a Rupert Brooke maniac, and it was a tremendous thrill to be
> invited to attend evenings with him at Grays Inn. […] after you
> had spent a warm and gloriously stimulating evening with him, he
> would escort you to the door and suddenly slam it with *ferocious*
> vigour! […] At first I used to think that I had in some mysterious
> way offended him at the last moment, but later I began definitely
> to look forward to it, as another little engaging manifestation of
> his abundantly engaging personality.[56]

Marsh and Hamilton stayed in touch for many years. Marsh was thrilled when Hamilton congratulated him on the publication of his translation of the *Odes of Horace* which he thought was 'crammed through & through with poetry of the very highest order',[57] and it is clear from Marsh's correspondence that they would occasionally meet up: 'Being now 78, I'm no longer more than twice your age as I was when we first met, & I've worn pretty well – My little joke when I'm asked "How are you?" is "sound in everything except wind and limb" – Looking forward vy [*sic*] much to seeing you – Yours ever, Eddie'[58]

Hamilton was one of the most talented and successful writers of his generation: both *Rope* and his play *Gaslight* were made into films. But in spite of his success he suffered from depression and alcoholism. Heavy drinking throughout his adult life led to his early death of cirrhosis of the liver at the age of fifty-eight.

Another writer whose alcoholism contributed to his premature death was Dylan Thomas. His reputation for drunken brawls in the pubs and bars of Fitzrovia and Soho was legendary. At the outset of the Second World War Thomas was desperate to get a job, as he believed all those who were unemployed would be conscripted and he had no intention of joining the war effort. Out of the blue Marsh received a letter from Thomas asking for his help to get a job:

> I have been earning just enough money to keep my family and myself alive by selling poems and short stories to magazines. These sources of income are now almost entirely dried up. It has occurred to me that you, with your connections with the Government, might be able to obtain some employment for me, either in the Ministry of Information – though that, I am told, is overrun with applicants, stampeded by almost every young man in London who has ever held a pencil or slapped a back – or elsewhere, any other place at all. […] I have never, even in my most desperate moments, begged or attempted to seek any employment outside my own limited and underpaid profession. But now I must have work – I want to be able to go on writing, and conscription will stop that, perhaps for ever – and I beg you to help me.[59]

Marsh responded with a gift of money, for which Thomas was extremely grateful: 'It was most generous of you to assist me. I had, as you know and said, no thought at all of asking anything other than advice, but

I am very grateful and your gift was welcome indeed and will help us *considerably* over a bad time.' He went on to say, 'I was afraid that the Ministry of Information would be crowded with staff and that it would be useless for me to apply, but I must thank you for mentioning my name there. I do hope that, if anything comes to your notice, you will let me know.'[60]

In the end Thomas was exempted from military service on physical grounds as he was diagnosed as an acute asthmatic. But he was continually in debt, and had no compunction about asking for money. At the outbreak of war he found himself in dire financial straits, needing to raise £70 (around £3,700 in today's money) in order to prevent him and his family having all their possessions seized and being evicted from their cottage in Laugharne, Wales. Thomas's literary champion, the poet Stephen Spender, organised an appeal, writing to the leading literary figures of the day, and to his friend Marsh. The money followed quickly, and Marsh was pleased to report, 'I got a letter from Dylan Thomas this morning, thanking me very sweetly for my contribution to Stephen's fund, which he says has enabled him to pay all his debts and leave his family assured of food and shelter for a long time to come.'[61]

Marsh, who was an occasional proofreader for Spender, would have been happy to support an appeal from him. He thought Spender had 'great good looks' and was 'most agreeable',[62] and he made 'tantalizing introductions'[63] for Marsh to a new generation of poets including Cecil Day Lewis and Louis Macneice. Interestingly, though, there is no mention of Spender in Hassall's biography of Marsh. There is, however, a reference to Graham Greene. There is no evidence that Marsh assisted Greene with his writing or was a particular friend, but Hassall records that a group of men which included Marsh, Somerset Maugham, Osbert Sitwell and Graham Greene were together in the lounge of Claridges Hotel at 9 p.m. on Friday 11 December 1936 listening to the BBC broadcast of Edward VIII's abdication speech on a radio Maugham had borrowed from one of the hotel porters.[64]

As well as supporting young writers, Marsh could be extremely critical of them. His friend Edith Sitwell had written the introduction to Denton Welch's memoir, *Maiden Voyage* (1943), and Marsh thought he ought to read it, even though – or perhaps because – a friend had said 'the book was reeking with homosexuality',[65] and felt that Edith Sitwell had shown a compromising naiveté in praising the book. Marsh's conclusion was

> I don't think much of it. It is true that the youth writes with great ease & vigour & vividness, but I did find his experiences terribly insignificant, & he is *such* an ass, & such an infernal little egotist, with a rather nasty mind. The camp atmosphere is certainly present, but not in any scandalous degree.[66]

His heartfelt criticisms were more difficult to deliver when they appertained to a friend's work. In a 'Most Private' letter to Christopher Hassall he set out his difficulty with Robert Nichols's play *Komusu*: 'I'm in a quandary [...] I've read it twice, and find it terribly bogus, and crammed with sins against good taste and common sense. *What* am I to say about it? I'm sure you'll sympathize with me, as Robert thinks the play a masterpiece, and is very sensitive.'[67]

There were times when Marsh regretted taking on a writer's work. One such writer was the academic and founder of the first birth control clinic in London, Dr Marie Stopes. Marsh and Stopes had first met at a Poetry Society dinner; her opening gambit was to tell Marsh that she had been told he did not like her. From that moment, he said, they got on 'like twin souls', and 'on the whole [he] thoroughly enjoyed her company' – although he did confer a rather backhanded compliment, stating that 'In spite of her blousy appearance and seeming ramshackle mentality, she is a remarkable woman.'[68] Following their meeting Dr Stopes sent Marsh a 'not very distinguished paper' on the subject of 'Real Poetry and Modern Poetry', but what perturbed him the most was her poem 'Ex-Moderns', 'explaining the aberrations of poets on *obstetrical* grounds'. Marsh's riposte was to say that 'Dryden had gone as far as was expedient in accounting for bad poetry on obstetrical grounds when he said of Shadwell, The midwife laid her hand upon his skull, / With this prophetic blessing: Be thou dull.'[69]

Stopes invited Marsh to visit her at home, which he greatly enjoyed, but he certainly seems to have had mixed feelings about her. On the one hand he thought he had never met anyone 'so completely devoid of taste': he was especially critical of the 'two enormous spires of garish paper hollyhocks' pasted over her mantelpiece in the sitting room. Nevertheless he admired her 'prodigious vitality', 'geniality and pugnacity' and her 'well-justified egocentricity', but only with regard to 'her line' of work, meaning her campaign for women's rights and birth control. Marsh came away from the visit tasked with organising an introduction for her to his former and final chief at the Colonial Office, Malcolm Macdonald, who she worried 'was on the point of decreeing the Pasteurization of Milk', which she thought 'turns it into a deadly poison'. However, he was relieved to have 'evaded a poem of 600 lines about love in every sense of the word'.[70]

Marsh had thought he had circumvented commenting on her new poem, but to his frustration she sent him the proof. 'It's really very difficult. [...] I found the most complimentary way of telling her what I thought was to compare the poem to a torrent of hot lava going straight ahead but not looking where it was going.' Marsh had made up his mind 'not to poke fun, but of course I couldn't stick to this.' He concluded, 'I'm afraid I've lost her for life.'[71] Evidently Marsh had not deterred her, as a few weeks later she joined him for tea and was 'very jolly as usual', although Marsh did wonder whether she was 'quite sane' after she related a story about Cardinal Bourne organising attempts on her life after she had started her campaign for birth control and that he had 'succeeded in having her elder son murdered before her eyes, and only just failed with the second'.[72] Marsh had his doubts as to the veracity of this story. At the age of thirty-eight Dr Stopes had given birth to a stillborn son; the pregnancy was overdue and Stopes had clashed with the staff in the nursing home about the way in which she wished to give birth. She was convinced her baby had been murdered.

Another unconventional character in Marsh's life was T. E. Lawrence. They enjoyed a long-standing acquaintance; Marsh described himself as feeling honoured to have been 'on the fringe of his friendship'.[73] They were in regular contact when Lawrence was appointed as a special adviser to Churchill when he was Colonial Secretary with Responsibility for the Middle East during the 1920s. Lawrence appeared in Marsh's office one day and deposited a pile of manuscript pages on his desk; these turned out to be an extract from *Seven Pillars of Wisdom*. Calling upon Marsh's critical powers, he said, 'I don't know that you read prose, except on official subjects: this is unofficial. They are objective extracts from a MS. story I wrote of Feisal's campaign [...] they can be minuted back to me saying "have seen" or "good" or "most amusing" or "I really think you ought to publish them."'[74]

Seven Pillars of Wisdom was privately published in 1926 and published for general circulation in 1935. Lawrence included in the text a note praising Churchill following the conference in Cairo in March 1921, which was an attempt to solve the problems in the Middle East after the First World War by the formation of the new state of Iraq:

> Mr Winston Churchill was entrusted by our harassed Cabinet
> with the settlement of the Middle East; and in a few weeks, at
> his conference in Cairo, he made straight all the tangle, finding
> solutions fulfilling (I think) our promises in letter and spirit
> (where humanly possible) without sacrificing any interest of our
> Empire or any interest of the peoples concerned. So we were quit
> of the war-time Eastern adventure with clean hands, but three
> years too late to earn the gratitude which peoples, if not states,
> can pay.[75]

High praise indeed for Mr Churchill; although later, when Lawrence asked Marsh to check the proofs, in particular his references to Churchill, Lawrence said, 'I haven't, of intention, said enough: because I feared that people might say that in praising him [Churchill] I was praising myself.'[76]

Marsh and Lawrence's friendship was augmented by their mutual friends, Ronald Storrs and Lord Lloyd. Marsh was best man at Storrs' wedding and rendered him another great service on his memoir, when he 'drove the penetrating tooth-comb of his judgement through the tangled proof-skeins of my *Orientations*, applying the ideal technique of a hostile but affectionate publisher's reader'.[77] Marsh and Storrs' friendship, as was the case with Lawrence, blurred the lines between work and play, politics and literature.

Lord Lloyd was High Commissioner in Egypt from 1925 to 1929, and much admired by Lawrence, who had worked closely with him during the Arab campaign in 1917. Lawrence described Lloyd as being 'understanding' and said he 'helped wisely'.[78] Lord Lloyd invited Marsh to complete his convalescence after his Corsican mishap in 1928 at the Residency in Cairo. Marsh had a splendid time. He enjoyed 'fervent sight-seeing' with Mrs George Keppel, which included a visit to Luxor where the renowned archaeologist Howard Carter showed him the tomb of Tutankhamen. He also played poker (with a sixpenny stake limit) with the Aga Khan, an inveterate gambler, who appeared to be 'just as much thrilled by the ups-and-downs of the play as if thousands had been at stake'.[79]

There were times when the eccentric Lawrence embarrassed the conventional Marsh. On one occasion in January 1919 Lawrence had been invited to a dinner at Claridges followed by a society party; having declined the dinner invitation, he arrived at the party wearing Arab dress. He was prompt to apologise to Marsh: 'Dear Marsh, This is owing, since I behaved like a lunatic yesterday. But I have been trying for three years to think like an Arab, and when I come back with a bump to British conventions, it is rather painful.'[80]

Marsh provided Lawrence not only with a connection to government but also with a link to the literary world. While Lawrence was based in Dorset he wrote to Marsh in January 1925 after having visited an ageing Thomas Hardy, whom he generally visited on alternate Sundays; he reported that Hardy had thought Marsh's translation of the *Fables of La Fontaine* was 'excellent reading', but later in the conversation Hardy 'had forgotten that he had read the fables'.[81] As Lawrence explained, 'a film seems to slip over his mind at times now: and the present is then obscured by events of his childhood.' In the same letter Lawrence thanked Marsh for 'seeing Winston for me', as he was keen to transfer out of the army and to re-enlist in the ranks of the RAF (he had said to the author and politician John Buchan 'It must be the ranks, for I'm afraid of being loose or independent'[82]) but he had been thwarted in his many attempts to do so.

Lawrence was an admirer of Churchill's achievements in the Middle East and also a fan of his writing. He wrote to a friend in 1927 stating that 'I have not met anything very new and good – except Winston's book which is a superb demonstration of power.'[83] (This was *The World in Crisis*, volume III, *1916–1918*.) He followed this up with a letter to Marsh:

> Winston wrote me a gorgeous letter. Called his *Crisis* a pot-boiler! Some pot! And probably some boil too. I suppose he realises that he's the only high person, since Thucydides & Clarendon, who has put his generation imaginatively in his debt. Incidentally neither T. nor C. was impartial! That doesn't matter, as long as you write better than anybody of your rivals.[84]

Marsh might also have been flattered by Lawrence's praise given his own significant contribution to Churchill's book.

In 1929 Marsh, who was a member of the Hawthornden Prize committee, invited Lawrence to present the prize to Siegfried Sassoon for *Memoirs of a Fox-hunting Man*. It was Marsh who had introduced Lawrence to Sassoon (at Lawrence's request); Marsh had organised dinner at the Savoy, and Sassoon arrived only knowing that he was meeting a 'somewhat distinguished Colonel who had done wonderful things in the Hejaz campaign'.[85] Sassoon was surprised to discover that the Colonel in question was Lawrence, who, in addition to being youthful, was unlike any other colonel he had known. The three men spent the evening happily discussing poetry, politics and peace. In his diary Sassoon simply wrote: 'Dined with Eddie Marsh and met Lawrence (the Hedjaz general – a little Oxford archaeologist).'[86] Sassoon came to idolise Lawrence, and they both harboured a deep admiration of Thomas Hardy. Although Lawrence held Sassoon's work in high regard and thought the award well deserved, he baulked at the idea of a very public prizegiving. In the end Sassoon did not attend the ceremony: his friend and fellow poet Edmund Blunden collected the award on his behalf.

Despite his own aversion to prizegiving, a few years later Lawrence was pressing Marsh to assist in having an honour conferred on Bertram Thomas. Thomas, a diplomat and explorer, was the first Westerner to cross the 'Empty Quarter', the Rub' al Khali (250,000 square miles of desert in the Arabian Peninsula) in 1930–31; he would go on to head the Middle East Centre for Arab Studies in Jerusalem during the Second World War. Lawrence considered Thomas's achievement 'the finest geographical feat since Shackleton', and he was very keen that the achievement should be recognised appropriately: 'Now something must be done for this most quiet and decent fellow, in the Birthday Honours, if not sooner. It may be all arranged; but if not I beg you to see to it. […] Give him a K. will you?'[87] Despite Lawrence's supplication and confidence in Marsh's influence, Thomas did not receive his CMG until 1949.

When David Garnett was compiling his edition of Lawrence's letters Marsh had no objection to Lawrence's correspondence to him being included. Churchill, on the other hand, refused to let Garnett make use of any of his letters from Lawrence. Garnett asked for Marsh's help: 'I should be very grateful if you could ask Churchill to reconsider the matter. It would be so much better from every point of view that he should help in what is really going to be an important book.'[88] Churchill was intransigent, and the letters do not appear in the volume.

One poignant literary task that befell Marsh was to advise his friend Lord Lytton on his memoir of his eldest son, *Antony* (1935). Antony Bulwer-Lytton was serving in the Royal Auxiliary Air Force, and had died in a flying accident in 1933 while rehearsing for an air pageant. His bereft father inscribed Marsh's copy with the words: 'To E. Marsh without whose help and encouragement this book would never have been produced, from his grateful friend the author, Lytton.'[89]

It was, however, for his protégé Christopher Hassall that Marsh worked above and beyond the call of duty. He would usually scribble notes in the margins of manuscripts or on scraps of paper, but in Hassall's case this was on reams of paper appended to his letters. Marsh's skill as a critic and wordsmith was invaluable to Hassall, who honed his craft as a poet and writer with Marsh's seemingly inexhaustible help. Marsh had begun the process merely as he said playing the part of *Advocatus Diaboli*, drawing attention to points that he felt were open to question. Henceforth Hassall dubbed Marsh as the 'diabolizer', a title which seemed to please Marsh. In his capacity as a translator he likened himself to 'a tailor fitting a coat' whereas an editor or diabolizer 'is rather a prinking lady's maid, fussing around with pins and curling tongs, and scrutinizing at angles from which her charge cannot see herself.' Marsh used the example of Clara Novello: she had twirled round to show off her dress to Sir Julius Benedict, who exclaimed 'your backside is even so beautiful as your frontside!' Marsh concluded 'till that can be said all is not well. I like to think that I have been of service to English letters in this literally ancillary capacity.'[90]

Marsh was modest about his contribution, putting it down to the 'governessy side of his nature' whereby he sought to create order with a 'passion for perfection'. His pleasure derived from having removed 'a blemish from a proof or manuscript before the book is published'.[91]

The enormous trouble that Marsh took in order to enhance the work of others cannot be overestimated. J. M. Barrie told Marsh: 'One can trace your helping hand here there everywhere, you never seem to give a thought to self when there are others whom you can encourage along the way. So many know this, and I just want you to understand that I know it also and have long had a deep regard for you.'[92] Frances Cornford declared, 'I do think you are one of the wonders of the world – both in the trouble you are prepared to take, and the brilliance and acuteness of the trouble when taken.'[93] Novelist and playwright Clemence Dane was enormously grateful to Marsh for proofreading her novel *He Brings Great News* (1944), which Marsh had found 'immensely enjoyable'; she wrote effusively, 'I send you a raft-load of thanks for your goodness in helping me so invaluably & at such cost of your time (!) & energy. I do really mean a raft-load, it's a wonderful thing to do for a fellow-writer.'[94] In gratitude for his services some writers dedicated their work to him, for example Noel Langley's novel *The Music of the Heart* (1946). Marsh was especially thrilled when Somerset Maugham prefaced his memoir, *Strictly Personal* (1942), with a letter addressed to him explaining his trepidation, as it was the first time in many years that Marsh had not corrected the proofs:

> I am pretty certain that you will find in it much to comment on
> with acidity, mitigated fortunately by humour, generosity and

kindliness, and humanized by a pleasant weakness for the colon, with which you are wont to castigate looseness of expression and faults of grammar. I am very well aware how much I owe to your keen eye for carelessness, impropriety of phrase and inaccurate punctuation, and it is a misfortune for me that the difficulties of the time have prevented me from taking my customary advantage of your direction. […] many of the best writers of English of our generation are indebted to you for such proficiency as they have acquired in the practice of writing our difficult language. […] it will be a bad day for English letters when you, dear Eddie, grow too feeble to hold a pen, to turn the pages of the *O. E. D.* or to scarify your grateful victims with a sarcastic reference to *Fowler's Dictionary of English Usage.*[95]

Robert Graves echoed Maugham's sentiments in summing up Marsh's critical principles: 'Everything must mean what it says; the ear must never be cheated, or the reason offended; punctuation must be exact, diction clean, metaphors and quotations accurate. Yet he [Marsh] believed in genius'; Graves probably spoke on behalf of all the writers that Marsh had mentored when he said, 'He was always on the side of honest work, good manners, and common sense, and I am proud to have gone to school under him.'[96]

Shortly after Marsh's death on 13 January 1953, James Lees-Milne wrote in his diary:

It is strange, in correcting the type-script of my book, to see Eddie Marsh's astringent pencil marks and notes in the first two chapters, and realize that that mind, so active a month ago, has disappeared overnight. […] I had received a letter from him that he could not continue correcting my book: the type was so faint it hurt his eyes; besides he said I was a bad writer. My use of words was odd. I could not express myself. For two days I was miserable; then on reading through his corrections and the book again I realized he was absolutely right. […] I truly believe I can improve my style on the lines he has shown me: i.e. to be natural. So I am grateful to the poor old deceased to that very real extent.[97]

Chapter Sixteen

'All his long life was serene'

By the end of 1952 Marsh's already frail health had deteriorated, hastened by his shock at the death of Novello. Novello had been suffering with chest and heart problems for some time, but being a die-hard trouper he insisted that the show went on regardless. After giving a performance in *King's Rhapsody* he suffered a coronary thrombosis and died at 2.15 a.m. on 6 March 1951. Christopher Hassall had the unenviable task of telling Marsh the news. Marsh's telephone was out of order, and Hassall did not want him to learn of Novello's demise from the radio news. Marsh must have known that something was badly amiss when Hassall appeared at his door in the early hours. His reaction to the death of his precious friend was that of anger. He was incandescent that he should have lived so long and in the belief that his had been an empty existence, when Novello had been taken in his prime and had contributed so much to life. Marsh had already started to feel the burden of his advancing years; he complained to a friend, 'It's as if all my past had been recorded in pencil and was now faded away',[1] and he was finding the present barely tolerable.

Following Novello's death Clementine Churchill was quick to extend her condolences to Marsh: 'My dear Eddie, I know that the death of your true & great friend will be a blow & a bitter grief to you. Please accept my sympathy. He gave joy & pleasure to count-less thousands. Yours affectionately, Clemmie.'[2] Frances Cornford also expressed her sympathy:

> But I see thinking at the time of your great loss in Ivor Novello [...] that is the way we all wish to die, but it doesn't make the gap for you any less deep & sad. You have never spoken of him much, but I feel that for years he's brought so much warmth, affection & pleasure into your life – and I am *so* sorry.[3]

Novello's funeral took place on 12 March 1951 at Golders Green crematorium; it was attended by his many friends from state, stage and screen, as well as over five thousand members of an adoring public who had come to mourn him. The funeral cortege had a mass of flowers including white lilacs, and the strains of his song, *We'll Gather Lilacs*, were heard as the service was relayed over loudspeakers. This was followed by a memorial service at St Martin-in-the-Fields on 29 March 1951, again attended by crowds of mourners who listened to Christopher Hassall's address over loudspeakers. Both the funeral and the memorial service were recorded on newsreels and broadcast in cinemas.

Gone were Marsh's weekly visits to the Aldwych flat. He visited Redroofs for the last time in June 1951 to make an inventory of the pictures he had loaned Novello, and brought them back to Walton Street; *September Moon* by Paul Nash took pride of place. On 28 January 1952 Marsh unveiled a bust of Novello at Golders Green crematorium and spoke of their 'thirty-six years of affection' and described Novello's 'genius for happiness, and for spreading happiness around him'. He paid tribute to Novello with lines from his translation of La Fontaine: 'Some few there be, spoilt darlings of Heaven, / To whom the magic grace of charm is given.'[4]

Christopher Hassall was still a big part of his life. Marsh had long made it clear to Hassall that the best way to keep him alive was to be needed by him.[5] Nonetheless the intensity of their early friendship had waned slightly as Hassall became more successful and was frantically busy trying to juggle the demands of his family and his career. He still visited Marsh in his Walton Street rooms for tea on a weekly basis whenever he could. Frances Cornford was convinced that Hassall's love was the one thing that kept Marsh alive. In spite of shortness of breath, tiredness and feeling generally unwell, Marsh rallied his strength, as he was determined to attend lectures and social occasions. He was still in demand as a guest of honour at various luncheons and dinners, but on 13 January 1953 his health finally failed him. Frances Cornford had seen him shortly before that and had perceived how 'deadly ill' he was. She eulogised Marsh in a long letter to Christopher Hassall:

As you'll know I keep thinking about Eddie (and therefore about you too) I hope he knew a little how I loved him, & valued him […] but all that can't prevent me missing him for the rest of my life & needing his friendship and reading his unfailing response to every turn of a letter, & every demand for help. […] I'm sure he was sometimes testy or exigent with you – That's how it is, Alas, with people we love the most. […] he was so steadfast in friendship & *so* generous – I think he was often hurt & bled inside – His face was bleakly tragic in repose wasn't it? That was what was perhaps most touching about him, the unassailable private courage behind his civilised social wit & urbanity. […] How glad I am he had you all those years.[6]

Marsh died on the cusp of the second Elizabethan Age; King George VI died shortly after Marsh on 6 February 1953, and the coronation of Queen Elizabeth II took place on 2 June 1953. Born in the reign of Queen Victoria, Marsh had witnessed tumultuous change during his lifetime, including two world wars. On hearing of his death Winston Churchill reflected, 'The death of Edward Marsh is a loss to the nation, and a keen personal grief to me. […] All his long life was serene, and he left this world, I trust, without a pang, and I am sure without a fear.'[7] Marsh may have given the appearance of 'serenity in all things',[8] but like a swan gliding on the water, beneath the surface he paddled furiously to support those he loved until he simply could not continue to do so. Marsh's friend 'Birdie', the artist Tristram Hillier, reflected, 'I think he found the post-war world more than he could bear.'[9] Frances Cornford remarked, 'I don't think he wanted to live.'[10]

Christopher Hassall organised Marsh's funeral, which took place on 17 January at St Mary-the-Virgin, Bourne Street, in Belgravia. He received many letters of condolence from Marsh's friends in all professions. Marsh's life had been populated not so much by 'a number of people' but by *numerous* people; he was well known by many – he was a public figure after all – and yet he was not known *well* by many. Marsh had enjoyed a large circle of acquaintances but had few truly close friends; as Noël Coward explained, 'although I knew him all those years, I never knew him really well and yet I can honestly say I was very fond of him.'[11]

In spite of twenty years of proofreading that Marsh performed for Maugham, not to mention all the parties they both attended, Maugham echoed Coward's sentiments when he said, 'though I knew him a very long time I don't think I can claim to have been more than a close acquaintance of his'; nonetheless Maugham acknowledged Marsh's 'rare generosity of spirit'.[12] Later in life Maugham was assiduous in destroying letters and papers, perhaps in an effort to preserve an untarnished reputation beyond the grave, and he claimed to have nothing of Marsh's correspondence. However Maugham's great friend the painter Gerald Kelly said that he possessed page proofs and 'astonishing letters' which Marsh had sent to Maugham.[13] Maugham responded, stating that he had 'no recollection of my having given Gerald Eddie's letters to me, and I have no recollection of them'.[14] Kelly does not mention Marsh in his memoir, and yet he said, 'I was fond of Eddie, and if one was fond of Eddie, one was very fond indeed.'[15]

One of Marsh's close friends, Lady Juliet Duff, also destroyed his letters; she put them on the garden bonfire in the belief that 'one keeps letters for ages, thinking one will one day read them again, and one never does'.[16]

Several other tributes to Marsh are worth noting. Paul Nash, who was a particular friend among the artists, described him as 'the most generous and hospitable person. […] he would use his influence not only on behalf of his friends, but of his friends' friends in distress. Where so many men would promise, Eddie would fulfil.'[17] Nash's wife, Margaret, described Marsh as 'Paul's greatest friend', and elaborated: 'he was infinitely good to me after Paul's death, most sympathetic and understanding, both over my difficulties and personal grief and loneliness.'[18]

Diana Mosley was equally appreciative of Marsh's kindness, but for different reasons:

> Eddie was the first grown-up person I ever met who treated me as an equal, in the sense of being ready to discuss a subject without the slightest trace of didacticism. This was a result of his exquisite politeness, and of course he taught us far more than do most of the usual run of dogmatic older people.[19]

Catherine Lascelles remarked, 'He was one of the people I admired very much, not only because he was so brilliantly clever and such good company but because one felt he had the same huge respect for each person he met whatever their walk in life.'[20]

There were times however when Marsh's sympathy backfired. He had read in a newspaper that a woman had been arrested for the murder of her husband, leaving behind a little girl to face a sad and lonely Christmas. The newspaper appealed to its readers to help give the child a happy Christmas, and being so moved by her plight, Marsh bought her an expensive doll. But a friend recalled: 'It was only when he was packing it that he found its chief attraction was that on pulling a string concealed in its clothing the doll said "Papa."'[21]

In spite of his many acts of kindness and impeccable manners, Marsh could also be tactless and insensitive, and would occasionally set his friends at odds with one another. Charles Graves asserted that 'He never gossips. He never gives away a secret – not even a dull one',[22] but Marsh found tittle-tattle irresistible. He described his correspondence with Christopher Hassall during the war as 'unilateral gossip'.[23] Early in his Cambridge days his friend G. E. Moore criticised him for being frivolous and taking a superficial interest in people; Marsh confessed, 'if you simply mean that one ought not to talk gossip I agree with you and admit that I do it too much.'[24] His propensity for gossip got him into trouble with Sir Alan Lascelles after dinner one evening: 'A good dinner; but walking home, E. M. chattered to me so indiscreetly about other people's indiscretions that I could have wrung his neck. He told me the last thing I should have wished to hear. I know now why some people think it worthwhile hating him.'[25]

Marsh had evoked an angry response from Lascelles, but there is no record of those reported 'indiscretions' in Lascelles' journal, and it remains a mystery as to who those individuals were who thought it worthwhile to hate Marsh.

Many of Marsh's letters to Hassall contain passages marked 'Private' and include snippets of spiteful comment. Marsh had helped the director Basil Dean early in his career but he was thoroughly disapproving of Dean's engagement to the actress Victoria Hopper: 'I've always been very good friends with Basil, but I *do* feel it's rather revolting – a man twice divorced, & that little mercenary bud.'[26] Marsh would never have said as much to Dean's face.

Apart from the spiteful gossip, Marsh was remembered fondly for his wit and his ability to regale any gathering with humorous anecdotes. James Lees-Milne noted in his diary that

> Eddie Marsh at luncheon at Brooks's told me three little stories
> in his clipped Edwardian manner. Someone congratulated
> Lady Tree on the colour of her hair which he supposed she had
> recently dyed. 'How sweet of you,' she replied, 'to say, *my* hair.'
> Winston Churchill when told that Mr Attlee had decided not to
> visit Australia remarked, 'he feared when the mouse was away the
> cats would play,' and described Socialism as 'Government of the
> duds, by the duds, for the duds'.[27]

The theatre critic James Agate after attending a luncheon party for Hamish Hamilton recorded in his diary:

> Eddie told us of a magnificent rebuke to a late-comer at a
> luncheon party, the host being Lord Brougham and the guest
> a famous society leader arriving half an hour late and pleading
> she had been buying a chandelier. Lord B., looking straight
> ahead, said, 'I once knew a man who bought a chandelier *after*
> luncheon.'[28]

Several of Marsh's favourite irreverent funny stories concerned God. In one of them, 'A child who was taken to see an Ascent in the early days of ballooning, said to his mother "Is God expecting those gentlemen?"'[29] Another he liked to relate was 'of a Bishop calling at Dartington. The door was opened by a little girl with nothing on. "Good God!" said the Bishop. "There isn't one," said the little girl, shutting the door in his face.'[30]

His sense of humour, often inappropriate by today's standards, was a huge part of his charm, although he was deemed silly or frivolous by some. Years after Marsh's death his old friend Siegfried Sassoon rather disloyally disparaged him when he said, 'Dear old Eddie was hollow inside [...] He did many good services to the arts; but was inwardly frivolous, and ended in despair – all his social world having collapsed.'[31] It is true to say that Marsh had embraced the superficial social scene that Sassoon had come to despise; but Marsh was desolate towards the end of his life not because he was 'hollow' through lack of feeling, but because those for whom he felt so deeply had been taken from him, notably Rupert Brooke in 1915 and Ivor Novello in 1951.

Throughout his life Marsh's most important relationships were his male friendships. His view of love and romance in relation to women had been formed early on. Writing to his friend Robert Trevelyan, Marsh considered the subject of love and women:

> Why is it harder to fall in love with women the more real they are? It is easiest with purely imaginary ones, such as Beatrice Esmond or Balzac's duchesses, next easiest with people who really existed long ago, such as Mary Queen of Scots or whoever you please, next with an actress in a part and hardest of all with actual women in real life. I suppose it's chiefly want of imagination, because we can't see in the women we meet what the writers saw in the people they wrote about.'[32]

He went on to describe a revealing, in all senses of the word, encounter with a very young boy:

> You'll be glad to hear I have an anecdote which is the strongest argument for the Return to Nature. If a little child, fresh from the Ideas, approves of it, who is to object? We had a kid staying with us in Yorkshire (3½ years old) who happened to come into my room one day when I had nothing on, and professed great pleasure at the sight. 'Oh I like to see you like that' he said. 'You look so pretty' – and next day at lunch he asked me in a loud voice, 'Why don't you come down naked? You really must *not* wear clothes.'[33]

Fortunately Marsh did not take the child's suggestion literally.

In a letter to Neville Lytton he described a half-hearted flirtation he had attempted with a girl, admitting that he 'wasn't an absolute failure, but I couldn't help feeling how much better you'd have managed it'.[34]

Marsh was very popular with women, but a relationship beyond friend-ship with a woman was simply not an attraction for him. Cecil Beaton described a similar dilemma in his diary:

> My attitude to women is this – I adore to dance with them and take them to theatres and private views and talk about dresses and plays and women, but I'm really much more fond of men. My friendships with men are much more wonderful than with women. I've never been in love with women and I don't think I ever shall in the way that I have been in love with men.[35]

In spite of his predilection for the company of handsome young men, Marsh did not appear to have any more interest in sexual rela-tionships with men than he had with women. He described one occa-sion when Novello was 'convinced' that Marsh's cinema companion was 'trying to get off' with him, and Marsh had agreed: 'I can't think of any other explanation – but all I can say is that anyone less qualified for a tart I never saw.'[36] And Marsh did not respond to the advances.

James Lees-Milne recalled the first occasion when he had met Marsh, at a weekend house party in Windsor during the early 1930s. Marsh had the next room; he described how Marsh had 'sat in a col-larless shirt and dressing-gown on the end of my bed before we said goodnight. A brass stud bobbled up and down his Adam's apple.'[37] Platonic relationships, though some with romantic overtones, were all that Marsh appears to have indulged in. Later in his diaries Lees-Milne recounts a meeting that James Pope-Hennessy had with Christopher Hassall after Marsh's death:

> Jamesey asked him outright if Eddie had ever loved anyone physically. And H. [Hassall] replied that the furthest he ever went, as far as he knew, was to take his, H's, foot, and polish it with his handkerchief while holding it against his bosom. Oddly enough Harold Nicholson told me only last week that before the first war Eddie was said to delight in taking off the hunting boots of his young men friends.[38]

Whether Nicholson's tale is true or not, one can imagine Marsh oblig-ing Edward Horner and his young Oxford coterie in this manner.

During Marsh's lifetime it was certainly not unusual for a man to be regarded publicly as a confirmed bachelor while his homosexuality was an open secret. Nineteenth-century sexologists such as Havelock Ellis and Sigmund Freud defined two types of homosexuality: inverts and perverts. 'Inverts' were essentially born different from the heterosexual type; 'perverts' were corrupted into homosexuality. During the early part of the twentieth century London's West End at night was a relatively easy place to engage in homosexual encounters: the Lyons Corner House café, the Alhambra Theatre and the upstairs bar at the Trocadero were popular meeting places for the gay community. Although they were still running great risks by importuning, it was relatively easy to find partners. According to one witness, soldiers (guardsmen) in Hyde Park were surprisingly obliging for two shillings.[39] However exceptions to conventional behaviour were less acceptable after the Second World War, when Britain was rebuilding itself. British society celebrated the notion of family, and the Metropolitan Police announced a 'clean up the West End' campaign. The view that homosexuals were corrupters of public morals was reinforced in 1951 by the defection of spies Donald Maclean and Guy Burgess, the latter known to be a homosexual. Homosexuality became a very public topic, fuelled by the British press during the infamous Montagu trial in 1954, when Lord Montagu of Beaulieu, Peter Wildeblood and Major Michael Pitt-Rivers were put on trial and imprisoned for gross offences and 'conspiracy to incite certain male persons to commit serious offences with male persons'. Marsh had not lived to witness this.

Throughout his life Marsh had moved seamlessly between the strata of high society and the bohemian world of writers, artists and performers. A constant friend, he lived vicariously through others. Christopher Hassall was perceptive in his conclusion that Marsh 'belonged nowhere, always feeling at home, yet always a guest, as if having no private life but what he was invited to share in the private lives of others'.[40] Marsh had been especially eager to be a part of Hassall's life, but of all the romantic attachments that he formed with poets, painters and players none eclipsed the love that Marsh felt for Rupert Brooke, who had died so young, on the brink of fulfilling his promise. Rupert Hart-Davis described Novello as 'a pale shadow' by comparison to Brooke.[41] Due to Marsh's persistent devotion Brooke had become a cultural icon on the lines of Peter Pan in J. M. Barrie's play, the boy who never grew up and who symbolised innocence and escapism. Brooke had been very taken with the play, and went to see it several times. Like Peter Pan, Brooke had not grown old. Nor had he lived long enough to frustrate, irritate, disappoint or fall from the burnished pedestal that Marsh had constructed for him. He remained unsurpassed in Marsh's life and memory, beyond human fallibility, perfect in every respect.

Notwithstanding Marsh's great love for Brooke, it is true to say that no one benefited more from Marsh's patronage than Christopher Hassall, who once admitted to Marsh, 'It seems I can't take a step in life without your assistance; so be it.'[42] Nicholas Hassall confirmed, 'My father would have been unable to make any progress as a writer, penniless and unknown as he was, without the enormous amount of help from Eddie.'[43]

There are several instances of expressions of gratitude to Marsh from Hassall in the course of their correspondence. On one occasion he remarked 'So much love; – if I hadn't met you I should now be a different and poorer person. You have literally "made" a great deal of the character that is I – or me!'[44] On re-reading some of their early letters Hassall observed,

> I am reminded afresh of my indebtedness to you Eddie. Some
> of these pages are actually stained with grease-paint from my
> make-up box! How I used to read, and re-read them, during my
> long 'waits' in the dressing-room! And what 'magic casements'
> you were opening for me then! My mother gave me my life,
> but you gave me my mind. […] I treasure my collection of your
> letters more than anything that is not flesh and blood.[45]

Marsh had openly discussed making his will with Hassall and made it clear that he would be a beneficiary. Hassall had responded by saying

> I don't like the thought of your signing a Will at all, even when
> it leaves me so spiritually enriched. […] you are as essential a
> part of my fabric as the Dome of St. Paul's, so I can't imagine

the consequence of your dying. The thought of ever possessing anything that was yours, apart from something of your mind and personality is so unreal to me, that I therefore send you an unsubstantial shadow of my thanks for your archives.[46]

As Marsh's beneficiary Hassall received £2,000 (around £45,000 in today's money), all Marsh's books, including the bound volumes of correspondence with Rupert Brooke and autographed poems by various poets, as well as all Marsh's personal correspondence 'for disposal by him as he may think fit'. Marsh had already given Hassall the pick of his library in 1946 when his funds (and storage space) were running low and he had been obliged to sell many of his books. Hassall sold the majority of Marsh's books at Sothebys on 19 May 1953, making a total of £452 10s (around £10,000 in today's money). Hassall also sold books to Bertram Rota Booksellers and authorised them to sell Marsh's papers, for which in 1954 Bertram Rota anticipated getting in excess of $20,000 USD[47] (around $226,000 in today's money). Hassall was also vested with all copyrights held by Marsh at the time of his death in any published or unpublished work, including his correspondence, together with all the royalties due from Marsh's published work. When Somerset Maugham commented on the fact that Hassall had been left a sum of money by Marsh and said, 'I hope you are pleased',[48] little did he know how pleased.

Fortunate financially, but unlucky in love: Hassall's fractured marriage fell apart after Marsh's death. From the start of his marriage to Eve there had been endless rows between them, fuelled by Hassall's devotion to Novello and Marsh. According to Novello's biographer James Harding, Novello would indulge in long telephone conversations with Christopher Hassall using passionate terms of endearment which distressed Eve.[49] Eve Hassall resented not only the affection bestowed on Hassall by the two men but also the time he spent away from home in their company. Hassall's friends and career were his priorities over his wife and children, and to a large extent he lived the life of a bachelor. The insinuation that Hassall was bisexual or homosexual undermined their relationship even further, though according to Nicholas Hassall in relation to Novello and Marsh 'affection it was, sex it wasn't'.[50] In turn, Eve could be volatile and chaotic. The couple eventually separated; Christopher Hassall moved to Tonford Manor near Canterbury while his wife continued to live in London. Hassall's health concerns surfaced again, and he began to suffer heart problems. Frances Cornford, who had become close to Hassall through their mutual friendship with Marsh, urged him to rest:

> Why not consult that doctor again?? In any case remember always how terribly your life matters to your children, and paradoxically I believe in another way to Eve. Her independence like a real child's, is rooted & grounded in you. Without you *there* it wouldn't be fun. It would be just chaos. Isn't this true?[51]

The correspondence between Frances Cornford and Hassall is very frank. He confided in her about his problems with Eve and the children; he was troubled by Nicholas and proud of Jenny. Frances took him under her wing, and he was welcomed as part of her family. Her daughter, Clare Chapman, wrote to Hassall expressing their affection in the warmest terms: 'you are a person so unwilling to believe that you are loved, that I hope it's worth telling you how much we all love you.'[52] Hassall had a deep-rooted sense of insecurity which for many years had been counteracted by Marsh's love and devotion; Marsh had boosted his ego and self-esteem whenever necessary. In the time that Hassall had known Marsh he had changed from a needy young man with dreams of becoming a poet to an ambitious, hard-working writer determined to build a literary reputation. It seems that Marsh was a Pygmalion as well as a Maecenas.

Hassall continued to work hard and enjoyed moderate success as a poet and librettist. He worked with William Walton as the librettist for *Troilus and Cressida*, but it was a difficult collaboration. The writer Osbert Sitwell, a great friend of Walton's, had been offended when he had chosen Hassall, as he 'despised Christopher for his association with Ivor Novello'.[53] (It is ironic that Walton went on to win an Ivor Novello Award for Services to British Music in 1981.) Susana Walton recalled:

The libretto remained a continuous problem. [...] William just could not come to terms with the words that Christopher had sent him. [...] Their correspondence could fill a book; William used to say that Christopher was maddening, because he could not distinguish between a trite line of verse and an inspired one. He came to believe that Ivor Novello had taken possession of Christopher's soul. [...] But when Christopher came to visit, all would be immediately forgiven. He would take my mother out to the village cafe for steaming cups of chocolate. He would quiz me about spaghetti – he believed that I actually grew spaghetti, like asparagus [...] Christopher was very good-tempered. [...] He had been extremely good-looking in his younger days but, by the time I met him, he had allowed himself to get quite chubby. However, he still had the most beautiful speaking voice.[54]

Hassall went on to write a biography of Marsh, *Edward Marsh: Patron of the Arts* (1959), for which he was awarded the James Tait Black Memorial Prize. That was followed by *Rupert Brooke: A Biography* (1964) and *Ambrosia and Small Beer: The Record of a Correspondence between Edward Marsh and Christopher Hassall* (1964). Both of the latter were published posthumously, as Hassall suffered a heart attack on a train and died in hospital on 25 April 1963. He had asked his friends John Guest and Laurence Whistler to be his joint literary executors. In a letter to Guest he had specified:

The function should involve preventing my family from ignorantly destroying my MS papers, correspondence etc – which are enthralling – many of them valuable – ditto my books. [...] For this I would instruct my solicitor to give you each £100 & to you individually my heavenly 4 vol Chaucer (recently valued at £80) (around £1,700 and £1,300 respectively in today's money) and originally E.M.'s. I do hope you will consider this seriously, and enable me to have a really enjoyable and care-free demise. I'm in excellent health, thank you very much. C.H.[55]

Sadly Hassall was not in excellent health, nor did he manage to organise a will: he died intestate. His funeral took place in Canterbury Cathedral, where a stained glass window is dedicated to his memory with the inscription 'Remember Christopher Hassall, Beloved Friend and Poet, MCMLXII'. It was followed by a memorial service at St Martin-in-the-Fields on 20 May 1963. Hassall had outlived Marsh by just ten years.

The story of Edward Marsh's life holds a mirror up to Britain in the turbulent first half of the twentieth century. It not only reflects the politics, society and culture of the time: it also shines a light on the necessity of patronage for the arts if they are to flourish. Marsh described himself as an 'acolyte of literature, painting and the drama'.[56] Max Beerbohm thought that 'he was undeniably one of the ornaments of his time'.[57] James Agate said, 'Any millionaire can be a Maecenas; Eddie has been that richer thing, an unmoneyed Maecenas.'[58] Jacques Raverat was right when he described Marsh as 'a valet to his heroes': from Winston Churchill to countless poets, painters and players, he served them all with loyalty, encouragement and generosity. But it is not simply a past generation that benefited from Marsh's munificence: present and future generations are beneficiaries too by way of the many literary works that he brought to fruition as 'the poet's midwife' and 'diabolizer', and through the gift of pictures that still adorn the walls of our public galleries.

Notes

FOREWORD

1 Marsh, *A Number of People*, p. xi.

INTRODUCTION

1 Marsh, *A Number of People*, p. 28.
2 Westminster School Archives.
3 Flora Russell to Hassall, 22 Aug. 1954; CUL, Hassall, MS Add. 8905/1/1.
4 Flora Russell to Hassall, 6 Sept. 1954; CUL, Hassall, MS Add. 8905/1/1.
5 Marsh, *A Number of People*, p. 15.
6 *Ibid.*, p. 7.
7 Moore to Hassall, 17 Aug. 1954; CUL, Hassall, MS Add. 8905/1/1.
8 Russell, *Autobiography*, p. 65.
9 *Ibid.*, p. 107.
10 Marsh to Hassall, 12 Nov. 1937; CUL, Hassall, MS Add. 8905/2/1/3.
11 Marsh to Lady Gladstone, n.d.; Hassall, *Edward Marsh, Patron of the Arts*, p. 167.
12 Marsh, *A Number of People*, p. 103.
13 *Ibid.*
14 *Ibid.*, p. 116.
15 Sassoon, *Siegfried's Journey*, p. 87.
16 Marsh, *A Number of People*, p. 115.
17 Hassall, *Edward Marsh, Patron of the Arts*, p. 130.
18 *Ibid.*
19 Marsh, *A Number of People*, p. 131.
20 *Ibid.*, p. 129.

THE POETS

CHAPTER ONE

1 Marsh, *A Number of People*, p. 274.
2 *Ibid.*, p. 275.
3 Benson, diary entry, 30 Nov. 1906; University of Cambridge, Magdalene College Archives, A. C. Benson Diaries, F/ACB, vol. 87, f. 72.
4 Marsh, *Rupert Brooke: The Collected Poems*, p. 24.
5 Brooke to St John Lucas, Nov. 1906; Brooke, *Letters*, pp. 65–6.
6 Hassall, *Edward Marsh, Patron of the Arts*, p. 147.
7 Brooke to Mrs Brooke, 9 Nov. 1906; Brooke, *Letters*, p. 66.
8 Holroyd, *Lytton Strachey*, p. 125.
9 Garnett, *The Golden Echo*, p. 169.
10 Brooke, *Letters From America*, p. xix.
11 Hassall, *Rupert Brooke: A Biography*, p. 187.

12 Benson, diary entry, 9 Nov. 1910; University of Cambridge, Magdalene College Archives, A. C. Benson Diaries, F/ACB, vol. 131, ff. 42–3.
13 Cornford, *Selected Poems*, p. 4.
14 Frieda Lawrence to Hassall, 14 April 1954; CUL, Hassall, MS Add. 8905/1.
15 Hassall and Mathews, *Eddie Marsh*, p. 18.
16 Benson, diary entry, 2 Dec. 1906; University of Cambridge, Magdalene College Archives, A. C. Benson Diaries, F/ACB, vol. 87, f. 64.
17 Hassall and Mathews, *Eddie Marsh*, p. 29.
18 Hassall, *Edward Marsh, Patron of the Arts*, p. 23.
19 Marsh, *A Number of People*, p. 153.
20 Hassall, *Edward Marsh, Patron of the Arts*, p. 23.
21 *Ibid.*, p. 66.
22 Keynes to Hassall, 19 June 1959; CUL, Hassall, MS Add. 8905/1/5.
23 Bettany Hughes, *Venus & Aphrodite: History of a Goddess* (London: Weidenfeld & Nicolson, 2019), pp. 90–91.
24 Newsome, *On the Edge of Paradise*, p. 192.
25 Brooke to Strachey, 10 July 1912; Hale, *Friends and Apostles*, pp. 249–52.
26 Strachey to Grant, 1909; *ibid.*, p. 50.
27 In 1932 Noel Oliver went on to conduct a long-term love affair with James Strachey. Jones, *Rupert Brooke*, p. 538.
28 Brooke to Marsh, 7 Feb. 1914; Brooke, *Letters*, p. 564.
29 *Ibid.*, 7 March 1914; *ibid.*, pp. 564–5.
30 Read, *Forever England*, pp. 268–9, 274–8.
31 *The Listener* Historical Archive, 1929–91. http://tinyurl.galegroup.com/tinyurl/9YUzT6
32 Marsh, *A Number of People*, p. 275.
33 Trevor-Roper, *The Secret World*, p. 171.
34 G. E. Moore, *Principia Ethica* (Cambridge: Cambridge University Press, 1903).
35 Brooke to Olivier, 28 Aug. 1912; Pippa Harris, ed., *Song of Love: The Letters of Rupert Brooke and Noel Olivier 1909–1915* (London: Bloomsbury, 1991), p. 213.
36 Brooke to Strachey, 28 Nov. 1908; Hale, *Friends and Apostles*, p. 47.
37 Hassall, *Edward Marsh, Patron of the Arts*, p. 142.
38 *Ibid.*
39 Marsh to Brooke, 26 March 1909; *ibid.*, p. 144.
40 Brooke to Marsh, 15 April 1909; Brooke, *Letters*, p. 166.

41 Hassall, *Edward Marsh, Patron of the Arts*, p. 145.
42 *Ibid.*, p. 188.
43 Marsh to Brooke, 21 July 1909; University of Cambridge, King's College Archives, Papers of Rupert Chawner Brooke, Schroder Coll., RCB/S/5/1.
44 Marsh, *A Number of People*, p. 177.
45 *Ibid.*, p. 179.
46 *Ibid.*, p. 181. The Bullingdon Club is an all-male private dining club for members of Oxford University which over the years has had a reputation for boisterous bad behaviour.
47 Violet Asquith to Venetia Stanley, 15 Oct. 1912; Bonham Carter, *Lantern Slides*, p. 338.
48 Brooke to Marsh, Aug. 1909; Brooke, *Letters*, p. 174.
49 *Ibid.*, p. 3.
50 Marsh, *A Number of People*, p. 305.
51 *Ibid.*, p. 1.
52 Hassall, *Edward Marsh, Patron of the Arts*, p. 9.
53 Marsh, *A Number of People*, pp. 22–3.
54 Benson, diary entries, 28 Feb.–14 April 1912, F/ACB, vol. 129, f. 5, and 10 June–14 Aug. 1912, F/ACB, vol. 131, ff. 42–3; University of Cambridge, Magdalene College Archives, A. C. Benson Diaries.

CHAPTER TWO
1 Marsh, *A Number of People*, p. 149.
2 Hassall, *Edward Marsh, Patron of the Arts*, p. 120.
3 Bonham Carter, *Winston Churchill As I Knew Him*, pp. 149–50.
4 Hassall, *Edward Marsh, Patron of the Arts*, p. 138.
5 Marsh to Cynthia Charteris, 11 Dec. 1907; *ibid.*, p. 139.
6 Brendon, *Winston Churchill: A Brief Life*, p. 46.
7 Churchill to Marsh, 20 Aug. 1908; University of Cambridge, Churchill Archives Centre, Papers of Sir Edward Marsh, GBR/0014/EMAR/ 2.
8 Hassall, *Edward Marsh, Patron of the Arts*, p. 151.
9 Mosley, *A Life of Contrasts*, p. 57.
10 Hassall, *Edward Marsh, Patron of the Arts*, p. 132.
11 Clementine Hozier to Marsh, n.d; University of Cambridge, Churchill Archives Centre, Papers of Sir Edward Marsh, GBR/0014/EMAR/ 3.
12 Randolph Churchill to Marsh, n.d.; *ibid.* According to Marsh the accident took place in Aug. 1928.
13 Brooke to Marsh, 12 April 1910; Brooke, *Letters*, p. 234.
14 *Democracy and the Arts*, paper read by Brooke to the Cambridge University Fabian Society in his room at King's College, *c.* 1909; CUL, GB 12, MS Add. 8479.
15 Brooke to Marsh, 26 Sept. 1909; Brooke, *Letters*, p. 189.
16 *Ibid.*, 3 March 1910; *ibid.*, p. 224.
17 *Ibid.*, 12 April 1910; *ibid.*, pp. 233–4.

18 *Ibid.*, 9 May 1910; *ibid.*, p. 236.
19 *Ibid.*, 5 July 1911; *ibid.*, p. 311.
20 Hassall, *Edward Marsh, Patron of the Arts*, pp. 149–50.
21 Brooke to Mrs Brooke, April 1910; Brooke, *Letters*, p. 235.
22 Brooke to Cornford, 7 July 1910; *ibid.*, p. 248.
23 Brooke to Cox, Sept. 1912; *ibid.*, p. 399.
24 Marsh, *A Number of People*, p. 276.
25 Hassall, *Rupert Brooke: A Biography*, p. 279.
26 Rogers, *Georgian Poetry 1911–1922*, p. 7.
27 Hassall, *Rupert Brooke: A Biography*, p. 535.
28 Hassall, *Edward Marsh, Patron of the Arts*, p. 176.
29 Brooke to Marsh, 22 Dec. 1911; Brooke, *Letters*, pp. 327–9.
30 Brooke to Olivier, 28 Aug. 1912; Harris, *Song of Love*, p. 212.
31 Brooke to Marsh, 22 Dec. 1911; Brooke, *Letters*, pp. 327–9.
32 Hassall, *Edward Marsh, Patron of the Arts*, pp. 174–5.
33 Marsh, *A Number of People*, p. 319.
34 Grant, *Harold Monro and the Poetry Bookshop*, p. 43.
35 Monro to Marsh, 6 Feb. 1912; Hassall, *Edward Marsh, Patron of the Arts*, p. 182.
36 Marsh to Hassall, 25 May 1940; CUL, Hassall, MS Add. 8905/2/1/5.
37 Marsh, *A Number of People*, p. 312.
38 Strachey to Brooke, 24 Feb. 1912; Hale, *Friends and Apostles*, p. 223.
39 At the outset the Poetry Society guaranteed Monro a market for the *Poetry Review* among its members of 1,000 copies a month at a cover price of sixpence (equivalent to £2.50 in value today).
40 Brooke to Marsh, 25 Feb. 1912; Brooke, *Letters*, pp. 359.
41 Hassall, *Edward Marsh, Patron of the Arts*, p. 183.
42 Marsh to Brooke, 4 Feb. 1912; Hassall, *Edward Marsh, Patron of the Arts*, pp. 182–4.
43 Marsh to Bridges, 12 Feb. 1912; *ibid.*, p. 185.
44 Brooke to Marsh, 28 Sept. 1912; *ibid.*, pp. 403–4.
45 *Ibid.*, 29 June 1913; *ibid.*, pp. 477–9.
46 *Ibid.*, 25 Feb. 1912; *ibid.*, pp. 359–62.
47 Hassall, *Edward Marsh, Patron of the Arts*, p. 186.
48 Brooke to Cornford, May–June 1912; Brooke, *Letters*, pp. 385–8.
49 Brooke, fragments of a poem to be entitled 'The Sentimental Exile'; University of Cambridge, Fitzwilliam Museum, MS/1/1917.
50 Brooke to Marsh, 11 July 1912; Brooke, *Letters*, p. 389.
51 Hassall, *Edward Marsh, Patron of the Arts*, p. 188.
52 Hassall, *Ambrosia and Small Beer*, p. 70.

CHAPTER THREE
1 Hassall, *Edward Marsh, Patron of the Arts*, p. 215.
2 *Ibid.*, p. 216.
3 *Ibid.*, p. 217.

4 Marsh to Hassall, 25 May 1940; CUL, Hassall, MS Add. 80905/2/1/5.

5 Hassall, *Edward Marsh, Patron of the Arts*, p. 189.

6 Brooke to Cornford, 25 Sept. 1912; Brooke, *Letters*, p. 402.

7 Brooke, *Democracy and the Arts*, p. 13.

8 Marsh, *A Number of People*, p. 328.

9 Brooke to Marsh, 4 Oct. 1912; Brooke, *Letters*, p. 405.

10 Marsh, *A Number of People*, p. 321.

11 *Ibid.*, p. 322.

12 Hassall and Mathews, *Eddie Marsh*, pp. 20–21.

13 Project Gutenberg EBook of Georgian Poetry 1911–12. http://www.gutenberg.org/files/9484/9484-h/9484-h.htm

14 Ross, *The Georgian Revolt*, p. 29.

15 *Ibid.*, p. 117.

16 Brooke to Olivier, 12 Feb. 1913; *Song of Love*, p. 234.

17 Grant, *Harold Monro and the Poetry Bookshop*, p. 81.

18 Brooke to Marsh, 9 Nov. 1912; Brooke, *Letters*, p. 406.

19 Brooke to Cox, Sept. 1912; *ibid.*, p. 400.

20 Ross, *The Georgian Revolt*, p. 128.

21 Hassall, *Edward Marsh, Patron of the Arts*, p. 269.

22 *Ibid.*, p. 236.

23 *Ibid.*, p. 255.

24 Catherine Carswell, *The Savage Pilgrimage: A Narrative of D. H. Lawrence* (Cambridge: CUP, 1981), p. 11.

25 Hassall, *Edward Marsh, Patron of the Arts*, p. 200.

26 Brooke was hoping to purchase a piece of Gill work. Brooke to Keynes, 9 Jan. 1913; Brooke, *Letters*, pp. 416–17.

27 MacCarthy, *Eric Gill*, p. 112.

28 Bonham Carter to Hassall, 9 Sept. 1954; CUL, Hassall, MS Add. 8905/1/1.

29 Hassall, *Edward Marsh, Patron of the Arts*, p. 209.

30 *Ibid.*, p. 213.

31 *Ibid.*, p. 251.

32 Hassall, *Edward Marsh, Patron of the Arts*, pp. 241–2.

33 Mrs Lascelles [Catherine] Abercrombie, 'Memories of a Poet's Wife', *The Listener*, 15 Nov. 1956, pp. 793–4.

34 Brooke to Russell Loines, American lawyer and poet, 6 July 1914; Brooke, *Letters*, pp. 597–8.

35 Brooke, *Rupert Brooke: The Collected Poems with a Memoir by Edward Marsh*, p. 79.

36 Bonham Carter, *Winston Churchill As I Knew Him*, p. 265.

37 Hassall, *Edward Marsh, Patron of the Arts*, p. 212.

38 'The Prime Minister's Cruise', *The Times*, 10 May 1913, p. 6.

39 *Ibid.*, p. 222.

40 *Ibid.*, pp. 225–8.

41 *Ibid.*, p. 241.

42 Marsh, *A Number of People*, p. 246.

43 University of Cambridge, Churchill Archives Centre, Papers of Sir Edward Marsh, GBR/0014/EMAR/5.

44 Hassall, *Edward Marsh, Patron of the Arts*, p. 226.

45 *Ibid.*, p. 252.

46 *Ibid.*, p. 254.

47 Brooke to Marsh, 22 July 1913; Brooke, *Letters*, p. 485.

48 *Ibid.*, 7 March 1914; *ibid.*, pp. 567–9.

49 Hassall, *Edward Marsh, Patron of the Arts*, p. 277.

50 Brooke to Marsh, 24 May 1914; Brooke, *Letters*, pp. 588–90.

51 *Ibid.*

52 Hassall, *Edward Marsh, Patron of the Arts*, pp. 280–81.

53 *Ibid.*, p. 282.

54 *Ibid.*, p. 270.

55 Nesbitt to Hassall, 17 Jan. 1953; CUL, Hassall, MS Add. 8905/3/2.

56 Hassall, *Rupert Brooke: A Biography*, p. 448.

57 Hassall, *Edward Marsh, Patron of the Arts*, p. 287.

CHAPTER FOUR

1 Brooke to Marsh, 2 Aug. 1914; Brooke, *Letters*, p. 604.

2 Brooke to Spencer, 31 July 1914; *ibid.*, p. 601.

3 Brooke to Marsh, 2 Aug. 1914; *ibid.*, p. 604.

4 Hassall, *Rupert Brooke: A Biography*, p. 461.

5 Asquith to Stanley, 13 Oct. 1914; Asquith, *H. H. Asquith: Letters to Venetia Stanley*, p. 275.

6 Hassall, *Edward Marsh, Patron of the Arts*, p. 297.

7 Brooke to Leonard Bacon, 11 Nov. 1914; Brooke, *Letters*, pp. 631–3. Bacon was an American poet and literary critic.

8 Brooke to Cathleen Nesbitt, Nov. 1914; *ibid.*, p. 630.

9 Brooke to Violet Asquith, Dec. 1914; *ibid.*, p. 645.

10 Hassall, *Rupert Brooke: A Biography*, p. 473.

11 Hassall, *Edward Marsh, Patron of the Arts*, p. 305.

12 Brooke to Marsh, 7 Dec. 1914; Brooke, *Letters*, p. 639.

13 Grant, *Harold Monro and the Poetry Bookshop*, p. 81.

14 Brooke to Mrs Brooke, 22 Feb. 1915; Brooke, *Letters*, pp. 661–2.

15 Hassall, *Edward Marsh, Patron of the Arts*, p. 309.

16 Violet Asquith, diary entry, 25 Feb. 1915; Bonham Carter, *Champion Redoubtable*, p. 27.

17 *Ibid.*, 28 Feb. 1915; *ibid.*, p. 30.

18 Brooke to Violet Asquith, 8 March 1915; Brooke, *Letters*, p. 667.

19 Brooke to Nesbitt, April 1915; Brooke, *Letters*, p. 676.

20 Browne to Marsh, 25 April 1915; *ibid.*, pp. 682–7.

CHAPTER FIVE

1 Brooke, *Poetical Works*, p. 23.

2 Hynes, *A War Imagined*, p. 338.

3 Lascelles Abercrombie, 'After Fifteen Years – An Appreciation of Rupert Brooke', *The Listener*, 30 April 1930, pp. 775–6.

4 Brittain, *Testament of Youth*, p. 133. This was first published by Victor Gollancz in 1933.

5 Bonham Carter, *Champion Redoubtable*, p. 40.

6 Bonham Carter to Hassall, 23 Aug. 1954; CUL, Hassall, MS Add. 8905/1/1.

7 Woolf to Bell, 22 April 1916; Woolf, *Letters*, p. 91.

8 Marsh, *A Number of People*, p. 247.

9 *Ibid.*, June 1915; *ibid.*, p. 688.

10 Pamela Blevins, 'William Denis Browne (1888–1915)'. http://www.musicweb-international.com/classrev/2002/May02/WDBrown.htm

11 Hassall, *Edward Marsh, Patron of the Arts*, p. 352.

12 Bonham Carter, *Winston Churchill As I Knew Him*, p. 381.

13 Hassall, *Edward Marsh, Patron of the Arts*, p. 329.

14 Violet Asquith to Churchill, 26 April 1915; University of Cambridge, Churchill College Archives Centre, CHAR 1/117/45.

15 Bonham Carter, *Champion Redoubtable*, pp. 41–3.

16 Strachey to Norton, 3 May 1915; Hale, *Friends and Apostles*, p. 284.

17 Asquith to Stanley, 23 April 1915; Asquith, *H. H. Asquith: Letters to Venetia Stanley*, p. 569.

18 Asquith, *Margot Asquith's Great War Diary*, p. 94.

19 Mrs Lascelles [Catherine] Abercrombie, 'Memories of a Poet's Wife', *The Listener*, 15 Nov. 1956, pp. 793–4.

20 In Wilfrid Wilson Gibson, *Friends* (London: Elkin Mathews, 1916). The book was dedicated to the memory of Rupert Brooke.

21 Duff Cooper, diary entry, 26 April 1915; *Duff Cooper Diaries*, p. 7. NB: Brooke had suffered sunstroke, but the cause of his death was septicaemia.

22 Roberts, *Siegfried Sassoon*, pp. 60–61.

23 Russell, *Autobiography*, pp. 211–12.

24 James to Marsh, 24 April 1915; James, *Henry James: Selected Letters*, p. 424.

25 Brooke to Marsh, 9 March 1915; Brooke, *Letters*, p. 669.

26 Marsh, *A Number of People*, p. 308.

27 These papers were given to Geoffrey Keynes and deposited at King's College, Cambridge.

28 Marsh, *A Number of People*, pp. 306–7.

29 Gertler to Marsh, 17 Aug. 1915; Gertler, *Mark Gertler: Selected Letters*, p. 100.

30 Cornford to Marsh, 2 July 1915; CUL, GB 12, MS Add. 9280/5.

31 Hassall and Mathews, *Eddie Marsh*, p. 22.

32 Cornford to Marsh, n.d; CUL, GB 12, MS Add. 9280/6.

33 Hassall and Mathews, *Eddie Marsh*, pp. 22–3.

34 Cornford to Marsh, n.d; CUL, GB 12, MS Add. 9280/7.

35 *Ibid.*; CUL, GB 12, MS Add. 9280/14.

36 Woolf to Mrs Brooke, 21 Aug. 1918; Woolf, *Letters*, p. 271.

37 Woolf to Cox, 13 Aug. 1918; Woolf, *Letters*, p. 268.

38 Woolf, Review of *The Collected Poems of Rupert Brooke, with a Memoir*, by Edward Marsh, *The Times Literary Supplement*, 8 Aug. 1918; University of Cambridge, King's College Archives, Papers of Rupert Chawner Brooke, RCB/Xd/24, The Society of Authors as the Literary Representative of the Estate of Virginia Woolf.

39 Sieveking, *The Eye of the Beholder*, pp. 94–5.

40 Brittain, *Testament of Youth*, p. 134.

41 Sassoon, *Siegfried Sassoon: Diaries 1915–1918*, p. 173.

42 *Ibid.*, p. 179.

43 Woolf to Mrs Brooke, 21 Aug. 1918; Woolf, *Letters*, p. 271.

44 Woolf, diary entry, 22 March 1921; *Virginia Woolf: The Complete Collection*, p. 4174.

45 Lady Ottoline Morrell to Gertler, 11 June 1919; Gertler, *Mark Gertler: Selected Letters*, p. 171.

46 Marsh to Browne, 24 April 1915; University of Cambridge, King's College Archives, Papers of Rupert Chawner Brooke, Schroder Coll., RCB/S/5.

47 Nesbitt to Hassall, 17 Jan. 1953; CUL, Hassall, MS Add. 8905/3/2.

48 Anecdote told to me on 7 Aug. 2019 by David Scrase, former Keeper of Paintings and Drawings at the Fitzwilliam Museum, Cambridge, and friend of Geoffrey Keynes. This story is confirmed by Keynes in his memoir, Keynes, *The Gates of Memory*, p. 319.

49 *Ibid.*, p. 165.

50 Delany, *Fatal Glamour*, p. 209.

51 Nesbitt to Hassall, 17 Jan. 1953; CUL, Hassall, MS Add. 8905/3/2.

52 Marsh to Hassall, 15 Oct. 1941; CUL, Hassall, MS Add. 8905/2/1/8.

53 Brooke to Jacques Raverat, 1 Dec. 1913; Brooke, *Letters*, pp. 538–40.

54 Jones, *Rupert Brooke*, pp. 242, 448.

55 Delany, *Fatal Glamour*, p. 209.

56 Brooke to Marsh, 8 Sept. 1913; Brooke, *Letters*, p. 507.

57 Beckett, *The Second I Saw You*, p. 52.

58 Mrs Brooke to Violet Asquith, 28 April 1915; Bonham Carter, *Champion Redoubtable*, p. 44.

59 Spencer to Marsh, 1918; Hassall, *Edward Marsh, Patron of the Arts*, p. 446.

60 Hassall, *Edward Marsh, Patron of the Arts*, p. 299.

61 Lee, *Penelope Fitzgerald*, p. 300.

62 Swinnerton, *The Georgian Literary Scene*, p. 208.

63 Hassall and Mathews, *Eddie Marsh*, p. 25.

64 Reeves, *Georgian Poetry*, p. xviii.
65 Sassoon, *The Weald of Youth*, pp. 221–3.
66 Lascelles to Guendolen Osborne, 7 July 1915; Lascelles, *End of an Era*, p. 174.
67 Keynes to Marsh, 16 Oct. 1915; University of Cambridge, King's College Archives, Papers of Rupert Chawner Brooke, RCB/S/9.
68 Keynes, *The Gates of Memory*, pp. 164–5.
69 Coward, *The Noël Coward Diaries*, p. 573.
70 Marsh, *A Number of People*, p. 330.
71 Marsh to Hassall, 26 April 1945; CUL, Hassall, MS Add. 8905/2/1/14.
72 Hassall, *Edward Marsh, Patron of the Arts*, p. 652.
73 *Ibid.*
74 Dickinson to Marsh, 5 Aug. 1952; CUL, Hassall, MS Add. 8905/1/3.
75 Brooke, *Rupert Brooke: The Collected Poems with a Memoir by Edward Marsh*, p. 139.
76 Hassall, *Edward Marsh, Patron of the Arts*, p. 470.

THE PAINTERS
CHAPTER SIX

1 Marsh, *A Number of People*, p. 351.
2 The Contemporary Art Society was founded in 1909 to foster the work of British contemporary artists by purchasing and exhibiting their work. It was officially registered as a charity in 1931.
3 Pamela Lytton to Hassall, March 1958; CUL, Hassall, MS Add. 8905/1.
4 Marsh, 'Patronage in Art To-day III', p. 487.
5 Noel Anthony Lytton (son of Neville and Judith Lytton) to Hassall, 3 March 1958; CUL, Hassall, MS Add. 8905/1/1.
6 Hassall, *Edward Marsh, Patron of the Arts*, p. 91.
7 Elizabeth Longford, *A Pilgrimage of Passion: The Life of Wilfrid Scawen Blunt* (London: Weidenfeld and Nicolson, 1979), p. 339.
8 *Ibid.*, p. 340.
9 Lady Wentworth to Hassall, 17 April 1954; CUL, Hassall, MS Add. 8903/1/1.
10 *Ibid.*, 14 July 1957; CUL, Hassall, MS Add. 8905/1.
11 Marsh, *A Number of People*, p. 9.
12 Ede, *Savage Messiah*, p. 142.
13 Mosley, *A Life of Contrasts*, p. 77.
14 Marsh, *A Number of People*, p. 355.
15 Hassall, *Edward Marsh, Patron of the Arts*, p. 114.
16 *Ibid.*, p. 179.
17 Marsh, *A Number of People*, p. 356.
18 Lytton to Connard, 15 Dec. 1945; London, Royal Academy, Letter PC/4/2.
19 Hassall, *Edward Marsh, Patron of the Arts*, p. 218.
20 Marsh, *A Number of People*, p. 171.
21 Mosley, *A Life of Contrasts*, p. 89. The conversation took place in 1932 at Diana Mosley's twenty-second birthday party.
22 Marsh, *A Number of People*, p. 49.
23 *Ibid.*, p. 54.
24 *Ibid.*, p. 55.
25 *Ibid.*, p. 55.
26 It now hangs in the National Portrait Gallery, London.
27 Marsh, 'Patronage in Art To-day III', p. 487.
28 Marsh to Hassall, Jan. 1942; Hassall, *Ambrosia and Small Beer*, p. 193. He was referring to Robert Emmons, *The Life and Opinions of Walter Richard Sickert* (London: Faber and Faber, 1941), which was published shortly before Sickert's death.
29 Sir Alec Martin to Marsh, 14 May 1934; University of Cambridge, Churchill Archives Centre, CHAR 2/575 A-B/83.
30 Marsh to Churchill, 15 May 1934; University of Cambridge, Churchill Archives Centre, CHAR 2/575 A-B/82.
31 Churchill to Marsh, 16 May 1934; University of Cambridge, Churchill Archives Centre, CHAR 2/575 A-B/84.
32 Matthew Sturgis, *Walter Sickert: A Life* (London: Harper Perennial, 2005), p. 615.
33 *Ibid.*, p. 617.

CHAPTER SEVEN

1 Marsh, *A Number of People*, p. 355.
2 MacDougall, *Mark Gertler*, p. 34.
3 Spalding, *Vanessa Bell*, p. 92.
4 Haycock, *A Crisis of Brilliance*, p. 162.
5 *The London Salon of the Allied Artists' Association, Ltd.*, July 1911, exhibition catalogue. National Art Library, Victoria and Albert Museum.
6 Hassall, *Edward Marsh, Patron of the Arts*, p. 241.
7 Marsh to Brooke, July 1913; Hassall, *Edward Marsh, Patron of the Arts*, p. 241.
8 *Ibid.*, 26 Aug. 1913; *ibid.*, p. 244.
9 Nash, *Paul Nash: Outline*, p. 115.
10 Woodeson, *Mark Gertler*, p. 107.
11 Parker, 'The man who enjoyed everything', pp. 79–83.
12 Hassall, *Edward Marsh, Patron of the Arts*, p. 563.
13 Carrington to Gertler, Dec. 1915; Carrington, *Carrington's Letters*, p. 28.
14 Woodeson, *Mark Gertler*, p. 68.
15 *Ibid.*, p. 121.
16 The Eiffel Tower restaurant in Percy Street was a favourite haunt of *haut* Bohemia. 'In the days of his prosperity, Rudolf Stulik, the Viennese proprietor, made his restaurant irresistible to London's "illuminati" – Beaton, Sickert, Gilman, Firbank, Iris Tree, Eddie Marsh, Horace Cole, Nina Hamnett, Viva King, Anthony Powell, Marchesa Casati, Tallulah Bankhead, Brenda Dean Paul.' Virginia Nicholson, *Among the Bohemians: Experiments in Living 1900–1939* (London: Penguin, 2003), p. 268.
17 Woodeson, *Mark Gertler*, p. 108.
18 *Ibid.*, p. 113.
19 *Ibid.*, p. 115.

20 Nash, *Paul Nash: Outline*, p. 74.
21 Woodeson, *Mark Gertler*, p. 109.
22 Marsh, *A Number of People*, p. 356.
23 Hassall, *Edward Marsh, Patron of the Arts*, p. 603.
24 Spencer to Jacques and Gwen Raverat, Oct./ Nov. 1913; Spencer, *Looking to Heaven*, p. 97.
25 Spencer to Jacques and Gwen Raverat, Oct./ Nov. 1913; Spencer, *Looking to Heaven*, pp. 97–8.
26 Gertler to Marsh, 1913; Gertler, *Mark Gertler: Selected Letters*, p. 56.
27 Spencer to Jacques and Gwen Raverat, Oct./ Nov. 1913; Spencer, *Looking to Heaven*, p. 98.
28 Spencer to Jacques and Gwen Raverat, Oct./ Nov. 1913; Spencer, *Looking to Heaven*, pp. 97–8.
29 Gertler to Marsh, Nov. 1913; Hassall, *Edward Marsh, Patron of the Arts*, p. 257.
30 Spencer to Lamb, 7 Nov. 1913; Spencer, *Looking to Heaven*, p. 99.
31 Spencer to Lamb, 1 Dec. 1913; Spencer, *Looking to Heaven*, p. 100.
32 Hassall, *Edward Marsh, Patron of the Arts*, p. 283.
33 Brooke to Marsh, 8 Sept. 1913; Brooke, *Letters*, p. 507.
34 Spencer to Jacques and Gwen Raverat, 17 July 1914; Spencer, *Looking to Heaven*, p. 119.
35 *Ibid.*, 15 Dec. 1913; *ibid.*, pp. 102–3.
36 Gertler to Carrington, 1 April 1914; Gertler, *Mark Gertler: Selected Letters*, p. 64.
37 Spencer to Jacques and Gwen Raverat, 19 April 1914; Spencer, *Looking to Heaven*, p. 112.
38 Hassall, *Edward Marsh, Patron of the Arts*, p. 302.
39 Nash, *Paul Nash: Outline*, p. 115.
40 *Ibid.*, p. 116.
41 Marsh, *A Number of People*, p. 360.
42 Gaudier-Brzeska to Sophie, Nov. 1912; Ede, *Savage Messiah*, p. 139.
43 *Ibid.*, p. 177.
44 Gertler to Marsh, 1913; Gertler, *Mark Gertler: Selected Letters*, p. 57.
45 *Ibid.*, June 1914; *ibid.*, p. 69.
46 Marsh, *A Number of People*, p. 361.
47 Hassall, *Edward Marsh, Patron of the Arts*, p. 265.
48 Marsh, *A Number of People*, p. 361.
49 *Ibid.*, pp. 361–2.

CHAPTER EIGHT

1 Gaudier-Brzeska to Alfred Schiff, 26 Feb. 1915; Ede, *Savage Messiah*, p. 201.
2 Hassall, *Edward Marsh, Patron of the Arts*, p. 263.
3 *Ibid.*, p. 271.
4 Haycock, *A Crisis of Brilliance*, p. 281.
5 Paul Nash to Marsh, Dec. 1915; Hassall, *Edward Marsh, Patron of the Arts*, p. 302.
6 Spencer to Jacques and Gwen Raverat, 8 May 1915; Spencer, *Looking to Heaven*, p. 144.
7 Haycock, *A Crisis of Brilliance*, p. 235.
8 Spencer to Jacques and Gwen Raverat, 18 July 1917; Spencer, *Looking to Heaven*, p. 283.

9 Spencer to Florence Spencer, July 1917; *ibid.*, p. 289.
10 Gaudier-Brzeska to Marsh, 1 Oct. 1914; Ede, *Savage Messiah*, pp. 198–9.
11 Hassall, *Edward Marsh, Patron of the Arts*, p. 288.
12 Rosenberg to Marsh, 8 Aug. 1914; Rosenberg, *Isaac Rosenberg*, p. 261.
13 *Ibid.*, Dec. 1915; *ibid.*, p. 286.
14 Hassall, *Edward Marsh, Patron of the Arts*, p. 439.
15 Marsh, *A Number of People*, p. 326.
16 Gertler, *Mark Gertler: Selected Letters*, p. 76.
17 Quoted from Gertler to Brett, 16 Sept. 1914; *ibid.*, p. 101.
18 Gertler to Carrington, 4 March 1915; *ibid.*, p. 87.
19 Marsh, *A Number of People*, p. 229.
20 Gertler to Marsh, Nov. 1914; Gertler, *Mark Gertler: Selected Letters*, p. 75.
21 Gertler to Dorothy Brett, Jan. 1915; *ibid.*, p. 78.
22 Gertler to Carrington, Jan. 1915; *ibid.*, p. 79.
23 Gertler to Marsh, Jan. 1915; *ibid.*, p. 79.
24 Gertler to Carrington, Jan. 1915; *ibid.*, p. 81.
25 *Ibid.*, Feb. 1915; *ibid.*, p. 83.
26 Marsh to Browne, 20 March 1915; Hassall, *Edward Marsh, Patron of the Arts*, pp. 312–13.
27 Gertler to Marsh, 1915; Gertler, *Mark Gertler: Selected Letters*, p. 90.
28 Gertler to Strachey, 23 May 1915; Gertler, *Mark Gertler: Selected Letters*, p. 92.
29 Marsh, *A Number of People*, pp. 247–8.
30 Gertler to Strachey, 23 May 1915; Gertler, *Mark Gertler: Selected Letters*, p. 92.
31 Gertler to Marsh, May 1915; *ibid.*, pp. 92–3.
32 Marsh to Gertler, 26 May 1915; *ibid.*, p. 93.
33 Gertler to Carrington, 1 July 1915; *ibid.*, p. 96.
34 Gertler to Marsh, July 1915; *ibid.*, p. 99.
35 Marsh to Gertler, 8 Aug. 1915; *ibid.*, p. 101.
36 *Ibid.*, 15 Aug. 1915; *ibid.*, p. 100.
37 *Ibid.*, 17 Aug. 1915; *ibid.*, pp. 100–101.
38 Gertler to Marsh, 19 Oct. 1915; *ibid.*, p. 102.
39 MacDougall, *Mark Gertler*, p. 127.
40 Marsh to Gertler, 26 May 1915; Gertler, *Mark Gertler: Selected Letters*, p. 93.
41 Gertler to S. S. Koteliansky, 3 Feb. 1916; *ibid.*, p. 108.
42 Lawrence to Gertler, 20 Jan. 1916; *ibid.*, p. 109.
43 Shearman to Gertler, 12 Oct. 1916; *ibid.*, p. 126.
44 Lawrence to Gertler, 9 Oct. 1916; *ibid.*, p. 129.
45 Lady Ottoline Morrell to Gertler, 11 June 1919; *ibid.*, p. 171.
46 Marsh to Sieveking, 17 Nov. 1915; Sieveking, *The Eye of the Beholder*, p. 87.
47 Bonham Carter, *Winston Churchill As I Knew Him*, p. 430.
48 Lady Juliet Duff to Marsh, n.d.; Hassall, *Edward Marsh, Patron of the Arts*, p. 407.
49 Marsh, *A Number of People*, p. 250.
50 *Ibid.*, p. 247.

CHAPTER NINE

1 Hassall, *Edward Marsh, Patron of the Arts*, p. 406.
2 *Ibid.*, pp. 545–6.
3 *Ibid.*, p. 549.
4 Marsh, *A Number of People*, p. 363.
5 W. MacQueen-Pope, *Ivor: The Story of an Achievement* (London: W. H. Allen, 1952), p. 459.
6 Grant to Hassall, 7 March 1937; CUL, Hassall, MS Add. 8905/3/4.
7 Hassall, *Edward Marsh, Patron of the Arts*, p. 601.
8 Marsh, 'Patronage in Art To-day III', pp. 487–9.
9 Marsh to Hassall, 28 May 1937; Hassall, *Ambrosia and Small Beer*, p. 47.
10 *Ibid.*, 21 March 1944; CUL, Hassall, MS Add. 8905/2/1/13.
11 Hassall, *Ambrosia and Small Beer*, p. 353.
12 Gertler to Marsh, 8 May 1939; Gertler, *Mark Gertler: Selected Letters*, p. 247.
13 *Ibid.*, 11 May 1939; *ibid.*, p. 248.
14 MacDougall, *Mark Gertler*, p. 327.
15 *Ibid.*, 11 May 1939; *ibid.*, p.248.
16 Marsh to Hassall, n.d.; Hassall, *Ambrosia and Small Beer*, p. 318.
17 Eric Newton, 'Mark Gertler', *Sunday Times*, 19 Nov. 1944, p. 2.
18 *Ibid.*, p. 2.
19 Deborah Devonshire to Diana Mosley, 24 June 1941; Mosley, *The Mitfords*, p. 179.
20 Devonshire, *Wait For Me!*, pp. 124–5.
21 Lascelles, *King's Counsellor*, p. 418.
22 Novello to Marsh, 4 March 1942; CUL, Hassall, MS Add. 8905/2/3/40.
23 Hassall, *Edward Marsh, Patron of the Arts*, p. 634, and Tate Archive, TG 1/6/19/57.
24 *Ibid.*, p. 365.
25 Malcolm Mackenzie, 'Sir Edward Marsh', *The Times*, 16 Jan. 1953, p. 8.
26 Hassall to Joan Hassall, n.d.; CUL, Hassall, MS Add. 8905/11/7.
27 Hitchens to Marsh, n.d.; quoted in Marsh to Hassall, 27 May 1944; CUL, Hassall, MS Add. 8905/2/1/13.
28 Marsh to Hassall, 27 May 1944; CUL, Hassall, MS Add. 8905/2/1/13.
29 *Ibid.*, 26 Aug. 1951; CUL, Hassall, MS Add. 8905/2/1/15.
30 Pope-Hennessy to Hassall, 30 April 1953; CUL, Hassall, MS Add. 8905/3/2.
31 Marsh to Hassall, 1 July 1940; CUL, Hassall, MS Add. 8905/2/1/5.
32 Pope-Hennessy, 'Eddie Marsh', *The Spectator*, 14 Nov. 1952, pp. 7–8.
33 Pope-Hennessy to Hassall, 24 Jan. 1953; CUL, Hassall, MS Add. 8905/3/2.
34 https://hadrury-artist.tripod.com/bio.htm (16/12/20).
35 Marsh to Hassall, 8 May 1952; CUL, Hassall, MS Add. 8905/2/1/15.

36 Hassall and Mathews, *Eddie Marsh*, p. 15.

THE PLAYERS

CHAPTER TEN

1 Mosley, *A Life of Contrasts*, p. 57.
2 Caption to a photograph of 'Eddie' Marsh in *The Bystander*, 24 April 1940.
3 Walpole, diary entry, 14 Oct. 1920, unpublished and copied from the original by Rupert Hart-Davis; CUL, Hassall, MS Add. 8905/1/1, Hart-Davis to Hassall, 6 Jan. 1958.
4 Rupert Hart-Davis, *Hugh Walpole: A Biography* (London: Macmillan & Co., 1952), p. 36.
5 Asquith to Stanley, 11 Jun 1914; *H. H. Asquith: Letters to Venetia Stanley* (Oxford: OUP. 1985) p. 85.
6 Gordon Beckles, 'King of the First-Nighters', *Leader Magazine*, 19 July 1947.
7 Charles Graves, 'After You, Who…? Celebrities in Cameo, no. 11. Edward Marsh, C.M.G., C.V.O.', *The Bystander*, 11 March 1936, p. 425.
8 Coward, *Present Indicative*, p. 251.
9 Marsh, *A Number of People*, p. 269.
10 Hassall and Mathews, *Eddie Marsh*, p. 34.
11 Marsh, *A Number of People*, p. 367.
12 Hassall and Mathews, *Eddie Marsh*, p. 11.
13 *Ibid.*, p. 35.
14 Mosley, *A Life of Contrasts*, p. 77.
15 Marsh, *A Number of People*, pp. 367–8.
16 Hassall and Mathews, *Eddie Marsh*, p. 28.
17 Hassall, *Edward Marsh, Patron of the Arts*, p. 536.
18 Hassall, *Ambrosia and Small Beer*, p. 321.
19 Hassall and Mathews, *Eddie Marsh*, p. 35.
20 Hassall, *Ambrosia and Small Beer*, p. 204.
21 Marsh to Hassall, 19 Feb. 1944; CUL, Hassall, MS Add. 8905/2/1/13.
22 Hassall, *Edward Marsh, Patron of the Arts*, p. 31.
23 *Ibid.*, p. 44.
24 *Ibid.*, p. 37.
25 *Ibid.*, p. 152.
26 *Ibid.*, p. 157.
27 Marsh to Mrs Gladstone, 22 May 1910; *ibid.*
28 Lady Diana Cooper to Hassall, 9 Oct. 1954; CUL, Hassall, MS Add. 8905/1/1.
29 Hassall, *Edward Marsh, Patron of the Arts*, p. 231.

CHAPTER ELEVEN

1 Coward, *Present Indicative*, p. 94.
2 Marsh, *A Number of People*, p. 369.
3 CUL, Hassall, MS Add. 8905/1/4.
4 Sieveking, *The Eye of the Beholder*, p. 84.
5 Hassall, *Edward Marsh, Patron of the Arts*, p. 394.
6 *Ibid.*, p. 379.
7 *Ibid.*, p. 394.
8 Paul Sieveking, ed., *Airborne: Scenes from the Life of Lance Sieveking, Pilot, Writer & Broadcasting Pioneer* (London: Strange Attractor Press, 2013), p. 48.
9 *Ibid.*, pp. 48–9.
10 *Ibid.*, p. 57.

11 Marsh, *A Number of People*, p. 207.
12 *Ibid.*, p. 378.
13 Hassall, *Edward Marsh, Patron of the Arts*, p. 402.
14 *Ibid.*, p. 400.
15 Sieveking, *Airborne* (cit. at n. 8), p. 49.
16 Hassall, *Edward Marsh, Patron of the Arts*, p. 478.
17 Hassall, *Ambrosia and Small Beer*, p. 6.
18 Hassall, *Edward Marsh, Patron of the Arts*,
    pp. 478–9.
19 Coward, *Present Indicative*, p. 94.
20 *Ibid.*, p. 76.
21 *Ibid.*, p. 122.
22 Hassall, *Edward Marsh, Patron of the Arts*,
    p. 477.
23 Coward to Hassall, 8 Sept. 1954; CUL, Hassall,
    MS Add. 8905/1/1.
24 Hassall, *Edward Marsh, Patron of the Arts*,
    p. 477.
25 *Ibid.*, p. 534.
26 Virginia Potter to Virginia Dickinson Reynolds,
    4 Aug. 1941; Angela Potter, ed., *Shared Histories:*
    Transatlantic Letters between Virginia Dickinson
    Reynolds and her Daughter, Virginia Potter,
    1929–1966 (Athens, Ga.: University of Georgia
    Press, 2006), p. 110.
27 Marsh to Hassall, 10 Aug. 1941; CUL, Hassall,
    MS Add. 8905/2/1/8.
28 *Ibid.*, 3 Aug. 1941.
29 Coward, *Present Indicative*, p. 314.
30 *Ibid.*, pp. 316–17.
31 *Ibid.*, p. 318.
32 *Ibid.*, p. 322.
33 Valerie Grove, *Dear Dodie: The Life of Dodie Smith*
    (London: Chatto & Windus, 1996), p. 76.
34 Philip Hoare, 'Ivor Novello and Noël Coward's
    flirtation with fascism'. theguardian.com/books/
    2014/jul/04/ivor-novello-noel-coward-fascism
35 Marsh, *A Number of People*, p. 227.
36 Barnes to Hassall, 12 April 1954; CUL, Hassall,
    MS Add. 8905/1/1.
37 Marsh to Hassall, 23 Aug. 1943; CUL, Hassall,
    MS Add. 8905/2/1/12.
38 *Ibid.*, 15 May 1937; CUL, Hassall, MS Add.
    8905/2/1/3.
39 Beaton, diary entry, 9 Oct 1923; Vickers, *Cecil*
    Beaton, p. 39.
40 *Ibid.*, Oct. 1947; *ibid.*, p. 310.
41 Channon, diary entry, 6 Jan. 1926; Channon,
    Henry 'Chips' Channon, p. 195.
42 Sieveking, *The Eye of the Beholder*, p. 91.
43 Holroyd, *Lytton Strachey*, p. 658.
44 Hastings, *The Secret Lives of Somerset Maugham*,
    p. 345.
45 Harding, *Ivor Novello*, p. 142.
46 Marsh to Hassall, 1 June 1937; CUL, Hassall, MS
    Add. 8905/2/1/3.
47 Clara Novello-Davies to Marsh, fragment, n.d.;
    CUL, Hassall, MS Add. 8905/2/3/41.

48 Marsh to Hassall, 7 Oct. 1940; CUL, Hassall, MS
    Add. 8905/2/1/6.
49 *Ibid.*
50 *Ibid.*, 3 Dec. 1940.
51 *Ibid.*, 4 April 1941; CUL, Hassall, MS Add.
    8905/2/1/7.
52 *Ibid.*, 20 Jan. 1942; CUL, Hassall, MS Add.
    8905/2/1/9.
53 *Ibid.*, 16 Jan. 1943; CUL, Hassall, MS Add.
    8905/2/1/11.
54 *Ibid.*, 28 Oct. 1942; CUL, Hassall, MS Add.
    8905/2/1/10.
55 *Ibid.*, 7 Feb. 1943; CUL, Hassall, MS Add.
    8905/2/1/11.
56 *Ibid.*, 12 Feb. 1943.
57 *Ibid.*
58 Harding, *Ivor Novello*, p. 51.
59 Phyllis Bottome to Hassall, 9 Sept. 1959; CUL,
    Hassall, MS Add. 8905/1/5.
60 Noel Anthony Lytton to Hassall, 3 March 1958;
    CUL, Hassall, MS Add. 8905/1/1.
61 *Ibid.*, 22 March 1958; CUL, Hassall, MS Add.
    8905/1/2.
62 Marsh to Hassall, 11 Aug. 1938; CUL, Hassall,
    MS Add. 8903/2/1/4.
63 Dorothy Colston-Baynes to Hassall, 1 Nov. 1957;
    CUL, Hassall, MS Add. 8905/1/1.
64 Marsh to Hassall, 31 Dec. 1944; CUL, Hassall,
    MS Add. 8905/2/1/13.
65 *Ibid.*, 1 Sept. 1943; CUL, Hassall, MS Add.
    8905/2/1/12.
66 Marsh, *A Number of People*, p. 372.

CHAPTER TWELVE

1   CUL, Hassall, MS Add. 8905/1/4.
2   Hassall, *Ambrosia and Small Beer*, p. xiii.
3   CUL, Hassall, MS Add. 8905/1/4.
4   Conrad Russell to Flora Russell, 4 Sept. 1927;
    Conrad Russell, *The Letters of Conrad Russell,*
    1897–1947, ed. Georgiana Blakiston (London:
    John Murray, 1987), p. 92.
5   Graves, 'After You, Who…?', p. 425.
6   Hassall, *Ambrosia and Small Beer*, p. xiv.
7   CUL, Hassall, MS Add. 8905/1/4.
8   Hassall, *Ambrosia and Small Beer*, p. 1.
9   *Ibid.*, p. 4.
10 Hassall to Marsh, 6 April 1934; CUL, Hassall, MS
    Add. 8905/2/2/1.
11 Hassall, *Ambrosia and Small Beer*, p. 6.
12 *Ibid.*
13 Hassall to Marsh, 23 April 1934; CUL, Hassall,
    MS Add. 8905/2/2/1.
14 *Ibid.*, 1 May 1934.
15 *Ibid.*, 15 Jan. 1935.
16 *Ibid.*, 18 Jan. 1935.
17 *Ibid.*, 27 Nov. 1935.
18 A play based on the life of Gaudier-Brzeska
    by Gordon Daviot (Josephine Tey). The first

production took place at the New Theatre, London, in April 1934.

19 Hassall, *Edward Marsh, Patron of the Arts*, p. 586.
20 *Ibid.*, p. 589.
21 Haggard to Marsh, 12 April 1934; CUL, Hassall, MS Add. 8905/5/3.
22 Hassall, *Ambrosia and Small Beer*, p. 89.
23 Hassall, *The Timeless Quest*, p. 74.
24 Hassall to Marsh, 18 May 1935; CUL, Hassall, MS Add. 8905/2/2/1.
25 Marsh to Hassall, 14 April 1936; CUL, Hassall, MS Add. 8905/2/1/2.
26 Hassall to Marsh, 15 April 1936; CUL, Hassall, MS Add. 8905/2/2/2.
27 Marsh to Hassall, 30 Dec. 1935; CUL, Hassall, MS Add. 8905/2/1/1.
28 *Ibid.*, 2 May 1936; CUL, Hassall, MS Add. 8905/2/1/2.
29 Sackville-West to Marsh, 23 Nov. 1934; CUL, Hassall, MS Add. 8905/3/5.
30 Lady Ottoline Morrell to Marsh, 18 June 1935; CUL, Hassall, MS Add. 8905/2/3/37.
31 Hassall to Mrs Constance Hassall, n.d.; CUL, Hassall, MS Add. 8905/11/6.
32 Hassall to Marsh, 20 June 1935; CUL, Hassall, MS Add. 8905/2/2/1.
33 Hassall to Mrs Constance Hassall, n.d.; CUL, Hassall, MS Add. 8905/11/6.
34 Marsh to Hassall, 6 May 1936; CUL, Hassall, MS Add. 8905/2/1/2.
35 Marsh to Hassall, 3 June 1937; CUL, Hassall, MS Add. 8905/2/1/3.
36 Marsh to Hassall, 26 and 29 Aug. 1936; CUL, Hassall, MS Add. 8905/2/1/2.
37 *Ibid.*, Feb. 1936.
38 *Ibid.*, 13 July 1936.
39 Hassall to Marsh, 24 Sept. 1935; CUL, Hassall, MS Add. 8905/2/2/1.
40 *Ibid.*, 3 Oct. 1935.
41 Hassall, *Devil's Dyke*, p. 91.
42 Hassall to Marsh, 12 April 1936; CUL, Hassall, MS Add. 8905/2/2/2.
43 Constance Hassall to Hassall, 6 Dec. n.d.; CUL, Hassall, MS Add. 8905/11/1.
44 *Ibid.*, 16 June 1939.
45 *Ibid.*, 28 Dec. 1938.
46 Marsh to Evelyn Chapman, 18 Oct. 1938; CUL, Hassall, MS Add. 8905/2/1/4.
47 Hassall, *Edward Marsh, Patron of the Arts*, pp. 613–14.
48 Hassall to Marsh, 16 Jan. 1939; CUL, Hassall, MS Add. 8905/2/2/2.
49 *Ibid.*, 18 Jan. 1939.
50 John Counsell, *Counsell's Opinion* (London: Barrie and Rockliff, 1963), p. 81.
51 *Ibid.*, p. 82.
52 Hassall, *Ambrosia and Small Beer*, p. 101.
53 Counsell, *Counsell's Opinion* (cit. at n. 50), p. 82.

THE THEATRE OF WAR
CHAPTER THIRTEEN

1 Sassoon to Marsh, 8 Jan. 1941; CUL, Hassall, MS Add. 8905/2/3/52.
2 Hassall, *Ambrosia and Small Beer*, p. 206.
3 *Ibid.*, pp. 210–11.
4 Beaton, diary entry, 6 Nov. 1922; Vickers, *Cecil Beaton*, p. 31.
5 Rylands to Vickers, 16 Dec. 1983; *ibid.*, p. xxvii.
6 Vickers, *Cecil Beaton*, p. 43.
7 Frances Partridge, *Memories* (London: Phoenix, 1996), p. 138.
8 Woolf to Jacques Raverat, 29 Nov. 1924; Emily Kopley, 'Virginia Woolf's Conversations with George Rylands', *Review of English Studies*, vol. 67, no. 282, 2016, p. 4.
9 Woolf, diary entry, 14 May 1925; *ibid.*, pp. 10–11.
10 Rothschild, *Rylands*, p. 65.
11 *Ibid.*, pp. 66–7.
12 Hastings, *The Secret Lives of Somerset Maugham*, p. 382.
13 Marshall, *Life's Rich Pageant*, p. 133.
14 Maugham to Marsh, 22 Feb. 1937; CUL, Hassall, MS Add. 8905/3/5.
15 Hastings, *The Secret Lives of Somerset Maugham*, p. 497.
16 Hassall, *Ambrosia and Small Beer*, p. 216.
17 *Ibid.*, p. 126.
18 *Ibid.*, p. 281.
19 Hastings, *The Secret Lives of Somerset Maugham*, p. 262.
20 Maugham to Knoblock, 24 Feb. 1918, Berg Collection, New York Public Library; *ibid.*, p. 236.
21 Knoblock, 'A National Theatre', *The Times*, 7 Sept. 1937, p. 8.
22 'News in Brief', *The Times*, 22 May 1924, p. 13.
23 Hassall, *Ambrosia and Small Beer*, p. 167.
24 *Ibid.*, p. 266.
25 'Obituary', *The Times*, 20 July 1945, p. 7.
26 Knoblock, *Round the Room*, p. 353.
27 Hayward to Greene, 16 Sept. 1939; Smart, *Tarantula's Web*, pp. 139–40.
28 Marsh to Hassall, 23 Jan. 1944; CUL, Hassall, MS Add. 8905/2/1/13.
29 Smart, *Tarantula's Web*, p. 29.
30 Hassall, *Ambrosia and Small Beer*, p. 121.
31 *Ibid.*, p. 182.
32 *Ibid.*, p. 237.
33 Hassall, *Edward Marsh, Patron of the Arts*, p. 591.
34 Smart, *Tarantula's Web*, p. 132.
35 Hassall, *Ambrosia and Small Beer*, p. 217.
36 Marsh to Hassall, 18 October 1944; CUL, Hassall, MS Add. 8905/2/1/13.
37 Hassall, *Ambrosia and Small Beer*, p. 294.
38 Smart, *Tarantula's Web*, p. 182.
39 Marsh to Hassall, 19 March 1944; CUL, Hassall, MS Add. 8905/2/1/13.

40 Hassall, *Ambrosia and Small Beer*, p. 304.

CHAPTER FOURTEEN

1 Marsh to Hassall, 22 May 1940; CUL, Hassall, MS Add. 8905/2/1/5.
2 *Ibid.*, 25 May 1940.
3 *Ibid.*, 5 June 1940.
4 *Ibid.*, 5 Feb. 1941; CUL, Hassall, MS Add. 8905/2/1/7.
5 *Ibid.*, 16 Feb. 1941.
6 *Ibid.*, 29 March 1941.
7 Hassall to Marsh, 3 Feb. 1941; CUL, Hassall, MS Add. 8905/2/2/4.
8 Eve Hassall to Marsh, 15 Feb. 1943; CUL, Hassall, MS Add. 8905/2/2/6.
9 Hassall to Marsh, 8 March 1941; CUL, Hassall, MS Add. 8905/2/2/4.
10 *Ibid.*, 29 May 1941.
11 Hassall to Marsh, 5 June 1941; CUL, Hassall, MS Add. 8905/2/2/4.
12 *Ibid.*, 10 June 1942; CUL, Hassall, MS Add. 8905/2/2/5.
13 Leissner, *Tuesday's Child*, p. 21.
14 Marsh to Hassall, 25 July 1943; CUL, Hassall, MS Add. 8905/2/1/12.
15 Hassall, *Ambrosia and Small Beer*, p. 248.
16 Haggard to Hassall, 26 May (presumably 1942); CUL, Hassall, MS Add. 8905/10/H/2.
17 Hassall, *Ambrosia and Small Beer*, p. 254.
18 *Ibid.*, p. 257.
19 Hassall to Marsh, 30 Aug. 1944; CUL, Hassall, MS Add. 8905/2/2/7.
20 Hassall, *The Timeless Quest*, p. 218.
21 Hassall to Marsh, 4 Oct. 1941; CUL, Hassall, MS Add. 8905/2/2/4.
22 *Ibid.*, 31 March 1942; CUL, Hassall, MS Add. 8905/2/2/5.
23 *Ibid.*, 1 May 1943; CUL, Hassall, MS Add. 8905/2/2/6.
24 *Ibid.*, 29 March 1944; CUL, Hassall, MS Add. 8905/2/2/7.
25 Marsh to Hassall, 3 May 1943; CUL, Hassall, MS Add. 8905/2/1/11.
26 Hassall to Marsh, 2 May 1942; CUL, Hassall, MS Add. 8905/2/2/5.
27 Marsh to Hassall, 7 May 1942; CUL, Hassall, MS Add. 8905/2/1/9.
28 Hassall to Marsh, 12 Oct. 1946; CUL, Hassall, MS Add. 8905/2/2/9.
29 *Ibid.*, 15 Nov. 1946; CUL, Hassall, MS Add. 8905/2/2/9.
30 *Ibid.*, 30 Aug. 1944; CUL, Hassall, MS Add. 8905/2/2/7.
31 *Ibid.*, 16 Aug. 1944.
32 Neville and June Braybrooke, *Olivia Manning: A Life* (London: Chatto & Windus, 2004), p. 250.
33 Marsh to Hassall, 10 April 1945; CUL, Hassall, MS Add. 8905/2/1/14.
34 Devonshire, *Wait For Me!*, p. 125.
35 Marsh to Hassall, 16 March 1941; CUL, Hassall, MS Add. 8905/2/1/7.
36 *Ibid.*, 21 March 1942.
37 *Ibid.*, 15 July 1942.
38 *Ibid.*, 15 July 1942.
39 *Ibid.*, 1 April 1942.
40 *Ibid.*, 20 May 1942.
41 *Ibid.*, 24 Jan. 1943.
42 *Ibid.*, 21 April 1944.
43 *Ibid.*
44 Marsh to Hassall, 25 April 1944; CUL, Hassall, MS Add. 8905/2/1/13.
45 *Ibid.*
46 *Ibid.*
47 *Ibid.*
48 *Ibid.*, 13 May 1944.
49 *Ibid.*, 10 May 1944.
50 Hassall to Marsh, 26 April 1944; CUL, Hassall, MS Add. 8905/2/2/7.
51 Marsh to Hassall, 16 May 1944; CUL, Hassall, MS Add. 8905/2/1/13.
52 *Ibid.*, 19 May 1944.
53 *Ibid.*, 20 May 1944.
54 *Ibid.*, 27 May 1944.
55 *Ibid.*, 2 June 1944.
56 *Ibid.*, 17 June 1944.
57 *Ibid.*, 7 Sept. 1944.
58 Hassall, *Ambrosia and Small Beer*, p. 339.

LEGACY

CHAPTER FIFTEEN

1 Hassall, *Edward Marsh, Patron of the Arts*, p. 217.
2 Marsh, *The Fables of Jean de La Fontaine* (London: William Heinemann, 1933), p. xxiv.
3 Channon, diary entry, 11 March 1925; Channon, *Henry 'Chips' Channon*, pp. 142–3.
4 Hassall, *Edward Marsh, Patron of the Arts*, p. 526.
5 *Ibid.*
6 *Ibid.*, p. 528.
7 L. P. Wilkinson, 'A free version of Horace's Odes', *The Classical Review*, vol. 55, 1941, p. 87.
8 Hassall, *Ambrosia and Small Beer*, p. 164.
9 Marsh to Hassall, 16 Jan. 1941; CUL, Hassall, MS Add. 8905/2/1/7.
10 Hassall, *Ambrosia and Small Beer*, p. 212.
11 G. Grigson, 'E. M. of the Anthologies', *New Verse*, May 1939, quoted in *Georgian Poetry 1911–1922: The Critical Heritage*, pp. 348–50.
12 Marsh to Hassall, 29 April 1948; CUL, Hassall, MS Add. 8905/2/1/15.
13 *Ibid.*, 15 Nov. 1944; CUL, Hassall, MS Add. 8905/2/1/13.
14 *Ibid.*, 11 Feb. 1936; CUL, Hassall, MS Add. 8905/2/1/2.
15 Hassall and Mathews, *Eddie Marsh*, p. 21.
16 Marsh to Hassall, June 1938; CUL, Hassall, MS Add. 8905/2/1/4.

17 *Ibid.*, 5 May 1944; CUL, Hassall, MS Add. 8905/2/1/13.
18 Maugham to Hassall, 23 June 1958; CUL, Hassall, MS Add. 8905/1/2.
19 nobelprize.org (accessed 17 Feb. 2021)
20 Churchill to Marsh, 27 Sept. 1923; University of Cambridge, Churchill Archives Centre, Papers of Sir Edward Marsh, GBR/0014/EMAR.
21 *Ibid.*, 30 Aug. 1947; University of Cambridge, Churchill Archives Centre, CHUR/4/20/157–8.
22 Hassall and Mathews, *Eddie Marsh*, p. 29.
23 *Ibid.*, p. 23.
24 Churchill to Marsh, 10 Aug. 1930; University of Cambridge, Churchill Archives Centre, Papers of Sir Edward Marsh, GBR/0014/EMAR.
25 *Ibid.*, 16 May 1933.
26 Hassall and Mathews, *Eddie Marsh*, p. 9.
27 Hastings, *The Secret Lives of Somerset Maugham*, p. 365.
28 Hassall, *Edward Marsh, Patron of the Arts*, p. 572.
29 Hastings, *The Secret Lives of Somerset Maugham*, p. 231.
30 H. G. Wells, *Men Like Gods* (London: Cassell and Co., 1923), p. 19.
31 *Ibid.*, pp. 29–30.
32 *Ibid.*, p. 84.
33 *Ibid.*, p. 145.
34 Joyce Grenfell to Hassall, 4 Aug. 1959; CUL, Hassall, MS Add. 8905/1/5.
35 Churchill to Marsh, 27 Sept. 1923; University of Cambridge, Churchill Archives Centre, Papers of Sir Edward Marsh, GBR/0014/EMAR.
36 Hassall, *Edward Marsh, Patron of the Arts*, p. 591.
37 Sir Kenneth Clark, 'Obituary' of Hugh Walpole, *The Times*, 4 June 1941, p. 7.
38 Hassall, *Edward Marsh, Patron of the Arts*, p. 186.
39 *Ibid.*, p. 270.
40 *Ibid.*, p. 486.
41 Hassall and Mathews, *Eddie Marsh*, p. 11.
42 Harold Nicolson to Christopher Hassall, n.d.; CUL, Hassall, MS Add. 8905/1/4.
43 Marsh to Hassall, 8 Sept. 1937; CUL, Hassall, MS Add. 8905/2/1/3.
44 *Ibid.*, 23 Jan. 1944.
45 Graves, *Goodbye to All That*, p. 48. The book was first published in 1929 by Cape in London.
46 Hassall, *Edward Marsh, Patron of the Arts*, p. 528.
47 Graves, *Goodbye to All That*, p. 48.
48 Hassall, *Edward Marsh, Patron of the Arts*, p. 588.
49 Hassall, *Ambrosia and Small Beer*, p. 29.
50 *Ibid.*, p. 52.
51 *Ibid.*, p. 354.
52 *Ibid.*, p. 219.
53 *Ibid.*, p. 222.
54 *Ibid.*, p. 244.
55 Leigh-Fermor to Hassall, 31 March 1953; CUL, Hassall, MS Add. 8905/1/1.
56 Hamilton to Hassall, 18 Sept. 1954; CUL, Hassall, MS Add. 8905/1/2.
57 Marsh to Hassall, 29 Aug. 1941; CUL, Hassall, MS Add. 8905/2/1/8.
58 Marsh to Hamilton, 5 Sept. 1951; CUL, Hassall, MS Add. 8905/1/1.
59 Thomas to Marsh, 14 Sept. 1939; Hassall, *Edward Marsh, Patron of the Arts*, pp. 616–17.
60 *Ibid.*, 19 Sept. 1939; *ibid.*, p. 617.
61 Hassall, *Ambrosia and Small Beer*, p. 91.
62 *Ibid.*, p. 330.
63 *Ibid.*, p. 342.
64 Hassall, *Edward Marsh, Patron of the Arts*, p. 596.
65 Hassall, *Ambrosia and Small Beer*, p. 257.
66 Marsh to Hassall, 31 May 1943; CUL, Hassall, MS Add. 8905/2/1/11.
67 Hassall, *Ambrosia and Small Beer*, pp. 255–6.
68 *Ibid.*, p. 85.
69 *Ibid.*, p. 90.
70 *Ibid.*, p. 96.
71 *Ibid.*, p. 105.
72 *Ibid.*, p. 107.
73 Marsh, *A Number of People*, p. 234.
74 Hassall, *Edward Marsh, Patron of the Arts*, p. 485.
75 Lawrence, *Seven Pillars of Wisdom*, p. 283.
76 Hassall, *Edward Marsh, Patron of the Arts*, p. 439.
77 Hassall and Mathews, *Eddie Marsh*, p. 43.
78 Lawrence, *Seven Pillars of Wisdom*, p. 410.
79 Marsh, *A Number of People*, p. 405.
80 Lawrence to Marsh, 7 Jan. 1919; Lawrence, *Selected Letters*, p. 114.
81 *Ibid.*, 12 April 1925; *ibid.*, p. 212.
82 Lawrence to Buchan, 19 May 1925; *ibid.*, p. 214.
83 Lawrence to H. H. Banbury, Regimental Sergeant Major, Royal Tank Corps, 20 April 1927; *ibid.*, p. 236.
84 Lawrence to Marsh, 10 June 1927; *ibid.*, p. 239.
85 Sassoon, *Siegfried's Journey*, p. 86.
86 Sassoon, *Siegfried Sassoon: Diaries 1915–1918*, p. 280.
87 Lawrence to Marsh, 10 March 1931; Lawrence, *Selected Letters*, p. 329.
88 Garnett to Marsh, 10 March 1938; University of Cambridge, Churchill Archives Centre, CHUR 4/2.
89 John Schroder, *Catalogue of Books and Manuscripts by Rupert Brooke, Edward Marsh & Christopher Hassall*, p. 104.
90 Marsh, *A Number of People*, p. 337.
91 *Ibid.*, p. 337.
92 Barrie to Marsh, 6 April 1932, copied out by Hassall, 14 April 1942; CUL, Hassall, MS Add. 8905/2/2/5.
93 Hassall, *Ambrosia and Small Beer*, p. 206.
94 Marsh to Hassall, 5 May 1944; CUL, Hassall, MS Add. 8905/2/1/13.

95 Maugham, *Strictly Personal*, pp. v–vi.

96 Hassall and Mathews, *Eddie Marsh*, pp. 25–6.

97 Lees-Milne, *A Mingled Measure*, pp. 4–5.

CHAPTER SIXTEEN

1 Hassall, *Edward Marsh, Patron of the Arts*, p. 662.

2 Clementine Spencer-Churchill to Marsh, 6 March 1951; University of Cambridge, Churchill Archives Centre, Papers of Sir Edward Marsh, GBR/0014/EMAR.

3 Cornford to Marsh, 6 March 1951; CUL, GB12, MS Add. 9280/24.

4 Hassall, *Edward Marsh, Patron of the Arts*, pp. 663-4.

5 Marsh to Hassall, 28 Sep. 1944; CUL, Hassall, MS Add. 8905/2/1/13.

6 Cornford to Hassall, 15 Jan. 1953; CUL, Hassall, MS Add. 8905/10/C/90.

7 Hassall, *Edward Marsh, Patron of the Arts*, pp. 680.

8 Hassall and Mathews, *Eddie Marsh*, p. 9.

9 Hillier to Hassall, 24 Jan. 1958; CUL, Hassall, MS Add. 8905/1/2.

10 Cornford to Hassall, 15 Jan. 1953 (cit. at n. 6).

11 Coward to Hassall, 8 Sept. 1954; CUL, Hassall, MS Add. 8905/1/1.

12 Hassall and Mathews, *Eddie Marsh*, pp. 27–30.

13 Kelly to Hassall, 9 April 1954; CUL, Hassall, MS Add. 8905/1/1.

14 Maugham to Hassall, 27 July 1954; CUL, Hassall, MS Add. 8905/1/2.

15 Kelly to Hassall, 9 April 1954; CUL, Hassall, MS Add. 8905/1/1.

16 Lady Juliet Duff to Hassall, 6 Aug. 1954; CUL, Hassall, MS Add. 8905/1/1.

17 Nash, *Paul Nash: Outline*, p. 115.

18 Margaret Nash to Hassall, 21 July 1954; CUL, Hassall, MS Add. 8905/1/1.

19 Mosley, *A Life of Contrasts*, p. 57.

20 Mrs Lascelles [Catherine] Abercrombie, 'Memories of a Poet's Wife', *The Listener*, 15 Nov. 1956, pp. 793–4.

21 Barbara Agar née Lutyens to Hassall, 31 Aug. 1959; CUL, Hassall, MS Add. 8905/1/5.

22 Graves, 'After You, Who…?', p. 425.

23 Hassall, *Ambrosia and Small Beer*, p. ix.

24 Hassall, *Edward Marsh, Patron of the Arts*, p. 55.

25 Lascelles, diary entry, 2 June 1911; Lascelles, *End of an Era*, pp. 100–101.

26 Marsh to Hassall, 21 April 1934; CUL, Hassall, MS Add. 8905/2/1/1.

27 Lees-Milne, diary entry, 12 Dec. 1947; Lees-Milne, *Caves of Ice*, pp. 255–6.

28 Agate, diary entry, 25 Nov. 1938; Agate, *The Selective Ego*, p. 113.

29 Marsh to Hassall, 27 Oct. 1944; CUL, Hassall, MS Add. 8905/2/1/13.

30 *Ibid.*, 27 June 1944.

31 Siegfried Sassoon to Dame Felicitas Corrigan, 28 July 1965; Corrigan, *Siegfried Sassoon: Poet's Pilgrimage*, p. 66.

32 Hassall, *Edward Marsh, Patron of the Arts*, p. 42.

33 *Ibid.*, p. 42.

34 *Ibid.*, p. 91.

35 Beaton, diary entry, 9 Oct. 1923; Vickers, *Cecil Beaton*, p. 40.

36 Marsh to Hassall, 16 Jan. 1943; CUL, Hassall, MS Add. 8905/2/1/11.

37 Lees-Milne, diary entry, 27 Jan. 1953; Lees-Milne, *A Mingled Measure*, p. 5.

38 *Ibid.*, diary entry, 22 April 1954; *ibid.*, p. 59.

39 *Being Gay in the Thirties*, London Weekend Television. https://player.bfi.org.uk/free/film/watch-being-gay-in-the-thirties-gay-life-1981-online (accessed 3 May 2021)

40 Hassall, *Edward Marsh, Patron of the Arts*, p. 66.

41 Hart-Davis to Hassall, 7 July 1959; CUL, Hassall, MS Add. 8905/1/5.

42 Hassall to Marsh, 10 June 1942; CUL, Hassall, MS Add. 8905/2/2/5.

43 Leissner, *Tuesday's Child*, p. 21.

44 Hassall to Marsh, 25 Feb. 1943; CUL, Hassall, MS Add. 8905/2/2/6.

45 *Ibid.*, 17 Sept. 1944; CUL, Hassall, MS Add. 8905/2/2/7.

46 *Ibid.*, 26 Sept. 1944.

47 Rota to Hassall, 10 Sept. 1954; CUL, Hassall, MS Add. 8905/3/5.

48 Maugham to Hassall, 10 May 1953; CUL, Hassall, MS Add. 8905/1/1.

49 Harding, *Ivor Novello*, p. 143.

50 Leissner, *Tuesday's Child*, p. 21.

51 Cornford to Hassall, n.d.; CUL, Hassall, MS Add. 8905/10/C/86-241.

52 Chapman to Hassall, n.d.; CUL, Hassall, MS Add. 8905/10/C/86-241.

53 Susana Walton, *William Walton: Behind the Façade* (Oxford: OUP, 1988), p. 102.

54 *Ibid.*, pp. 135–6.

55 Hassall to Guest, n.d.; CUL, Hassall, MS Add. 8905/15/2.

56 Hassall and Mathews, *Eddie Marsh*, p. 41.

57 *Ibid.*, p. 51.

58 Agate, diary entry, 12 Feb. 1937; Agate, *The Selective Ego*, p. 54.

Sources and Bibliography

ARCHIVES

CAMBRIDGE

FITZWILLIAM MUSEUM
Rupert Brooke, Fragments of a poem to be entitled 'The Sentimental Exile', MS/1/1917

UNIVERSITY OF CAMBRIDGE
CAMBRIDGE UNIVERSITY LIBRARY SPECIAL COLLECTIONS (CUL)
Rupert Chawner Brooke: *Democracy and the Arts*, GB12, MS Add. 8479
Christopher Hassall: Correspondence and Papers, GB 12 MS Add. 8905
Frances Cornford: Letters to Sir Edward Marsh, GB 12, MS Add. 9280

CHURCHILL COLLEGE ARCHIVES CENTRE
Papers of Sir Edward Marsh: GBR/0014/EMAR
Chartwell Papers: CHAR 1/392/24–27, CHAR 1/117/26–33, CHAR 1/117/45, CHAR 1/392/48–55, CHAR 2/65/32, CHAR 2/66/21, CHAR 2/141/105–106, CHAR 2/152/1, CHAR 2/152/129, CHAR 28/84/3
Churchill Papers: CHUR 4/2

KING'S COLLEGE ARCHIVES
Papers of Rupert Chawner Brooke: GB 272 RCB (1869–1915)
RCB/L/11, RCB/L/8/28b, RSB/Ph/303, RCB/S/6, RCB/S/9, RCB/Xf/10, RCB/Xd/24
Edward Marsh's Visitors' Book 1914–1937: RCB/S/10
Schroder Collection: RCB/S/5/1

MAGDALENE COLLEGE ARCHIVES
A. C. Benson Diaries: F/ACB

LONDON

ROYAL ACADEMY OF ARTS ARCHIVE
PC/4/2, RAA/SEC/6/33

TATE ARCHIVE
TG 1/6/19, TGA 923/4/2/1108–1111, TGA 7050/3951, TGA 8221/6/59, TGA8313/1/2/130–150, TGA 9215

WESTMINSTER SCHOOL ARCHIVES
Biographical Entry in The Record

THE NATIONAL ARCHIVES, ROYAL NAVAL DIVISION
Service Record, Rupert Chawner Brooke, ADM 337/117/370 p. 187

BOOKS

Agate, James, *The Selective Ego: The Diaries of James Agate*, ed. Tim Beaumont (London: Harrap, 1976)
Alpers, Antony, *The Life of Katherine Mansfield* (Oxford: Oxford University Press, 1982
Asquith, H. H., *H. H. Asquith: Letters to Venetia Stanley*, ed. Michael and Eleanor Brock (Oxford: OUP, 1985)
Asquith, Margot, *Margot Asquith's Great War Diary 1914–1916: The View from Downing Street*, ed. Michael and Eleanor Brock (Oxford: OUP, 2014)

Barnes, James Strachey, *Half a Life* (London: Eyre and Spottiswoode, 1933)

Beckett, Lorna C., *The Second I Saw You: The True Love Story of Rupert Brooke and Phyllis Gardner* (London: British Library, 2015)

Bell, Clive, *Old Friends: Personal Recollections* (London: Chatto and Windus, 1956)

Bonham Carter, Violet, *Champion Redoubtable: The Diaries and Letters of Violet Bonham Carter 1914– 1945*, ed. Mark Pottle (London: Weidenfeld & Nicolson, 1998)

— *Lantern Slides: The Diaries and Letters of Violet Bonham Carter 1904–1914*, ed. Mark Bonham Carter and Mark Pottle (London: Phoenix Orion Books, 1997)

— *Winston Churchill As I Knew Him* (London: Reprint Society, 1966)

Braybrooke, Neville and June, *Olivia Manning: A Life* (London: Chatto & Windus, 2004)

Brendon, Piers, *Winston Churchill: A Brief Life* (London: Pimlico, 2001)

Brittain, Vera, *Testament of Youth: An Autobiographical Study of the Years 1900–1925* (London: Virago Press, 2014)

Brooke, Rupert, *Rupert Brooke: The Collected Poems, with a Memoir by Edward Marsh* (London: Sidgwick & Jackson, 3rd edn, 1942, reprinted 1983)

— *Democracy and the Arts* (London: Rupert Hart-Davis, 1946)

— *The Letters of Rupert Brooke*, ed. Geoffrey Keynes (London: Faber and Faber, 1968)

— *Letters From America with a Preface by Henry James* (London: Sidgwick & Jackson, 1931, reprinted 1971)

— *The Poetical Works of Rupert Brooke*, ed. Geoffrey Keynes (London: Faber and Faber, 1970)

Carrington, Dora, *Carrington's Letters: Her Art, Her Loves, Her Friendships*, ed. Anne Chisholm (London: Chatto & Windus, 2017)

Channon, Henry, *Henry 'Chips' Channon: The Diaries 1918–38*, ed. Simon Heffer (London: Penguin, 2021)

Clark, Keith, *The Muse Colony: Rupert Brooke, Edward Thomas, Robert Frost and Friends, Dymock 1914* (Bristol: Redcliffe, 1992)

Cole, Sarah, *Modernism, Male Friendship, and the First World War* (Cambridge: CUP, 2003)

Cooper, Artemis, *Cairo in the War, 1939–1945* (London: Hamish Hamilton, 1989)

Cornford, Frances, *Selected Poems*, ed. Jane Dowson (London: Enitharmon Press, 1996)

Corrigan, Dame F., *Siegfried Sassoon: Poet's Pilgrimage* (London: Gollancz, 1973

Counsell, John, *Counsell's Opinion* (London: Barrie and Rockliff, 1963)

Coward, Noël, *Autobiography: Present Indicative, Future Indefinite and the uncompleted Past Conditional* (London: Methuen, 1986)

— *The Noël Coward Diaries*, ed. Graham Payn and Sheridan Morley (Boston: Little Brown and Company, 1982)

— *Present Indicative* (London: William Heinemann, 1937)

De la Mare, Walter, *The Collected Poems of Walter de la Mare* (London: Faber and Faber, 1979)

Delany, Paul, *Fatal Glamour: The Life of Rupert Brooke* (Quebec: McGill-Queen's University Press, 2015)

Devonshire, Deborah, *Wait For Me! Memoirs of the Youngest Mitford Sister* (London: John Murray, 2010)

Duff Cooper, Alfred, *The Duff Cooper Diaries 1915–1951*, ed. John Julius Norwich (London: Weidenfeld and Nicolson, 2005)

Ede, H. S., *Savage Messiah: A Biography of the Sculptor Henri Gaudier-Brzeska* (Cambridge/Leeds: Kettle's Yard/Henry Moore Institute, 2011)

Fenwick, Simon, *The Crichel Boys: Scenes From England's Last Literary Salon* (London: Constable, 2021)

Frayn Turner, John, *Rupert Brooke: The Splendour and the Pain* (London: Breese Books, 1992)

Fussell, Paul, *The Great War and Modern Memory* (Oxford: OUP, 1975)

Gardiner, Juliet and Wenborn, Neil, eds., *The History Today Companion to British History* (London: Collins & Brown, 1995)

Garnett, David, *The Golden Echo* (London: Chatto & Windus, 1953)

Gertler, Mark, *Mark Gertler: Selected Letters*, ed. Noel Carrington (London: Rupert Hart-Davis, 1965)

Grant, Joy, *Harold Monro and the Poetry Bookshop* (London: Routledge and Kegan Paul. 1967)

Graves, Charles, 'After You, Who...? Celebrities in Cameo, No. 11, Edward Marsh, C.M.G.,C.V.O.', *The Bystander*, 11 March 1936, p. 425

Graves, Robert, *Goodbye to All That* (London: Penguin, 1960)

Hale, Keith, ed., *Friends and Apostles: The Correspondence of Rupert Brooke and James Strachey 1905–1914* (New Haven & London: Yale University Press, 1998)

Harding, James, *Ivor Novello* (Cardiff: Welsh Academic Press, 1997)

Harris, Pippa, ed., *Song of Love: The Letters of Rupert Brooke and Noel Olivier, 1909–1915* (London: Bloomsbury, 1991)

Hassall, Christopher, *Ambrosia and Small Beer: The Record of a Correspondence between Edward Marsh and Christopher Hassall* (London: Longmans, 1964)

— *Devil's Dyke* (London: William Heinemann, 1936)

— *Edward Marsh, Patron of the Arts: A Biography* (London: Longmans, 1959)

— *Rupert Brooke: a Biography* (London: Faber and Faber, 1964)

— *The Timeless Quest: Stephen Haggard* (London: Arthur Barker, 1948)

— and Denis Mathews, *Eddie Marsh. Sketches for a Composite Literary Portrait of Sir Edward Marsh, K.C.V.O., C.B., C.M.G.* (London: Lund Humphries for the Contemporary Art Society, 1953)

Hastings, Selina, *The Secret Lives of Somerset Maugham* (London: John Murray, 2010)

Haycock, David Boyd, *A Crisis of Brilliance: Five Young British Artists and the Great War* (London: Old Street Publishing, 2010)

Hepburn, Nathaniel, *Cedric Morris and Christopher Wood: A Forgotten Friendship* (London: Unicorn Press, 2012)

Hibberd, Dominic, *Harold Monro: Poet of the New Age* (Basingstoke: Palgrave, 2001)

Hollis, Matthew, *Now All Roads Lead to France: The Last Years of Edward Thomas* (London: Faber and Faber, 2011)

Holroyd, Michael, *Lytton Strachey* (London: Pimlico, 2011)

Hynes, Samuel, *A War Imagined: The First World War and English Culture* (London: Pimlico, 1992)

Hynes, Samuel, *The Edwardian Turn of Mind* (London: Oxford University Press, 1968)

Isherwood, Christopher, *Lions and Shadows: An Education in the Twenties* (London: Vintage, 2013)

James, Henry, *Henry James: Selected Letters*, ed. Leon Edel (London: Belknap/Harvard University Press, 1987)

Jones, Nigel, *Rupert Brooke: Life, Death and Myth* (London: Head of Zeus, 2014)

Kaylor, Michael Matthew, *Secreted Desires, The Major Uranians: Hopkins, Pater and Wilde* (Brno, CZ: Masaryk University Press, 2006)

Keynes, Geoffrey, *The Gates of Memory* (Oxford: Clarendon Press, 1982)

Knoblock, Edward, *Round the Room: An Autobiography* (London: Chapman & Hall, 1939)

Langley, Noel, *The Music of the Heart* (London: Arthur Barker, 1946)

Lascelles, Alan, *End of an Era: Letters and Journals of Sir Alan Lascelles 1887–1920*, ed. Duff Hart-Davis (London: Hamish Hamilton, 1986)

— *King's Counsellor, Abdication and War: The Diaries of Sir Alan Lascelles*, ed. Duff Hart-Davis (London: Weidenfeld &Nicolson, 2006)

Lawrence, T. E., *Selected Letters of T. E. Lawrence*, ed. David Garnett (London: World Books, 1941)

— *Seven Pillars of Wisdom* (London: Jonathan Cape, 1940)

Lee, Hermione, *Penelope Fitzgerald: A Life* (London: Chatto & Windus, 2013)

Lees-Milne, James, *Caves of Ice* (London: Chatto & Windus The Hogarth Press, 1983)

— *A Mingled Measure: Diaries 1953–1972* (London: John Murray, 1994)

Lehmann, John, *Rupert Brooke: His Life and Legend* (London: Weidenfeld & Nicolson, 1980)

Leissner, Dan, *Tuesday's Child: The Life and Death of Imogen Hassall* (Baltimore: Midnight Marquee Press, 2002)

MacCarthy Fiona, *Eric Gill* (London: Faber and Faber, 1990)

MacDougall, Sarah, *Mark Gertler* (London: John Murray, 2002)

Mackrell, Judith, *Flappers: Six Women of a Dangerous Generation* (London: Macmillan, 2013)

Marsh, Edward, *A Number of People: A Book of Reminiscences* (London: William Heinemann in association with Hamish Hamilton, 1939)

— 'Patronage in Art To-day III', *The Listener*, vol. 14, no. 349, 18 September 1935, pp. 487–9

Marshall, Arthur, *Life's Rich Pageant* (London: Hamish Hamilton, 1984)

Maugham, William Somerset, *Strictly Personal* (London: William Heinemann, 1942)

Miller, Alisa, *Rupert Brooke in the First World War* (Liverpool: Clemson University Press in association with Liverpool University Press, 2017)

Mosley, Charlotte, ed., *The Mitfords: Letters Between Six Sisters* (London: Fourth Estate, 2007)

Mosley, Diana, *A Life of Contrasts: An Autobiography* (London: Hamish Hamilton, 1977)

Nash, Paul, *Paul Nash: Outline, An Autobiography*, ed. David Boyd Haycock (London: Lund Humphries, 2016)

Newsome, David, *On the Edge of Paradise: A. C. Benson: The Diarist* (Chicago: University of Chicago Press, 1980)

Pearsall, Robert Brainard, *Rupert Brooke: The Man and the Poet* (Amsterdam: Editions Rodopi, 1974)

Read, Mike, *Forever England: The Life of Rupert Brooke* (Edinburgh: Mainstream, 1997)

Reeves, James, *Georgian Poetry* (Harmondsworth: Penguin Books, 1962), pp. xi–xxiii

Reynolds, David, *In Command of History: Churchill Fighting and Writing the Second World War* (London: Penguin, 2005)

Roberts, John Stuart, *Siegfried Sassoon (1886–1967)* (London: Richard Cohen Books, 2000)

Rogers, Timothy, ed., *Georgian Poetry 1911–1922: The Critical Heritage* (London: Routledge & Kegan Paul, 1977)

Rosenberg, Isaac, *Isaac Rosenberg*, ed. Vivien Noakes (Oxford: Oxford University Press, 2008)

Ross, Robert H., *The Georgian Revolt: Rise and Fall of a Poetic Ideal 1910–22* (London: Faber and Faber, 1967)

Rothschild, Lord, *Rylands* (London: The Stourton Press, 1988)

Russell, Bertrand, *The Autobiography of Bertrand Russell, 1872–1914* (London: George Allen & Unwin, 1967)

Rutherford, Jonathan, *Forever England: Reflections on Race, Masculinity and Empire* (London: Lawrence & Wishart, 1997)

Sassoon, Siegfried, *Siegfried's Journey* (London: Faber and Faber, 1945)

— *Siegfried Sassoon: Diaries 1915–1918*, ed. Rupert Hart-Davies (London: Faber and Faber, 1983)

— *The Weald of Youth* (London: Faber and Faber, 1942)

Schroder, John, *Catalogue of Books and Manuscripts by Rupert Brooke, Edward Marsh & Christopher Hassall* (Cambridge: Rampant Lions Press, 1970)

Sellers, Leonard, *The Hood Battalion: Royal Naval Division: Antwerp, Gallipoli, France 1914–1918* (Barnsley: Pen & Sword Books, 2003)

Seymour, Miranda, *Robert Graves: Life on the Edge* (London: Doubleday, 1996)

Sieveking, Lance, *The Eye of the Beholder* (London: Hulton Press, 1957)

Sinclair, Andrew, *Dylan the Bard: A Life of Dylan Thomas* (London: Robinson, 2003)

Smart, John, *Tarantula's Web: John Hayward, T. S. Eliot and Their Circle* (Norwich: Michael Russell, 2013)

Spalding, Frances, *British Art Since 1900* (London: Thames & Hudson, 1986)

—, *Duncan Grant* (London: Chatto & Windus, 1997)

—, *Gwen Raverat: Friends, Family and Affections* (London: Vintage, 2004)

—, *Vanessa Bell* (London: Weidenfeld and Nicolson, 1983)

Spencer, Stanley, *Looking to Heaven*, ed. John Spencer (London: Unicorn Press, 2016)

St Clair, Hugh, *A Lesson in Art & Life: The Colourful World of Cedric Morris & Arthur Lett-Haines* (London: Pimpernel Press, 2019)

Frank Swinnerton, *The Georgian Literary Scene, 1910–1935: A Panorama* (London: Hutchinson & Co. Ltd, 1950)

Taylor, A. J. P., *The Struggle for Mastery in Europe 1878–1914: From Peace to War* (London,: The Folio Society, 1998)

— *The First World War and its Aftermath 1914–919* (London: The Folio Society, 1998)

Trevor-Roper, Hugh, *The Secret World: Behind the Curtain of British Intelligence in World War II and the Cold War* (London: I. B. Tauris, 2014)

Vickers, Hugo, *Cecil Beaton: The Authorised Biography* (London: Phoenix Press, 2003)

Watling, Sarah, *Noble Savages: The Olivier Sisters Four Lives in Seven Fragments* (London: Vintage, 2020)

Webb, Paul, *Ivor Novello: A Portrait of a Star* (London: Stage Directions, 1999)

Wells, H. G., *Men Like Gods* (London: Cassell and Co: 1923)

Woodeson, John, *Mark Gertler: Biography of a Painter* (London: Sidgwick & Jackson, 1972)

Woolf, Virginia, *The Letters of Virginia Woolf*, vol. 2, *1912–1922*, ed. Nigel Nicolson (New York: Harcourt Brace Jovanovich, 1976)

— *Virginia Woolf: The Complete Collection* (Co. Cork: Oregan Publishing, 2017)

ARTICLES

Abercrombie, Lascelles, 'After Fifteen Years – An Appreciation of Rupert Brooke', *The Listener*, 30 April 1930, pp. 775–6

Abercrombie, Mrs Lascelles, 'Memories of a Poet's Wife', *The Listener*, 15 November 1956, pp. 793–4

Cribb, T J., 'Obituary: George Rylands', *Independent*, 20 January 1999

Davison, Edward, 'Some Notes on Modern English Poetry', *The English Journal*, 15, no. 6, 1926, 407–14

Johnston, John H., 'Victorian Poetry', *Victorian Poetry*, 3, no. 3, 1965, 197–9

Jordan, John, 'Studies: An Irish Quarterly Review', *Studies: An Irish Quarterly Review*, 51, no. 202, 1962, 327–9

Laskowski, William, 'Georgians at Work and in Love', *English Literature in Transition, 1880–1920*, 37, (1994), 75–9

Marsh, Edward, 'Patronage in Art Today', *Listener*, 14, 18 September 1935, pp. 487–9

Parker, Derek, 'The man who enjoyed everything', *Slightly Foxed*, vol. 57, March 2018, pp. 79–83

Pope-Hennessy, James, 'Eddie Marsh', *The Spectator*, 14 November 1952, pp. 7–8

Simon, Myron, 'The Georgian Poetic', *Bulletin of the Midwest Modern Language Association*, 2, 1969, 121–35

Taddeo, Julie Anne, 'Plato's Apostles: Edwardian Cambridge and the New Style of Love', *Journal of the History of Sexuality*, vol. 8, no. 2, 1997, pp. 196–228

Wilkinson, L. P. 'A free version of Horace's Odes', *The Classical Review*, vol. 55, 1941

ONLINE RESOURCES

https://www.historyextra.com/period/victorian/the-victorians-surprisingly-liberal-attitude-towards-gay-men/ (accessed 01/03/19)

http://www.King's.cam.ac.uk/archive-centre/archive-month/january-2011.html (accessed 07/03/19)

https://www.warcomposers.co.uk/brownebio (accessed 07/03/19)

http://www.King's.cam.ac.uk/archive-centre/archive-month/june-2014.html (accessed 07/03/19)

https://en.wikipedia.org/wiki/Georgian_Poetry (accessed 15/03/19)

https://cudl.lib.cam.ac.uk/collections/schroder/1 (accessed 17/03/19)

https://winstonchurchill.org/publications/finest-hour/finest-hour-131/great-contemporaries-eddie-marsh-a-profile/ (accessed 23/03/19)

http://catholicencyclopedia.newadvent.com/cathen/08174a.htm (accessed 09/04/19)

http://www.victorianweb.org/religion/apocalypse/irvingite.html (accessed 09/04/19)

https://williampryor.wordpress.com/tag/frances-cornford/ (accessed 15/04/19)

https://www.washingtonpost.com/archive/entertainment/books/1981/01/25/rupert-brooke-the-red-sweet-wine-of-youth/13787fc4-8466-4c04-97a7-57a53125326e/?noredirect=on&utm_term=.a740202d3184 (accessed 18/04/19)

https://en.wikipedia.org/wiki/Spencer_Perceval (accessed 24/04/19)

http://www.glbtqarchive.com/ssh/cambridge_apostles_S.pdf (accessed 24/04/19)

https://en.wikipedia.org/wiki/Principia_Ethica (accessed 11/05/19)

https://en.wikipedia.org/wiki/Rhythm_(literary_magazine) (accessed 24/05/19)

https://www.bl.uk/collection-items/rhythm-art-music-literature-no-iv (accessed 24/05/19)

https://www.nytimes.com/1913/01/12/archives/phillips-attacks-masefields-poetry-sharply-criticises-the-award-of.html (accessed 24/05/19) http://www.gutenberg.org/files/9484/9484-h/9484-h.htm (accessed 29/05/19)

http://lawlit.net/lp-2001/loines.html (accessed 06/06/19)

http://www.nationalarchives.gov.uk/education/greatwar/g2/backgroundcs1.htm (accessed 10/06/19)

https://www.theguardian.com/world/2014/aug/05/england-declares-war-germany-1914 (accessed 10/06/19)

https://www.newyorker.com/books/page-turner/the-true-story-of-rupert-brooke (accessed 14/06/19)

http://exhibits.lib.byu.edu/wwi/poets/rbobituary.html (accessed 19/06/19)

http://ww1lit.nsms.ox.ac.uk/ww1lit/education/tutorials/intro/brooke/obituary (accessed 19/06/19)

https://www.stpauls.co.uk/worship-music/worship/read-sermons/sermon-preached-on-easter-day-5-april-2015-by-the-very-reverend-david-ison-dean (accessed 19/06/19)

https://www.theguardian.com/books/2015/apr/27/rupert-brooke-death-first-world-war-poet-1915 (accessed 22/06/19)

https://www.bl.uk/collections-items/copy-of-the-letter-from-samuel-johnson-to-the-earl-of-chesterfield (accessed 15/07/19)

https://www.oxfordbibliographies.com/view/document/obo-9780195399301/obo-9780195399301-0358.xml (accessed 20/07/19)

http://www.musicweb-international.com/classrev/2002/May02/WDBrown.htm (accessed 05/08/19)

http://www.therag.co.uk/the-club/history (accessed 23/03/20(

https://doi.org/10.1093/ref:ondb/34892 (accessed 10/09/18)

https://www.npg.org.uk/collections/search/portrait/mw01298/Winston-Churchill (accessed 17/10/18)

https://en.wikipedia.org/wiki/Leicester_Galleries (accessed 17/10/18)

http://www.19thc-artworldwide.org/fletcher/london-gallery/data/pages/as524.html accessed 18/10/18

https://artuk.org/discover/artists/tonks-henry-18621937# (accessed 18/10/18)

https://en.wikipedia.org/wiki/Rhythm_(literary_magazine) (accessed 19/10/18)

https://www.newenglishartclub.co.uk/about-new-english (accessed 20/10/18)

http://www.contemporaryartsociety.org/wordpress/wp-content/uploads/2008/11/1953-edward-marsh-collection.pdf (accessed 27/10/18)

http://archive.spectator.co.uk/article/14th-november-1952/7/eddie-marsh (accessed 27/10/18)

http://benuri100.org/archive-piece/two-pages-of-newspaper-cuttings-from-the-gertler-exhibition-2/ (accessed 02/11/18)

https://library.leeds.ac.uk/special-collections/research-spotlight/1521 accessed 02/11/18)

https://en.wikipedia.org/wiki/Michael_Sadler_(educationist) (accessed 02/11/18)

BROADCASTS

'Rupert Brooke', *Witness History* (BBC World Service, 30 April 2019)

Novello: The Handsomest Man in Britain, directed by Ian Jones (Fulmar Television & Film Ltd, BBC 4 & BBC Wales, 2002)

Picture Credits

Front Cover – National Portrait Gallery
Frontispiece – National Portrait Gallery

Plates:

H – (bottom) Image courtesy of The Potteries Museum & Art Gallery, Stoke-on-Trent; J – © Estate of Stanley Spencer. All Rights Reserved 2023 / Bridgeman Images/Tate; L – (top) National Portrait Gallery (NPG), (bottom) Heritage Image Partnership Ltd/Alamy Stock Photo; O – (top) NPG, (bottom) NPG; P – (top) NPG, (bottom) NPG

Acknowledgements

I am grateful for the assistance of the staff, archivists and librarians at Cambridge University Library Manuscripts Reading Room, in particular Louise Clarke, Allen Packwood and the team at the Churchill Archives Centre, Churchill College, Cambridge, King's College Archives, Cambridge, Magdalene College Archives, Cambridge, the Tate Gallery Archive, the Royal Academy of Arts Archive and Westminster School Archive.

My thanks are due to Professor Jane Ridley at the University of Buckingham for her guidance at the inception of this book. I am especially grateful to Dr Piers Brendon for his advice and guidance throughout the project.

My thanks to Ian Strathcarron, Lucy Duckworth and the team at Unicorn Publishing for bringing the book to print and to my editor Emily Lane for her astute observations.

I must acknowledge permission to quote from the following copyright material:
David Higham Associates for extracts from the unpublished letters of Christopher Hassall and Edward Marsh; copyright Siegfried Sassoon by kind permission of the Estate of George Sassoon; extracts from the unpublished letters from Patrick Hamilton and Noël Coward to Christopher Hassall by permission of Alan Brodie Representation Ltd; extracts from the letters of Clementine Churchill by permission of The Master, Fellows and Scholars of Churchill College, Cambridge; extracts from the letters of Frances Cornford reproduced with the permission of the trustees of the Frances Crofts Cornford Will Trust; Francis Chapman for permission to quote from the unpublished letters of Clare Chapman to Christopher Hassall; Professor Simon Keynes for extracts from the unpublished letters of Sir Geoffrey Keynes to Christopher Hassall; extracts from the unpublished letters of W. Somerset Maugham to Christopher Hassall reproduced by permission of United Agents Ltd (www.unitedagents.co.uk) on behalf of The Royal Literary Fund (Copyright © The Royal Literary Fund); the estate of James Pope-Hennessy c/o Artellus Ltd; copyright © Patrick Leigh Fermor 1954.

Finally, huge thanks to my children: Dan, Cat, and Jonny for their encouragement and to my husband Stephen for his infinite patience and unfailing support.

Index